# Dining in Baltimore
Food and drink in and around Charm City

# Other books from *The Sun*:

*Hometown Boy: The Hoodle Patrol and Other Curiosities of Baltimore*, by Rafael Alvarez

*The Wild Side of Maryland, An Outdoor Guide, 2nd Edition*

*The Great Game of Maryland Politics,* by Barry Rascovar

*Gaining A Yard: The Building of Baltimore's Football Stadium,* by Jon Morgan and Doug Kapustin

*Raising Kids & Tomatoes,* by Rob Kasper

*Motherhood Is A Contact Sport,* by Susan Reimer

*The 1996-1997 Maryland Business Almanac*

*Cal Touches Home*

*A Century In The Sun (September 1999)*

---

This *Sun* book is published by SunSource, the information service of *The Sun*. To order any of the above titles, or for information on research, reprints and other services SunSource offers, please call 410-332-6800.

# Dining in Baltimore
Food and drink in and around Charm City

THE BALTIMORE SUN

# Dining in Baltimore
Food and drink in and around Charm City

Bruce Friedland, *Copy Editor*
Jennifer Halbert, *Research, Design and Layout Editor*
Eugene Balk, *Researcher*

*Cover photos by, clockwise from top left:*
Nanine Hartzenbusch, George W. Holsey, Chiaki Kawajiri and Doug Kapustin.

© 1999 by The Baltimore Sun
All rights reserved under international copyright conventions. No part of the contents of this book may be reproduced or utilized in any form or by any means, electronic or mechanical, including photocopying, recording, or by any information storage or retrieval system without the written consent of the publisher.

Published by

The Baltimore Sun
A Times Mirror Co.
501 N. Calvert St.
Baltimore, Md. 21278

ISBN: 1-893116-02-6

Library of Congress Publication Data applied for.

Dining In Baltimore: a publication of The Baltimore Sun
— 1999 — Baltimore, Md.: Baltimore Sun Co., 1999

# Contents:

Introduction ......................................................................vii

Restaurant reviews ...............................................................1

Restaurants A to Z ...........................................................162

Community ......................................................................165

Cuisine .............................................................................171

Entree pricing .................................................................178

Live music .......................................................................186

Children's menus ............................................................187

Waterfront views .............................................................189

Wheelchair accessible .....................................................190

Reservations ...................................................................193

Area classics ...................................................................196

# Introduction

Where are we going to eat?

That's a question everyone has asked at one time or another: couples on a date, families with small children, office workers with limited time for lunch.

To help resolve this gustatory dilemma and make your decisions easier, we present *Dining in Baltimore*. Our goal is to provide you with a representative view of Baltimore-area restaurants. *Sun* reviewers Elizabeth Large and Kathryn Higham have been eating in and around Charm City for years, and we have collected 160 of their reviews in one handy reference.

The reviews in this book were originally published in *The Sun* from 1992 through 1998. We have updated the restaurants' vital statistics at the top of each review, and compiled easy-to-use indexes so you can check restaurants by area, cuisine, price and other helpful categories.

Most of the restaurants we've included accept all major credit cards. We have noted only the exceptions (it's a good idea to call ahead if you have any questions about credit cards, hours or reservations). One more note: We have decided not to use the star rating system as seen with reviews in The Sun. The reviews themselves give an excellent description of the restaurants and their strengths and weaknesses.

We also invite you to visit SunSpot CitySearch at http://citysearch.sunspot.net. There you will find directions, places to go before or after your meal, and much more.

So enjoy. Have fun looking through the indexes for whatever you're in the mood for: ribs in Ellicott City, seafood in Canton or an Indian meal in Pikesville.

Bon appetit!

# The Reviews

# Acropolis

*4714-4718 Eastern Ave., Greektown • 410-675-7882*
*Hours: Open every day for lunch and dinner*
*Prices: Appetizers, $2.50; entrees, $8.50-$23.95*
*Live music: No • Kid's menu: No • Waterfront views: No •*
*Wheelchair access: Yes • Reservations: Accepted*

The Acropolis is one of those Greektown restaurants that have been around forever but you never hear much about. Over the years it's been overshadowed by other Greek eateries.

This is a modest little restaurant of a certain mold: the neighborhood ethnic eatery where you're promised lots of food and a good time for not much money.

These it delivers. Just don't hope for good food, too.

How can you have a good time and not have good food? you may ask. Well, the dining room, which was renovated not too long ago, is fresh and pretty. The staff is composed of nice people, and the service is excellent. Start drinking a little Greek wine with a piece of bread or two, and you might not notice that the eggplant salad has so much garlic it tastes bitter, or that the stuffed grape leaves are smothered in a sea of egg-lemon sauce.

Still, the meat-and-rice stuffing is sprightly. While so much sauce is somewhat unappetizing, it tastes fine. A tyropita, the traditional pastry made with flaky phyllo dough and softly melting Greek cheeses, is hot and crisp. No problem there.

But from then on our meal goes rapidly downhill. A lamb stew is a special this evening. It comes in a pretty little casserole, and the waitress arranges it gracefully on a plate at the table. But I'm dismayed by the unidentified cuts of lamb, bone in and quite fatty, cooked to the point of falling off the bones. The casserole includes a few cooked carrots and artichoke hearts. The whole thing is awash in egg-lemon sauce — more egg-lemon sauce than anyone could possibly eat — this time heavily flavored with dill.

A "Seafood Delite" sounds wonderful; but the phyllo pastry, shredded crab meat, fish and shrimp are covered in a thick blanket of imperial sauce. (Do I sense a trend?)

An enormous portion of moussaka has the requisite ground beef, potatoes, eggplant, bechamel and tomato sauce, but is heavily seasoned and tastes burnt. A pretty Greek salad comes with it, but the oregano-flavored salad dressing is as thick as mayonnaise.

Greek vegetables are usually cooked for a long time, but the Acropolis goes overboard with both its endive and its green beans in tomato sauce — supposedly fresh, but who can tell when they've been cooked to mush.

Oh well, on to dessert. How bad can dessert be? I find out when my baklava arrives. The pastry and nut confection is as soggy as a wet towel — a sign, I suppose, that it's been sitting around too long. The other choices, rice pudding and a custard pastry called galaktoboureko, are simply tasteless.

*Elizabeth Large*

# Akbar Palace

*3541 Brenbrook Drive, Randallstown • 410-655-1600*
*Hours: Open every day for lunch and dinner*
*Prices: Appetizers, $2.50-$7.95; entrees, $8.95-$16.95*
*Live music: Friday night • Kid's menu: No • Waterfront views: No •*
*Wheelchair access: Yes • Reservations: Accepted*

When Chandra Nigam bought the Randallstown Akbar and turned it into Akbar Palace, he expanded the menu to include some new specialties and some Southern Indian dishes, but what's noteworthy is that there are no great changes. And that's good when you start with as dependable a restaurant as the Akbar was.

Probably the biggest plus of the ownership change is the presence of this affable man in the dining room, with his very likable staff. The people here add a warmth that the large, open dining room lacks.

When the first Akbar opened many years ago, it specialized in Northern Indian food. Dishes like its signature crab Malabar (made with backfin and cream) set it apart in a city where Indian food was synonymous with curry.

We tried to sample what was new on the menu. Dosas (huge, paper-thin filled pancakes) are a new addition; but our waiter told us that for some reason, never fully explained, the kitchen couldn't make them that evening. We settled instead for another new dish, shrimp mustard.

One of the pleasures of eating Indian food is the chance to indulge in flavors you don't run into every day. So maybe we shouldn't have ordered a dish called shrimp mustard unless we wanted what we got, namely shrimp in a strongly mustard-flavored cream sauce. But somehow we assumed mustard would be only one of a complex of spices.

The lamb Xacutti, a curry with toasted coconut and layers of fiery flavor, was more to our taste. But the most appealing dish was a standard, chicken tikki masala. The chicken kept its distinct smoky flavor from being cooked in a tandoor oven, a pleasant contrast with the spicy, buttery sauce.

You can start with little appetizer bits of lamb ground with peppers and onions, or a thick, flavorful lentil soup; but our favorite first course was peshawri nan, unleavened bread stuffed with dried fruits and nuts and baked in the tandoor oven. That didn't stop us from ordering more breads to dip into our main-course sauces: whole-wheat chapati and the deep-fried, football-shaped puff called poori.

For dessert we tried the ice creams. The restaurant offers a cooling, creamy mango or pistachio ice cream; very appealing after a highly spiced meal. But I have a fondness for kulfi, the frozen dessert made in-house. The little, dense, icy-cold rectangles taste of condensed milk, pistachio and rose water and have none of the familiarity of the commercial ice creams. They have an odd appeal all their own.

*Elizabeth Large*

# Aldo's

*306 S. High St., Little Italy • 410-727-0700*
*Hours: Open every night for dinner*
*Prices: Appetizers, $7.50-$9.50; entrees, $14-$29*
*Live music: No • Kid's menu: No • Waterfront views: No •*
*Wheelchair access: Yes • Reservations: Accepted*

When Aldo's opened in Little Italy, the owner wisely decided to offer traditional southern Italian home cooking. But having done that, Aldo Vitale had to figure out how to differentiate his restaurant from all the other restaurants that offer traditional southern Italian home cooking. He's done it by creating the most beautiful restaurant in Little Italy.

You have to admire the cream and cappuccino facade with its decorative columns. You enter through an etched-glass doorway to a fin de siecle bar, then walk back to a center hallway with a dining room on either side. A simple vase of lush, peach-colored roses at the maitre d' station sets the tone. The dining rooms have windows opening onto the central corridor, which gives the restaurant a pleasant indoor-outdoor feeling.

The service is also excellent; the staff is attentive and friendly without being presumptuous. Our waiter handled a spilled glass of red wine beautifully — he simply moved us to another table without making anyone feel guilty.

With so much else going for Aldo's, the kitchen needs to get up to speed. What was good about our meal was very good. Sadly, what went wrong could easily have been avoided.

The tenderloin tips in a dark, flavorful red-wine sauce came from the kitchen stone cold. What could have been a delicious veal scaloppine with sauteed peppers and wild mushrooms suffered because the winey sauce hadn't been simmered long enough to get rid of the raw taste of alcohol. A beautiful fruitti di mare posillipo had a noteworthy tomato sauce and the shellfish were nestled on good pasta. But the featured lobster chunks tasted chewy and a bit dry.

The best of our main courses was the most modest, ear-shaped orecchiette pasta. It was tossed with pleasantly bitter broccoli rabe and mild Italian sausage sauteed in good, garlicky olive oil. In fact, all the pasta was excellent. My guest who ordered the cold tenderloin tips devoured her side dish of penne with its fresh tomato sauce and grated Parmesan.

First courses, too, made us happy: golden fried calamari; fat, garlicky shrimp sauteed in butter; a fresh-tasting plate of sauteed red, green and yellow peppers; a tangy arugula salad with balsamic vinaigrette. Also worthy of note was Aldo's excellent bread.

So we started well, and we would have ended well if we had all ordered the cannoli. It was a particularly good version of an old standard, with a thin, crisp shell and a creamy, just-sweet-enough ricotta filling. Alas, a lemon curd tart and a mille-feuille pastry both tasted a bit long in the tooth.

*Elizabeth Large*

# Ambassador Dining Room

*3811 Canterbury Road, Canterbury • 410-366-1484*
*Hours: Open Monday through Friday for lunch, Saturday and Sunday for brunch, every night for dinner*
*Prices: Appetizers, $1.75-$6.95; entrees, $9.95-$18.95*
*Live music: No • Kid's menu: No • Waterfront views: No •*
*Wheelchair access: No • Reservations: Required*

On a weeknight visit, almost every table was filled in the new Ambassador Dining Room, operated by Keir Singh, owner of Banjara in South Baltimore.

Why is this place doing so well? Well, while there are other Indian restaurants with food as good as the new Ambassador's, nowhere in the city will you find as perfect a setting for it.

Who would have guessed that with a few subtle changes, the dining room's faux Old English inn look could become a sophisticated setting reminiscent of the British Raj? This is now a handsome place to eat. (Yet it's very comfortable. Some of the dining-room seating is upholstered wing chairs.) The waiters wear black tie; customers are more casual.

The Ambassador's food isn't served family-style, as is usual for Indian restaurants around here. Plates are prepared in the kitchen. My tenderloin of lamb in a fennel and chive sauce, for instance, was arranged with individual helpings of basmati rice, sweet potatoes and sauteed zucchini.

Attention is paid to presentation. A delicate chicken shorba soup was lovely; a lime slice and a sprig of cilantro enlivened the flavorful golden broth and snippets of chicken.

Dinner at the new Ambassador begins happily, with an Indian bread, alu paratha, brought to the table with your drinks. It's something like hot whole-wheat pita with a soft center (actually a thin filling of whipped potatoes).

Dinner at the new Ambassador ends magnificently, with fresh fruit or sensuous homemade almond and mango ice cream or delicate Indian rice pudding.

But it's impossible to categorize our meal in between. One of the "Chef's Recommendations," murgh khumari — a chicken dish with apricots and a creamy sauce — was unusual and delicious. But thumbs down on the tenderloin of lamb. The meat was almost raw when I cut into it, and its fennel and chive sauce was unexpectedly and unpleasantly sweet.

A tandoori mixed grill with shrimp, chicken and minced lamb rolls satisfied. But crab Malabar wasn't made with the promised backfin crab and was over-salted to boot. Yet side dishes of raita (yogurt, cucumber and tomatoes) and dal (seasoned yellow lentils) couldn't have been better.

Perhaps the couple of clunkers we had weren't as typical of the Ambassador's menu as the truly excellent dishes we had. That's what I'm hoping, because the people there are so nice and I love the setting.

*Elizabeth Large*

# Annapurna

*204 Reisterstown Road, Pikesville • 410-484-2944*
*Hours: Open Tuesday through Sunday for lunch and dinner*
*Prices: Appetizers, $2.50-$6.25; entrees, $7.75-$13.50*
*Live music: No • Kid's menu: No • Waterfront views: No •*
*Wheelchair access: Yes • Reservations: Suggested*

Annapurna, the new Indian restaurant in Pikesville, is the ethnic version of the little mom-and-pop eating place that serves up good family-style food — the kind of inexpensive restaurant you visit when you're tired and don't feel like cooking.

The sauces are wonderful here, with a complexity of flavor that doesn't depend on fiery spicing for its appeal. If asked, the kitchen will make the food so hot your hair will stand on end; but the default mode is set for American tastes.

The restaurant is modest, to say the least. But it's cheerful enough inside, with mirrors to make the dining room appear a bit bigger, and fresh white tablecloths. The serving staff is friendly and eager to please.

There are no surprises on Annapurna's menu, except perhaps for the 12 types of bread: some baked in the tandoor oven, some deep fried, some grilled. One bread is stuffed with radishes; others with potatoes or cauliflower and peas.

You could simply fill up on bread, or you could start with a soothing, creamy lentil soup or fat little Nepalese dumplings filled with ground turkey and lamb. Alas, our samosas, vegetarian pastries filled with potatoes and peas, and meat pastries filled with ground lamb, were overcooked.

Bangan bharta is a great dish to share. This is a luscious concoction of roasted and pureed eggplant, fresh tomatoes, peppers and onions with a buttery edge and the texture of soft whipped potatoes. The sauce for shrimp masala was every bit as good, creamy and delicately spiced — superb over basmati rice or as a dip for one of the breads. Too bad there were so few, and such tiny, shrimp swimming in it.

Chicken seems to be a house specialty here; several of the chicken dishes are so designated. We loved the seductively spiced tomato-based sauce of the Annapurna Chicken Jalfrezi with notes of fresh ginger — so good it overshadowed the chunks of chicken and fresh vegetables, including broccoli.

To balance the rich sauces, we ordered Annapurna's tandoori platter, which sported intriguingly seasoned meatballs of ground lamb, tender grilled chicken and two shrimp, all roasted in the tandoor oven. Everything was good, but it seemed a little skimpy to me, mostly because we never got the promised cubes of shish kebab.

Annapurna makes exceptionally good Indian desserts. It isn't so surprising that the delicate rice pudding sprinkled with pistachios would appeal. But for the first time I noticed that the gulab jamun, balls made of dried milk powder, with honey and rose water syrup are no sweeter, say, than baklava — one of the world's great desserts.

*Elizabeth Large*

# Angelina's

*7135 Harford Road, Parkville • 410-444-5545*
*Hours: Open Tuesday through Sunday for lunch and dinner*
*Prices: Appetizers, $3.95-$9.95; entrees, $8.95-$20.95*
*Live music: Friday and Saturday nights • Kid's menu: No •*
*Waterfront views: No • Wheelchair access: Yes •*
*Reservations: Accepted for large parties*

Angelina's — like Haussner's and Maison Marconi — has been around so long it's taken on landmark status in Baltimore. The Irish pub now known for its crab cakes and Italian food opened 48 years ago as a small Italian restaurant.

In the early '70s, the bar opened downstairs from the dining room, added what has become Baltimore's most famous crab cake to the menu, and started making what some think is the best cheesecake in the city — if not the world. I'm tempted to agree. In recent times, some of the fried dishes have been taken off the menu and more broiled and sauteed ones added. The restaurant also started shipping the crab cakes as gifts, which has been a huge success.

What hasn't changed is the comfy, old-fashioned dining rooms of the corner rowhouse. Angelina's has become a tourist attraction for those who want a taste of Baltimore as it used to be. Many of them order those crab cakes, and they are as good as you'll get anywhere. Made with jumbo lump crab meat, they have a minimum of filler and are assertively spiced. My preference is to get them fried, so they have a light, golden crust to contrast with the snowy lumps of crab.

Just about everything is made on the premises, including the bread and the desserts. Soups taste fresh and homey. The kitchen makes its own coleslaw, good stewed tomatoes and a fabulous potato salad, and it pickles its own beets.

I love the mussels marinara, with their light, fresh tomato sauce and crusty garlic bread. Equally good is the shellfish spaghettini. Steamed clams, mussels, scallops and shrimp come nestled in tender pasta with a deliciously garlicky broth flecked with parsley. The fish of the day might be rockfish — a fine, fat fillet — and you can get it stuffed with lump crab meat and topped with an old-fashioned, thick blanket of imperial sauce (which I could do without).

I would stay away from the veal parmigiana. The waitress lovingly refers to it as "veal parm," and tells us it's a favorite among regulars. But the reality is thin veal, thick breading, uninteresting tomato sauce and rubbery cheese.

It's no surprise that fresh vegetables aren't a forte here, and green beans are cooked to a fare-thee-well.

I did think pies might be extra-good; the dessert display certainly looks tempting enough. Alas, fillings are decent, but pastry that I tried on two different nights was dreadful.

But who cares when you have cheesecake this good? No fussing with perfection here — no crust, no fruit, no exotic flavors. Just a heavy, incredibly creamy slice of pure bliss.

*Elizabeth Large*

# Antrim 1844 Country Inn

*30 Trevanion Road, Taneytown • 410-876-0237*
*Hours: Open daily for dinner*
*Prices: Five-course prix-fixe, $55*
*Live music: Weekends • Kid's menu: No • Waterfront views: No •*
*Wheelchair access: Yes • Reservations: Required*

The magic of our evening at Antrim 1844 started miles before we arrived at the gracious brick mansion in Taneytown. As we passed farms and meadows on a country road, our moods changed. We were on a dining adventure.

We were told to arrive at 6:30 p.m. for the hors d'oeuvre hour, before being seated for dinner at 7:30 p.m. We wandered through the inn, and trays of skewered lamb, tiny crab cakes, bacon-wrapped scallops and other morsels somehow found us. Sipping drinks and nibbling food, we admired parlors filled with antiques and strolled along gravel paths through the formal gardens.

In the smokehouse dining room, one of several options, the rooms were cool yet cozy. There were plump, high-back chairs in plaid, and paintings of Civil War generals on the walls. The staff moved silently, often anticipating our needs. First they brought us a chilled peach soup — sweet, but not as cloying as one might expect. The corn chowder was sublime.

A grilled vegetable and goat cheese terrine was served chilled on a coulis of yellow tomatoes. Layered with chopped tomatoes, eggplant and mushrooms, it had a mild, tangy taste. Salad choices were arugula or mesclun lettuce. The latter was better, with tiny cubes of cantaloupe and prosciutto tossed in a kiwi-lime vinaigrette. The arugula salad needed a stronger dressing. With bits of cucumber and bulgur wheat, it tasted like thinned-down tabbouleh on sharp greens.

Of the four dinner selections, the house-smoked fillet of Angus beef tenderloin was the most exquisite. Crusty black on the outside, rare and meltingly tender inside, it was full of smoky flavor. It came with a dried-cherry sauce and roasted new potatoes. Roasted pork tenderloin, brushed with a hoisin glaze, also was lovely and tender, matched with a creamy tropical risotto. Grilled salmon on top of a cold, wild-rice salad was encircled by lemony vinaigrette. Least impressive was the skinless, tequila-grilled spring chicken. Though laced with a nice lime-marinade, it was a bit dry. There was ancho chili butter to spread on top.

Dessert arrived on a large plate for two. Our favorites were rich cherry ice cream with nuggets of chocolate, and a crisp, lace tower filled with chocolate whipped cream and fresh strawberries. A creme brulee looked gray and tasted like burnt sugar, a lemony cheesecake was over-salted and a moist chocolate torte was bitter. If we had ordered any of them individually, we would have been disappointed.

We left after coffee, but we could have finished with port, a cigar and a walk on the grounds after dinner.

*Kathryn Higham*

# Ashley M's

*911 N. Charles St., Mount Vernon • 410-837-2424*
*Hours: Open Tuesday through Sunday for dinner*
*Prices: Appetizers, $4.50-$9; entrees, $9-$24*
*Live music: Weekends • Kid's menu: Yes • Waterfront views: No •*
*Wheelchair access: No • Reservations: Accepted*

This pleasant, moderately priced restaurant from Ed Rogers of La Tesso Tana has the relaxed feeling of a neighborhood spot; but with its white tablecloths and good-looking decor, Ashley M's is nice enough for a special occasion.

The menu is an odd but appealing combination of Italian, wild game and "old style" American dishes. In other words, it's a menu that ranges from flounder piccata to rattlesnake salad to a country-style fried-chicken platter. There's also a separate section of vegetarian entrees.

The second-floor dining room and bar is divided into several cozy spaces decorated in warm, earthy tones. The background music is worth listening to. There's original art on the walls. All in all, it's ambience with a little bit of soul to it.

The food works very well in this context. The show stopper was a first course of alligator. Thin slices of the most delicate white meat imaginable had a fragile golden crust and a light lemon-butter sauce sparked with dill. Arranged beside angel-hair pasta, it was nothing short of fabulous.

Our other first courses were less unusual, but nicely done. Baked brie came with a warm raspberry sauce and little toasts. "Minestra" soup, made with a fresh-tasting chicken stock, was filled with corkscrew pasta and bright vegetables. An Ashley salad was a pretty salad of mixed greens in a tangy-sweet raspberry vinaigrette.

Our main courses didn't let us down. Semi-boneless Muscovy duck was the star with its juicy meat, a complete lack of fat and crisp golden-brown skin. A fragrant Bing-cherry sauce was intensely flavorful without being cloyingly sweet. The baked half-tomato with a crumb topping was an unexpected but not unpleasant accompaniment.

Linguine alla Ashley featured shrimp and lump crab meat in a rich cream sauce over tender pasta. A succulent fillet of salmon sported a crust of poppy seeds and a pleasingly tart lime-butter sauce. Least successful was the chopped venison steak, a bit dry because it had so little fat. Still, it was cooked pink as ordered, and its red-wine sauce with peppers, onions and mushrooms was potently flavorful.

The kitchen let us down in only one instance: The vegetable that came with our dinners, yellow squash cooked with onion and tomatoes, tasted odd. It had been flavored with something acrid that I couldn't identify.

The dessert tray included pastries from Patisserie Poupon, so it's hard to go wrong there. Our favorite was a turtle cheesecake, a creamy slice with a thin layer of chocolate, caramel and pecans on top.

*Elizabeth Large*

# Azeb's Ethiopian Restaurant

*322 N. Charles St., downtown • 410-625-9787*
*Hours: Open Tuesday through Sunday for dinner*
*Prices: Entrees, $5.95-$10.95; samplers for two, $16.95-$24.95*
*Live music: Saturday night • Kid's menu: No • Waterfront views: No •*
*Wheelchair access: No • Reservations: Suggested*

When you eat Ethiopian, you eat an awful lot of enjera, the thin, spongy bread used to wrap up morsels of spicy stews. At Azeb's on Charles Street, the enjera is moist and delicate-tasting, quite unlike doughy, sour versions I've had before.

Owner Azeb Teklay said her enjera is so tasty because it's made from teff, a seed that grows in Ethiopia. She serves a basket full of enjera strips, rolled up into tight bundles, with each dinner. Enjera also lines the communal dinner tray — almost like a soft pizza crust — where different stews, salads and vegetables are arranged in a circle. Rip off a piece of bread and wrap up a bite of food; no forks allowed. It's a fun way to eat, if your friends are game — and if they wash their hands.

To make the experience even more authentic, we decided to eat in the upstairs loft, next to a deep-blue mural of sky. Here, chairs and cushioned stools are arranged around coiled baskets that serve as tables. At our feet were animal-skin rugs. If you're the kind of eater who inevitably drops something in your lap, choose a table downstairs.

There were no appetizers to speak of, so we moved directly to our dinner order. Azeb's specialty chicken, which featured chunks of breast meat cooked in awaze, a thin sauce with sauteed onions, peppers and wine, was our favorite dish — light-tasting and not too spicy-hot.

Beef in barbarre sauce was simmered to the point of disintegration, the shreds of meat coated in a thick, dark, hot sauce. There was so much going on in this complex dish, we could hardly identify the key players — cardamom, clove, paprika, turmeric, perhaps.

Our last choice was a vegetarian sampler, which allowed us to pick three entrees. We decided on gomen, a dish of spicy chopped collards, onions and garlic; missir, a seasoned porridge of red lentils, and tikel gomen, a bland mix of cabbage, potato, carrots and onion.

We also tried a red-ripe tomato salad with bits of fiery jalapeno peppers. That, too, we tried to wrap in pieces of enjera, but it was a bit slippery. Eating with your hands is an acquired skill, we learned. Small portions of split-pea puree, and limp house salad, with iceberg lettuce and tomatoes in vinaigrette, also came with our dinners.

The chocolate layer cake, the only dessert offered, wasn't made in-house. Straight from the refrigerator, it tasted dry, but the frosting was thick and had deep chocolate flavor.

Like some other things, the cake was slow to arrive. Our waitress was serene and helpful, if not especially fast. But with a hands-on meal like this, lingering is part of the experience.

*Kathryn Higham*

# Bandaloops

*1024 S. Charles St., Federal Hill • 410-727-1355*
*Hours: Open for lunch and dinner Monday through Saturday, brunch*
*and dinner on Sunday*
*Prices: Light fare, $4.95-$8.50; entrees, $12-$18.95*
*Live music: No • Kid's menu: No • Waterfront views: No •*
*Wheelchair access: Yes • Reservations: Preferred for large parties*

Since it opened more than a decade ago, Bandaloops has settled down and become an established presence in Federal Hill. You know you can come here for a good burger with green peppercorn mayonnaise or a meal-in-itself salad with the chef's own dressings. Touches like freshly baked muffins and unusual desserts made in the restaurant's kitchen set Bandaloops apart. The staff is young and casual, but knows how to wait tables.

And Bandaloops has aged well physically. Long and narrow, with the dining room in back of the bar, it looks newly renovated. It still has its signature stained glass, parquet floor, hanging plants, dark wood paneling below the chair rail and local art for sale on the off-white walls.

As for the food, the misses aren't terrible and the hits are right on target. First courses on the regular menu are limited to soups and snacks (like a dip and a cheese board), but the night we dined there we could also get Cajun-style mushroom caps. They were stuffed with spicy, minced andouille sausage and baked with a little cheese, which melted appealingly into the sausage. Excellent.

Not so excellent was the soup of the day, a sort of Maryland crab soup without the crab and with overcooked shrimp. A better starter was the house salad, made of fresh leaf lettuce, a few too many alfalfa sprouts, grated carrots, tomatoes and good house-made dressings. The salad also comes with a burrito, so you get a satisfying light meal for $7.75.

The flour tortilla is filled with a pleasant combination of smoked turkey cubes, kidney beans, cheese and chorizo sausage, with salsa on top. If that's too adventuresome, have the chicken salad, made with white meat, green grapes and almonds and tossed with a subtle tarragon mayonnaise. It comes with lots of greens, or you can have it stuffed in a pita.

Places that do casual food well don't always shine when it comes to more complicated dinners, but I had only one complaint about the special of the day, shrimp ratouille tournedos — the two good fillets were almost raw, even though I had ordered them medium rare. Each is topped with a fat shrimp and a red pepper and cream sauce. The seasoned rice and fresh asparagus were both perfectly cooked.

House-made desserts like a fudgy chocolate cake with butterscotch-liqueur icing and a raspberry sour cream tart with a streusel topping are good, if a bit overwhelming. But if you've eaten heartily, I recommend the homemade ice cream of the day. The flavors can be offbeat — sticky bun ice cream, anyone? — but this night it was a fine and simple vanilla.

*Elizabeth Large*

# Bare Bones

*9150 Baltimore National Pike, Ellicott City • 410-461-0770*
*Hours: Open daily for lunch and dinner*
*Prices: Appetizers, $2.50-$7.50; entrees, $6.95-$16.95*
*Live music: Saturday night • Kid's menu: Yes • Waterfront views: No •*
*Wheelchair access: Yes • Reservations: Accepted for large parties •*
*Other locations: 617 Frederick Ave., Gaithersburg • 301-948-4344*

A strip shopping center is about the most unlikely place for a microbrewery that I can imagine. But that's exactly where the Bare Bones in Ellicott City is located.

Inside, the rooms are attractive enough, but it's only in the dark, brick-walled bar area where stainless-steel brewing tanks are displayed you get the feeling that you're in a microbrewery. But ambience hardly matters when the beer and barbecue are on target, and they are at Bare Bones.

The easiest way to try the beers is to order the sampler — a round, wooden caddy holding five glasses of Bare Bones' brews, from the light Patapsco Valley Gold to the molasses-rich Savage Mill Porter.

The menu suggests either the Gold or the more robust Old Ellicott Ale to go along with a rib dinner. That's not the only choice rib lovers must make. There are ribs and chicken. Ribs and prime rib. Ribs and shrimp. We went with half a rack each of baby back and spareribs. Tender and smoky, they were terrific, with the meat pulling easily off the bone.

The barbecued chicken was just as delicious. It was started off in the oven, baked slowly to keep the meat moist. Then the two enormous chicken breast halves were slathered with tangy barbecue sauce and finished on the grill.

All our dinners were done to perfection, including a large salmon fillet and an oversized chicken breast cutlet on the teriyaki chicken sandwich. Drizzled with tarragon creme sauce, the salmon flaked into moist sections. The chicken breast was juicy under its light teriyaki glaze. It was served on an oversized kaiser roll with lettuce and tomato.

For appetizers, try the buffalo wings, which were crisp, light and tangy with hot sauce, or the massive loaf of shoestring fried onions. We also ordered potato skins with crisp, chopped bacon and melted Cheddar, but you can have them Southwest style, topped with chili, onion and cheese. The Cajun gumbo had lots of chicken and dime-thin slices of andouille sausage but was missing the shrimp the menu promised.

The best of what we sampled for dessert was the New York-style cheesecake, as thick as cream cheese. If the Key lime tart hadn't been such a bright pistachio green, or the apple pie heated to mush, we might have enjoyed them more.

Those are our only quibbles, given the fine food, drink and service we received. Our young waiter indulged us all night long, made us laugh and, most important, kept us in full supply of napkins: When you end up with a plate of bare bones after a messy rib dinner, napkins are essential.

*Kathryn Higham*

# Barn Restaurant & Crab House

*9527 Harford Road, Parkville • 410-882-6182*
*Hours: Open daily for lunch and dinner*
*Prices: Appetizers, $3.95-$9.95; entrees, $4.50-$21; crabs, $24-$45 a dozen*
*Live music: Every night • Kid's menu: Yes • Waterfront views: No •*
*Wheelchair access: Yes • Reservations: Accepted*

If you're a crab lover who prefers to hear more than cracking crab shells while dining, check out the Barn Restaurant & Crab House in Parkville. Bands play progressive tunes and rock and roll in the upstairs bar on weekends.

Downstairs, though, is for serious crab eating. The basement dining room, with gray-painted paneling, tile floors, stone foundation walls and an enviable collection of sports memorabilia, has a homey feel.

Tables are covered with a sheet of brown kraft paper and outfitted with a bucket full of mallets, knives and paper towels. The large crabs we tried, shipped in from Texas, were finger-stinging hot when they were dumped on the center of our table. Most were heavy, but our waitress had tossed in an extra one or two just in case some were light.

The Barn's own spice mix is a balanced blend of black and red pepper, rock salt and spices. A few crabs were caked heavy with spice, but most had a light dusting. The two options satisfied the different palates at our table. To wash down all that salt and spice, our waitress suggested pitchers of beer and ice tea, instead of individual glasses.

Everyone around us seemed to be eating crabs; most also had the foresight to order steamed corn, which is cooked husk, silk and all right in the pot with your crabs. When we asked for corn mid-dinner, our waitress said it would take 10-15 minutes. We didn't want to wait so we can't vouch for what the corn tasted like, but it looked beautifully fresh.

The Barn delivered great crabs, but the rest of our meal didn't fare well. To start, the soups we tried were incredibly salty. The Maryland crab tasted like concentrated beef broth, full of diced vegetables but little crab. There was more crab meat in the cream of crab, but it was as thick as cheese dip.

The baby back ribs were gray and tasted as if they had been reheated. The blackened chicken was coated so thickly with salt and herbs it was nearly inedible. Underneath, the boneless chicken breast meat was tender and juicy, so ordering the grilled chicken might be wiser.

Pass on water-logged mixed vegetables and pasty coleslaw, and order crisp coated fries as a dinner side. Or order some appetizers. We liked the buffalo chicken wings, called Barn Burners; they were crunchy under their tangy red coating. Best of all were the fried crab balls. Full of backfin with a hint of filler, they were sweet mouthfuls of Maryland.

Our waitress said staffers were sorting crabs in the kitchen and that put desserts out of reach. They had run out of everything but chocolate ice cream and cheesecake, anyway.

*Kathryn Higham*

# Bay Cafe

*2809 Boston St., Canton • 410-522-3377*
*Hours: Open daily for lunch and dinner, breakfast on Sunday*
*Prices: Appetizers, $2.95-$8.95; entrees, $6.95-$17.95*
*Live music: Weekends, summer only • Kid's menu: No • Waterfront views: Yes • Wheelchair access: Yes • Reservations: Accepted*

What stood out about our evening at the Bay Cafe were the dockside ambience, the desserts and the appetizers.

People mingle at the man-made beach with palm trees and tiki lights, and at several outdoor and indoor bars. There are dining tables in the sand, on the terrace, and inside.

We wouldn't have thought of the Bay Cafe as a dessert spot, but we now recommend sharing coffee and something sweet in the glow of a tiki light. None of the desserts is made in-house; all we tried, though, were delicious.

Strawberry shortcake stood 5 inches high, topped by a mammoth berry. Fresh and light, it was constructed of layers of soft spongecake and clouds of sweet whipped cream. The Snickers cheesecake was dense and sweet. A thick, chewy layer of chocolate, peanuts and caramel was topped by a thin coating of cheesecake. The mousse cake was more mousse than cake, with a fluffy texture and light chocolate flavor.

Appetizers were terrific, too, especially the crab balls. These were among the best we've tried, not doughy like some. Greaseless and delicate-tasting with lumps of crab, they were like eating a golf-ball-size crab cake.

A portion of jerk chicken was generous also. Boneless chicken tenders were marinated and rubbed with a thick coating of herbs. A honey mustard sauce, whipped so that it looked like banana pudding, was on the side for dunking.

The Bay Cafe serves a chunky version of Maryland crab soup with enough crab meat to satisfy. Big pieces of carrots, potatoes and cabbage gave it homemade flavor. But the jumbo lump crab cake platter was the only entree without problems. The fat crab cake was made with lots of lump crab and not a lot of filler.

The chicken stir-fry, one of six similar dishes on the menu, was full of lovely crisp-tender vegetables, but the sauce was bland enough for a baby. Our Italian pizza, with peppers, onions and pepperoni, had a nice crust. Too-sweet marinara, though, tasted like it came from a jar.

We liked being able to select pieces of yellowfin tuna to top our dinner salad and to request them blackened, charbroiled or dipped in Cajun spices. But the tuna was overcooked and the salad of romaine, cherry tomatoes and cucumber slices was small and uninteresting. The shrimp salad sandwich, a house specialty, was an eye-popper. Unfortunately, it lacked flavor. More troubling, some shrimp were mushy and underdone, others overcooked.

But the Bay Cafe is not about serious food. It's about tiki lamps, conversations and people-watching.

*Kathryn Higham*

# Bayou Blues Cafe

*8133-A Honeygo Blvd., The Avenue, White Marsh • 410-931-2583*
*Hours: Open daily for lunch and dinner*
*Prices: Appetizers, $3.99-$7.99; entrees, $7.99-$23.99*
*Live music: Every night • Kid's menu: Yes • Waterfront views: No •*
*Wheelchair access: Yes • Reservations: Accepted*

Bayou Blues is the real deal. I asked two friends who had just returned from New Orleans to help me assess the authenticity of the Cajun dishes. The result: Thumbs up.

But food is not the only draw at Bayou Blues. There's live jazz and blues every night until 2 a.m. Since the headliners start at 9 p.m., our advice is to skip the forgettable desserts, and finish your meal with a drink in the lounge where the musicians perform. There, a wall of iron scrollwork and ivy calls to mind the intricate porches of the French Quarter.

There are Southern touches in the dining room, too — plantation shutters, Big Easy chandeliers and a Mardi Gras-patterned carpet, loomed with confetti, beads and coins.

We ordered a round of Abita microbrews from New Orleans and appetizers that tasted as if they hailed from the same place. The smooth, shrimp-studded gumbo got its soul from a dark roux and authentic andouille sausage.

The menu warned that crispy pieces of fried alligator tail were chewy, but we found them manageable because they were cut so thinly. We dipped them into a sweet glaze, a cross between orange marmalade and horseradish sauce.

Our capable waiter suggested the Cajun quesadilla appetizer — tortilla wedges filled with spiced cream cheese, shrimp and crawfish. The fusion of flavors worked, helped by a zippy salsa garnish of corn, peppers and tomatoes.

That salsa is called maque choux, and we tried it in an entree served over rice. Grilled chicken cubes were tossed with a Cajun vegetable mix: fresh corn kernels, celery, red peppers, onions and tomatoes. We ordered ours with "New Orleans kick" rather than as "Maryland mild," and it had the perfect cayenne scorch for heat lovers.

The crawfish etouffee over rice was mild in contrast but had the nutty richness that comes from a good roux. Curled crawfish tails were coated in the brown gravy along with fat cuts of celery and green and red bell peppers.

Besides Cajun dishes and classics such as chicken Marsala and shrimp scampi, there's a full listing of hand-cut steaks on the menu. We tried the tender steak au poivre: two juicy tenderloins encrusted with cracked peppercorns on a satiny cushion of decadent brandy sauce. Instead of rice or a baked potato, we chose creamy "smashed" red-skin potatoes to go with the steak, and the same huge portion of steamed vegetables that came with our other dinners.

As for presentation of the dishes, the kitchen earned a star for its edible confetti — tiny bits of carrot and red cabbage that is the vegetable world's contribution to Mardi Gras.

*Kathryn Higham*

# Bill Bateman's Bistro

*7800 York Road, Towson • 410- 296-2737*
*Hours: Daily 11 a.m.-1 a.m.*
*Prices: $2.29-$12.95*
*Live music: No • Kid's menu: Yes • Waterfront views: No*
*Wheelchair access: Yes • Reservations: Not accepted •*
*Other locations: 1226 Bel Air Road, Bel Air • 410-879-7748*
*7620 German Hill Road, Dundalk • 410-282-7980*
*1803 Taylor Ave., Parkville • 410-668-7421*
*10101 Harford Road, Parkville • 410-665-4262*
*3101 Emmorton Road, Abingdon • 410-569-1366*

There's no magic to making it in the restaurant business. You just serve huge quantities of the food everybody knows you shouldn't eat, from loaded skins to ribs with fries to black bottom cheesecake. The more we hear we should be consuming a diet heavy on whole grains, vegetables and fruits, the more of us head for Bill Bateman's Bistro.

Not that you can't have a very nice salad at this college hangout/family restaurant/sports bar, but the closest most customers are going to get to a green vegetable is the celery sticks that come with the chicken wings.

Even though everybody knows a Buffalo wing dipped in blue cheese dressing has 8 trillion calories, people are lining up for the Bill Bateman version. On a Friday or Saturday night, the wait for a table can be as long as an hour and a half.

The dining rooms are so noisy you might as well give up any idea of talking and simply dive into the pile of wings, which are plump, fiery hot and deliciously greasy, with a generous amount of celery sticks and a thick blue cheese dressing to dip them in. We had the original wings, but there are 14 other choices, from "atomic" to "wings from hell."

Bateman knows that what sells well is food you can eat in your sweat clothes and dishes that cost under $10. The menu is a compendium of the '90s version of comfort food: quesadillas, hamburgers, fries with gravy, pizza.

Those pizzas are made with big, soft, bread-like crusts, topped with everything from seafood imperial to chili. I liked the comparatively modest "bianco," with ricotta cheese, lots of olive oil and garlic, broccoli florets and chopped fresh tomato.

Quesadillas also come in a variety of flavors. The 12-inch tortillas we tried were filled with melted cheese and sauteed onions with bits of grilled vegetables to add a little pizazz.

The baby back ribs were less interesting to me. They were fall-off-the-bone tender but had too much too-sweet barbecue sauce.

While nothing is very expensive here, it costs even less to eat on specials nights — all the wings you can eat on Mondays and half-price burgers on Sundays. This respect for the customer's pocketbook is the great drawing card of Bill Bateman's, and why everyone ends up here. That and the fact that it's fun food, the kind that makes your soul happy if not your bathroom scale.

*Elizabeth Large*

# The Black Olive

*814 S. Bond St., Fells Point • 410-276-7141*
*Hours: Open for dinner Tuesday through Sunday*
*Prices: Appetizers, $4-$8; entrees, $15-$32*
*Live music: No • Kid's menu: No • Waterfront views: No •*
*Wheelchair access: Yes • Reservations: Required on weekends*

The Black Olive is a rarity — a restaurant that doesn't try to do too much, but does what it does tastefully.

The eatery is nestled on a quiet block in Fells Point. The dining room, with its open kitchen in back, is deceptively simple and has lots of style. Tables are charmingly dressed in blue-and-white checked cloths. The waiter arranges a bowl of Greek olives on each one as carefully as he might place a vase of flowers. Brick walls painted white are hung with a few framed photographs; the wood floors are bare; ceiling fans revolve slowly. The look is fresh and very Mediterranean.

The Black Olive's menu and wine list have the same stylish simplicity as the setting. The Black Olive's selection of Greek wines offers customers a chance to explore. As for the menu, the house specialty is clearly whole grilled fish. Nine choices are listed; but expect only a few to be available any given night.

Judging from the whole red snapper, the fish is winningly fresh, with the smoky char setting off the firm, moist flesh beautifully. And the waiter fillets the fish for you tableside.

Try the superbly cleaned, deliciously plump mussels in the shell bathed in ouzo liqueur. Or a remarkable first course of charcoal-grilled portobello and oyster mushrooms with a buttery bit of grilled bread. (Attention is paid to the looks of each plate — a pretty garnish here, a careful arrangement of ingredients there.)

The Black Olive's equivalent of spanakopita is a vegetable pie made with flaky pastry and a zingy spinach filling. It's too dry for my taste, but the flavor is excellent.

Grilled lamb chops may be a special, but they aren't on the regular menu. Something called kleftico is. Tender cubes of marinated lamb and mushrooms are cooked in parchment with a mild sheep's cheese, which melts deliciously into the other ingredients. With it comes a fine couscous flavored with minced black olives and red pepper, and a winning concoction of zucchini and onions. Not so successful is the plain — and tasteless — couscous that accompanies the lamb.

All this assumes you haven't filled up on the irresistible bread, baked in the restaurant's brick oven. Order tzatziki, a tangy yogurt and cucumber dip, to eat with it. Brave souls can opt for the garlic-infused melitzanasalata, made with eggplant mashed with capers, olive oil and seasonings.

Finally, you must end your meal with the Black Olive's fruit plate. Ours consisted of juicy ripe chunks of mango, fat strawberries, blood-orange slices and a few plump blackberries. The baklava and banana nut cake, house-made to be sure and quite good, paled in comparison.

*Elizabeth Large*

# Blue Garden

*7523 Ritchie Highway, Glen Burnie • 410-761-1965*
*Hours: Open daily for lunch and dinner*
*Prices: Appetizers, $3.95-$8.95; entrees, $7.95-$24.95*
*Live music: No • Kid's menu: Yes • Waterfront views: No •*
*Wheelchair access: Yes • Reservations: Not accepted •*
*Credit cards: Diner's Club, MasterCard, Visa only*

The Blue Garden is a triple threat among Asian restaurants, specializing in Korean, Japanese and Chinese food, and handling each cuisine amazingly well.

Mr. and Mrs. Chong So have owned their restaurant on Ritchie Highway for over 16 years, serving mostly Chinese and Korean dishes. Recently, they've added a sushi bar and Korean barbecue tables, and expanded their menu to include more Korean and Japanese fare.

We sat in the front room of the Blue Garden, where tables are thick, lacquered slices of tree trunks, outfitted with stainless-steel grills for Korean barbecue. It turned out that we didn't get to use our grill, even though we ordered thinly sliced Korean barbecued beef. The dish was brought to our table already cooked, so all we had to do was wrap pieces of the tender, smoky-sweet meat in lettuce leaves along with jalapeno slices, garlic cloves and chili paste.

Noodles are outstanding at Blue Garden, and they're done many ways. We sampled them Japanese-style, with sauteed scallops and scallions in a delicate sauce. The thick, velvety strands were quite different from the springy, thin Chinese noodles. These were served plain in a large bowl, with a mahogany-dark pork and black bean sauce on the side.

Our other dinner came from the list of Korean chef specialties, an iron pot full of bubbling-hot, spicy seafood soup with shiitake slices, tofu and watercress. We only wished tough pieces of octopus hadn't been substituted for squid.

The octopus was better in a cold appetizer salad, dressed with a splash of vinegar. We picked up chewy pieces with our chopsticks and ate them along with Korean salads of bean sprouts, and watercress with ginger and sesame.

Man doo, Korean dumplings with pork and scallions, were equally good simmered in chicken broth with onions and carrots, and fried until they turned into golden puffs.

Among the Japanese starters on the menu, we chose greaseless shrimp tempura, served with an assortment of battered, fried vegetables, and the six-piece sushi platter, which included wonderfully fresh salmon, tuna and shrimp.

Service was attentive, although our waitress barely spoke English. Whenever we asked a question, Mrs. So or another waitress came over to help. But no one could tell us exactly what was in an exotic Korean salad of translucent slivers. Some sort of fish, we were told. Our imaginations wandered.

We also had fish for dessert, but we found out what kind before we ordered it — a fish-shaped wafer filled with red bean ice cream.

*Kathryn Higham*

# Bo Brooks

*5415 Belair Road, Gardenville • 410-488-8144*
*Hours: Open Monday-Friday for lunch; daily for dinner;*
*crabs served evenings only*
*Prices: Appetizers, $2.50-$12.95; entrees, $3.95-$15.95;*
*crabs, $20-$42 per dozen*
*Live music: No • Kid's menu: Yes • Waterfront views: No •*
*Wheelchair access: Yes • Reservations: Suggested for large parties •*
*Credit cards: Discover, MasterCard, Visa only*

Bo Brooks, serving steamed hard-shells for more than 30 years, satisfies all of Charm City's gastronomic rules for classic crab houses.

*Rule One: The best crab houses are not fancy.*

Bo Brooks scores on that front. The dining room is open and bright, like a cafeteria. There's lots of room to stretch out for serious crab eating. Plastic abounds, in the bright orange plastic chairs, molded plastic paneling and plastic buckets on the floor for shell overload. Tables are set in classic form, with brown paper, wooden mallets and plastic knives.

*Rule Two: At the best crab houses, the crabs are fresh, hot, and not too exorbitantly priced.*

Every time I've eaten at Bo Brooks, the crabs have been impressive, and this visit was no exception. We tried extra-large crabs from Texas for $34 a dozen. They were enormous, and heavy with sweet crab meat. Dumped off a plastic tray into the center of our table, they were almost too hot to handle at first. We've sampled more robust crab seasoning, but this mixture had enough heat and rock salt to keep us licking it off the shells.

*Rule Three: The best crab houses have at least a few side dishes worth eating.*

At Bo Brooks, it's the incredible cream of crab soup, a buttery cloud full of crab meat, and the freshly made chopped coleslaw, with just a touch of mayonnaise and sugar. In summer, I like an ear of Maryland sweet corn with my crabs, but in winter, I'll settle for the house salad, with crisp romaine, sliced radish and ribbons of carrot. Bracelet-sized onion rings are a specialty. Encased in heavy batter and fried golden, they felt as if they each weighed a pound.

*Rule Four: For dinner, stick to the crabs.*

That advice applies at Bo Brooks. Its fishy-tasting, dried-out fried oysters, and too-firm crab cakes don't deserve much attention. The baby back ribs were a surprise, though. The meat was so tender and the flavor so good, they deserved a better barbecue sauce.

That sauce also turned up in our barbecued shrimp appetizer, swamping tough shrimp, limp bacon and mozzarella.

As we expected, desserts aren't made by the staff. They're pretty simple and standard: dry, crumbly cheesecake; thick peanut butter pie. The best of the lot was the frozen Oreo pie, made with ice cream and cookie crumbs.

*Rule Five: As long as the crabs are good, diners leave happy.*

At Bo Brooks, we did.

*Kathryn Higham*

# Boomerang

*1110 S. Charles St., Federal Hill • 410-727-2333*
*Hours: Open daily 5 p.m. to 2 a.m.*
*Prices: Appetizers, $2.95-$8.50; entrees, $9.95-$21.95*
*Live music: No • Kid's menu: No • Waterfront views: No • Wheelchair access: Yes • Reservations: Accepted*

Remember that scene in "Crocodile Dundee" where Dundee fixes an authentic Australian meal for a woman (blackened alligator on a spit, yams, grilled slugs) and then says something like, "Actually, that stuff tastes terrible" and opens a can of chili for himself?

Well, you won't want to open a can of chili if you try the authentically ethnic food at Boomerang, Baltimore's new Australian pub. But you might want to order instead the Port Philip Bay fillet, a tender piece of beef as big as your fist, topped with fried oysters and a creamy red-pepper sauce.

I'm as adventuresome an eater as anyone; but there's the sweetest picture of a kangaroo on the menu, right near the kakadoo stew ("cubes of tender kangaroo and beef") and the Boomer fillet of kangaroo Polynesian. Still, a job is a job. I remind myself that as cute as little lambs are, there's nothing better than a loin lamb chop. Kangaroo, however, has the texture of chicken livers and none of the flavor — at least when it's fixed Polynesian style. Thumbs down.

The good news is that the other Aussie food is pretty decent. "Dishwasher soup" is a down-under version of French onion soup. Split pea soup with a meat pie floater is wonderfully smooth and flavorful. The meat pies are imported from Australia, our waiter tells us. To be authentic, we should open them up and pour ketchup in them. Noosa-style shrimp have a brown garlic sauce that's oddly reminiscent of Chinese food, but works well enough over pasta. And the shrimp are fine.

Still, what we enjoy most seems pretty American, like that gorgeous piece of beef. A first course of battered and fried artichoke hearts, served piping hot with butter sauce and a bit of grated cheese, is nothing short of spectacular. Oysters baked with spinach and finished with bearnaise also please us. Desserts are made in-house, the best one being a super bread pudding that's more custard than bread.

If all this sounds like more food than you might want, Boomerang does offer a separate light-fare menu; and there's plenty of bar food to be had.

But in spite of the kangaroo and other native food, what sets Boomerang apart from other bars in the area is the decor, which is eye-popping. The pub is in an empty bank building, with a high ceiling, huge windows and a mezzanine.

The walls are covered with extraordinary murals of the outback and the Great Barrier Reef. Giant boomerangs in festive colors separate tables on the mezzanine. Add to that wonderfully friendly service delivered in the best of all possible accents, mate, and you've got yourself a live one here.

*Elizabeth Large*

# The Brass Elephant

*924 N. Charles St., Mount Vernon • 410-547-8480*
*Hours: Open every night for dinner*
*Prices: Appetizers, $7-$9; main courses, $18-$28*
*Live music: No • Kid's menu: No • Waterfront views: No •*
*Wheelchair access: No • Reservations: Suggested*

I was struck by how exquisite the Brass Elephant's formal dining rooms are. Once an elegant townhouse, the restaurant seems to belong to a different era. The ornate double mantelpieces, carved woodwork, high ceilings, gold-framed mirrors and candlelit tables create a graceful setting for almost any occasion — from treating yourself to an evening out to getting engaged.

The Brass Elephant's menu has always been characterized as northern Italian. In Baltimore that seems to mean almost anything that doesn't involve a lot of red sauces and garlic. If I had to describe the menu, I'd say new American with an Italian grandmother standing in the background.

Appetizers range from a charming conceit like the escargot "cigars" to a dark, intense wild mushroom and asparagus soup filled with woodsy flavors. Those cigars are actually plump snails rolled in a crisp bit of phyllo pastry and sauced seductively with beurre blanc. A silky, buttery sauce also enhanced a remarkable concoction of portobello mushroom, spaghetti squash, lump crab meat, a bit of ham and tomato. A sampler of three pates made in-house is so good you'll be tempted to eat every bite and leave room for nothing else.

The two dishes people come back for, our waiter told us, are the filet mignon and the rack of lamb. The filet was everything he promised. Flavorful, butter-tender and rosy-centered, it was gently charred and had superb accompaniments: a dark, winy sauce; a savory bread pudding studded with dried cherries; baby carrots and slivers of red pepper. The lamb, alas, didn't live up to its billing. Although full of meaty flavor, it was served very rare instead of medium as ordered. But its timbale of wild rice and spinach was appealing.

As with our other dishes, the tuna with a burgundy shrimp sauce's accompaniments were as good as they were clever. In this case, herbed waffles added a savory bit of crunch while a "napoleon" of eggplant, spinach and squash provided a range of textures and tastes.

Until this point in the meal, the service was superb, with intelligent commentary, attentiveness and unobtrusiveness. Then things fell apart. Our up-till-then excellent waiter deposited dessert menus on our table as he raced by, and we didn't see him again until we finally complained.

Once we had given him our order, I could understand why it took so long to get our desserts to the table. (They were elaborate and beautiful.) But why we didn't get coffee mystified me. Oh well. The evening had been such a smashing success until then, it almost didn't matter.

*Elizabeth Large*

# Burke's Cafe

*Address: 36 Light St., downtown • 410-752-4189*
*Hours: Open daily for breakfast, lunch and dinner*
*Prices: Appetizers, $1.75-$16.75 (steamed shrimp); entrees, $3.55-$21.25*
*Live music: No • Kid's menu: Yes • Waterfront views: No •*
*Wheelchair access: Yes • Reservations: Accepted for large parties*

When a restaurant has been going strong for more than 60 years, it must be doing something right. At Burke's Cafe, it's the little things. Three-inch-wide onion rings and foot-long zucchini spears that are fried to a golden crisp, for instance.

We got the feeling that the kitchen has been doing things the old-fashioned way since the doors opened in 1934.

There are medieval touches in the dark, wood-paneled restaurant, like the diamond-pattern stained-glass windows and beamed ceiling. Don't get the idea that this is upscale dining, though. Burke's is a bar-restaurant with Formica-topped tables and high-backed booths.

It's also a restaurant with a menu that runs the gamut from grilled frankfurters to flounder with crab imperial. Start with a basket of fried zucchini and Burke's famous onion rings. Greaseless, crunchy-edged and golden, they are worth every calorie. We wished we had ordered the homemade potato chips, too, after seeing them being devoured at a nearby table. This restaurant knows how to fry.

Burke's potato pancakes — served with homemade cinnamon applesauce or sour beef — are also greaseless. With a creamy texture and soft, golden skin, they tasted almost as light as buttermilk pancakes. On our next visit, we'll try them with the sour beef, an old-time Baltimore favorite.

A lot of what we tried at Burke's had a homey appeal. The beef stew, in a bright-red tomato gravy, was full of long cuts of carrot and celery, and nearly whole pared potatoes. The home-style meatloaf featured two enormous slabs served as an open-faced sandwich on white bread. Made with beef and veal, the meatloaf was just this side of dry, but it was moistened with lots of ruby-colored Creole sauce.

The jumbo lump crab cake is a good choice at Burke's. It had a dose of hot, dry mustard that contrasted nicely with the sweet lumps of crab. That made for an assertive flavor that would stand up well under a bun.

Don't bother with chewy clams casino made with incinerated bacon, however, or giant fried chicken sticks wrapped in mozzarella. Skip the overdone baked salmon and the steaks, also. Our strip steak had a tough exterior, as if it had been pan-fried. A friend swears by Burke's strip-steak sandwich, though, which he calls the best deal in Baltimore.

Be sure to save room for warm cinnamon apples and ice cream, double chocolate layer cake or the nut-encrusted rum cake. This bundt cake was so moist and light, so balanced in its flavors, it made us want to take some home. We could have, too. Burke's sells whole rum cakes for $22.

*Kathryn Higham*

# Cactus Willies

*1125 Cromwell Bridge Road, Towson • 410-321-9833*
*Hours: Open Monday through Friday for dinner, Saturday and Sunday for lunch and dinner*
*Prices: Buffet $7.49 for adults; 45 cents times the age of the child for children ages 3-12; $6.99 for seniors over 60*
*Live music: No • Kid's menu: No • Waterfront views: No • Wheelchair access: Yes • Reservations: Accepted*

Some people favor quantity over quality. Cactus Willies is the place for them — an all-you-can-eat buffet for only $7.49 a person. That's $7.49 for all the steak you want, all the barbecued, baked or fried chicken, all the fried or broiled fish, vegetables, potatoes, stuffing, salads of every kind, breads and pies and ... well, you get the idea.

On a hilltop above Cromwell Bridge Road, Cactus Willies is part of a chain of restaurants owned by managing partners Robert Katz and Brett Austin. Their Towson restaurant is expansive and bright, dotted with desert gardens of plastic cacti. A staff of servers moves briskly throughout, bringing soda and coffee refills.

Don't expect haute cuisine — this is cafeteria food. What you'll find here that you won't find in most cafeterias, though, is steak. Cooked on a grill right in front of us, the small sirloins were cut to a quarter-inch thickness. They were surprisingly good for being that thin — tender, flavorful and faintly smoky. The steaks we tried were all done medium-well.

Our advice is to build your meal around the steak or chicken. We sampled both the baked chicken, which remained moist under its bronzed skin, and the fried, which was a little dry but admirably greaseless.

Skip the instant mashed potatoes, the sweet, mushy stuffing, the lumpy macaroni and cheese, the overcooked vegetable medleys. A baked potato or yam wrapped in foil is a safer choice. If you're lucky, there will be at least one vegetable that hasn't lost its bite. For us, it was the cabbage cooked with sliced carrots and butter.

No buffet would be complete without a salad bar. The bins are filled with iceberg lettuce and standard toppers. All looked fresh and well-maintained. There also are prepared salads and two kinds of soup. The Maryland crab soup should have been billed as tomato-vegetable.

There's hardly room to list everything that's on the buffet: the good (sliced ham, barbecued ribs, coleslaw); the bad (fried cod, sweet pizza, dried-out fettuccine); and the ugly (tacos and nachos). For dessert, there's soft-serve ice cream, sheet cakes cut into manageable squares, pies and, our favorite, moist bread pudding with rum sauce.

Yes, Cactus Willies is a glutton's paradise, where even a dozen trips to the buffet won't turn a single head.

*Kathryn Higham*

# Cafe Isis

*12240 Tullamore Road, Timonium • 410-666-4888*
*Hours: Open daily for lunch and dinner*
*Prices: Appetizers, $2-$7.95; entrees, $4.95-$14.95. No liquor license; bring your own beer or wine*
*Live music: Weekend nights • Kid's menu: Yes • Waterfront views: No •*
*Wheelchair access: Yes • Reservations: Suggested •*
*Credit cards: American Express, MasterCard, Visa only*

Egyptian pyramids and pizzas may seem like an odd duo, but they've been combined at Cafe Isis in Timonium, where Mediterranean pizza is the specialty. The Egyptian-temple decor looks like a backdrop for Cleopatra, with honey-colored blocks scaling the walls, and a border of faded hieroglyphics.

From curried shrimp to taco beef, there are almost three dozen varieties of Mediterranean pizza here, cooked in the beehive-shaped wood-burning oven that's open to view. The pizza is made on what is essentially a large pita bread crust. If you're a fan of thick, chewy crusts, you may not appreciate the fact that this crust is soft and thin, speckled underneath with toasty patches of brown.

We avoided the more unusual pizza selections and chose the Osiris, with roasted eggplant and red peppers, button mushrooms, pesto, mozzarella and feta. It was a little on the bland side. We wondered why the wood-fired oven hadn't added more flavor. We also expected more flavor from the lamb kebab casserole, one of Cafe Isis' Middle Eastern specialties. The big cubes of lamb were tender, though, served on basmati rice with nutty tahini sauce, slivered almonds and roasted onions, mushrooms and green peppers. A fresh salad of chopped romaine, carrots, cucumbers and other vegetables was also tucked into the oval casserole.

Pasta is not a good choice here, if the tandoori chicken fettuccine is any indication. The neon pink sauce tasted bland. The menu promised curry, walnuts, garlic and tandoori spices, but the sauce delivered none that we could detect.

Not everything was disappointing. The barbecued chicken sandwich was one of the best I've ever had — a Mediterranean re-creation of an American classic. Tender chicken breast fillets topped with a judicious amount of barbecue sauce and red onions filled two halves of a giant pita. Crisp-coated curly fries and the house chopped salad were served alongside.

For appetizers, skip the Middle Eastern scampi, and split the combination platter with friends. It has a little of everything: sesame-capped falafel patties, rice-stuffed grape leaves and chopped salad, along with airy, lemon-spiked hummus, a pink puree of fava beans, and the most flavorful eggplant baba ghannouj in memory.

Service was at first vigilant, less so later on. Our waiter did ask the kitchen to make Turkish coffee especially for us. The robust brew went well with a pyramid of simple chocolate cake and butter cream, a Middle Eastern custard topped with curly wheat pastry, and a syrup-soaked cornmeal cake called komasa.

*Kathryn Higham*

# Cafe Madrid

*505 S. Broadway, Fells Point • 410-276-7700*
*Hours: Open every day for dinner*
*Prices: Appetizers, $4.95-$10; entrees, $13.75-$23.95*
*Live music: No • Kid's menu: No • Waterfront views: No •*
*Wheelchair access: No • Reservations: Suggested*

When I first heard about the re-opening of the Tio Pepe-wannabe Madrid as the Cafe Madrid, I was skeptical. But dinner there won me over — unlike the original Madrid, Cafe Madrid isn't trying to be anything else but a good Spanish restaurant in its own right. And for the most part, it succeeds.

The romantic dining room has a few Spanish touches. Dark wood paneling, deep green wallpaper, an antique sideboard, sconces and candlelight give it a charming period air.

The Cafe Madrid's specialty is tapas. Could they bring us a selection? Yes, they could. Dishes begin to appear: first, a cold plate of delicious little squares of potato-based frittata, white asparagus, tomatoes, olives and hearts of palm in vinaigrette. Yum. Then small hot dishes, each better than the last: plump shrimp in an aromatic garlic sauce; dainty meatballs with an unusual and very good mint sauce; tender mussels in garlic, wine and parsley; slices of chorizo with an enticing tomato-based sauce; and artichoke hearts cooked with onion and sherry.

How about a veal chop for our main course? "I will fix you the best veal chop in America!" says Chef Pepe with boundless enthusiasm. Well, you can't turn that down, even though it's not on the menu and we can only guess they won't be giving it away. And it is a very fine veal chop, tender and pink with sauteed mushrooms and a dark, complex sauce.

But the star of the show is cazuela pescador — a medley of shrimp, calamari, scallops and tender chunks of fish in a blush-pink sauce as delicate as it is rich. Its shallow white bowl is garnished with paper-thin slices of pale green cucumber, making the dish as beautiful as it is good.

Roast duck is decent enough, but it doesn't have the wonderful crisp skin you sometimes get. The flavorful orange-cognac sauce, though, almost makes up for the duck's flaws.

Side dishes seem to be an afterthought. Neither the rice nor the mixed vegetables cooked with potatoes interests us.

Cafe Madrid has flaming baked Alaska for two — the sort of dessert that this evening should end with. But we weren't ready to commit ourselves at the beginning of the meal, and it must be ordered in advance. Instead, our waiter brings us a dessert sampler with custard and pieces of roll cake and a fabulous bread pudding made with oranges and orange liqueur.

Needless to say, we spend a bit of money here. More than a bit. But the good thing about the Cafe Madrid is that you don't have to. A selection of tapas, bread and a bottle of wine would be an excellent light meal — more than enough to satisfy most people if they weren't starving.

*Elizabeth Large*

# Cafe Normandie

*185 Main St., Annapolis • 410-263-3382*
*Hours: Open every day for breakfast, lunch and dinner*
*Prices: Appetizers, $3.75-$8.75; entrees, $7.25-$22.95*
*Live music: No • Kid's menu: Yes • Waterfront views: No •*
*Wheelchair access: No • Reservations: Suggested*

Annapolis' favorite French bistro, Cafe Normandie, is so warm and cozy and full of people having a good time that no one seems to notice how erratic the food is. But then at these prices, even a hardened food critic can afford to be forgiving.

If you like cozy, you'll love the lace curtains, the beamed ceiling, the pretty little bar in front, the center fireplace, the snug booths. If you like friendly, you'll enjoy the warm-hearted staff and the good-natured customers crowded in front waiting for a table.

If you like cheap, you'll make a dinner on the chicken and mushroom crepe and a small salad for $8.25. Or the charcuterie plate ($6.50) and bread ($1 extra) with a glass of wine or a beer. This includes a couple of kinds of European sausages; a delicious, rough-textured pate made on the premises; and a suave duck-liver mousse. All on enough lettuce with grated carrots to qualify as a salad.

Not quite enough for a meal? Add a bowl of smooth tomato bisque with lump crab meat. Or have a salad with the cafe's delicious blackened shrimp on top.

For those who want more than bistro food, Cafe Normandie had a chef's special for $22.95 the night we were there, which included a filet mignon, a small fillet of salmon, a fat little crab cake — almost all lump crab meat — and some shrimp. Pretty impressive. Too bad the salmon had a blueberry sauce better suited for cheesecake; the rest of it was quite good.

Then things started to go downhill. Beef burgundy over linguine was a generous, full-flavored meal for $14.75. But as the waitress pointed out when she placed the dish on the table, the kitchen had made a mistake and put the stew over rice instead of the promised homemade pasta.

Veal portobello with a dark, intense sauce was simply a bad idea. The mushrooms and sauce overwhelmed the meat. A crepe Annapolis filled with sea scallops, bits of shrimp, mushrooms and a thick lobster sauce was too heavy for my taste.

Crepes are supposedly a specialty, but I wasn't any happier with a crepe aux fraises for dessert than I was with the entree crepe. The pancake itself was fine, but the filling consisted of mounds of whipped cream with only four strawberries.

The kitchen got back on track with profiteroles au chocolat — tender cream puffs filled with ice cream and drizzled with chocolate sauce. But the piece de resistance was a slice of freshly baked tarte Tatin, with tender, short pastry and warm caramelized apples. Eat this and die happy.

*Elizabeth Large*

# Cafe Pangea

*4007 Falls Road, Hampden • 410-662-0500*
*Hours: Open Tuesday through Saturday for lunch and dinner,*
  *Sunday for brunch*
*Prices: Entrees vary from week to week, $8-$19*
*Live music: No • Kid's menu: No • Waterfront views: No •*
*Wheelchair access: No • Reservations: Suggested*

The Cafe Pangea made news when it opened because it was Baltimore's first Internet coffee and wine bar.

Hampden had never seen anything like it. The food, which played second fiddle to the computers, consisted of some Italian panini (sandwiches), a couple of salads, desserts from Vaccaro's. Now, the computers languish on top of carved mantels, untouched for the most part, while Cafe Pangea has become known for its good casual fare and hip surroundings.

The computers may be gathering dust, but Cafe Pangea has a new young chef and a real dinner menu. It may be that sandwiches will always be the best seller here. It's quite a switch for customers to start paying $15 for an entree. But judging from our dinner, the food is worth it.

Customers also have the pleasure of chic contemporary surroundings, a surprising contrast to the Victorian-gingerbread exterior of the white clapboard house. The dining room is all light wood, track lighting and art from La Terra.

Cafe Pangea doesn't have much in the way of appetizers, but you could start with a homemade soup of the day, like the Italian wedding soup with a fine homemade broth, tender pasta and fresh greens. We also had a mesclun-mix salad with a good balsamic vinaigrette in two versions: one with Gorgonzola cheese, yellow raisins and walnuts; the other with feta, kalamata olives and plum tomatoes. Both were fine.

The dinner menu is quite limited, usually four entrees and two sandwiches; we liked everything we tried. A fat beef fillet, full of meaty flavor and cooked rosy rare as ordered, towered over a crisp round of toast. Decorating its plate were excellent mashed potatoes and thin curls of zucchini.

Curried crab is apparently a staple at Cafe Pangea, and deservedly so. The dish consisted of lumps of crab meat baked in a rich, creamy sauce just touched with exotic spices. A small green salad was served on the side.

Baby coho salmon, fresh and cooked just long enough, had a crust of sliced potatoes and a zingy watercress sauce drizzled on top. The skin was kept on to keep the fish moist.

Cafe Pangea has various desserts, each richer than the last, like a chocolate turtle tart made with cashews, and a banana cake iced with thick chocolate. Both were good. Still, it would be nice to have at least one lighter choice.

And although everyone was pleasant, there's no getting around the fact that the wait staff had a laid-back attitude. It's just right for a coffee bar but not a restaurant, especially when a 20 percent tip is added to checks for parties of six or more.

*Elizabeth Large*

# Cafe Troia

*28 W. Allegheny Ave., Towson • 410-337-0133*
*Hours: Open Monday through Friday for lunch, every day for dinner*
*Prices: Appetizers, $5-$10.50; entrees, $9-$22.*
*Live music: No • Kid's menu: No • Waterfront views: No •*
*Wheelchair access: Yes • Reservations: Suggested*

Good restaurants have personalities all their own. If I tell you that Cafe Troia is an Italian restaurant, don't have any preconceptions. It's not like other Italian restaurants.

Cafe Troia is just that. A cafe. In spite of having three dining rooms and a sophisticated, expensive menu, it seems homey and unprepossessing — very much the neighborhood place to eat. Customers on both sides of us were regulars; they greeted our waiter by name.

So it comes as no surprise that Nonna's chicken soup is the zuppa del giorno. This is a lovely, fragile chicken soup: a soothing, homemade broth with snippets of white-meat chicken, rice and bits of carrot for color. Nonna is owner Gino Troia's mother — what could be homier?

But then what do you make of carpaccio di pesce spada? It's a spectacular composition of fresh arugula leaves draped with translucently thin slices of raw swordfish. Black caviar and the crunch of pine nuts are sensational additions, and the light, lemony dressing ties the ingredients together beautifully. Hardly home-style cooking.

Although Cafe Troia has some formal dinners, what they do best are the bistro dishes — not elaborate but relying on quality ingredients and a deft hand. These might be plump mussels served in an invigorating broth of white wine and tomato, with slices of grilled bread tucked around them. Or pastas with sauces like a fresh-tasting tomato and pancetta.

You could come here for supper and share a sampler of Troia's antipasti with your friends. With the cafe's good rolls and a glass of wine, it's a meal in itself. The plate might include thin slices of grilled eggplant, prosciutto, roasted sweet peppers and olives, fresh mozzarella, ruby-red plum tomatoes and creamy goat cheese.

If you do want something more elaborate, Cafe Troia's osso bucco captures the essence of the place: comforting peasant food reinvented with style. The veal shanks, meaty and flavorful, are winningly sauced. The accompaniment might be polenta or fresh vegetables like cauliflower with raisins and olives (a happy combination of sweet and salt) or the first tender-crisp asparagus of spring.

If there are any disappointments to be had here, they would be the desserts. Not that the tiramisu isn't perfectly presentable; it simply isn't any better or worse than other tiramisus. A homemade apple tart was heavier than you might expect, given the subtlety of the rest of the food.

If you haven't been, the Troia is worth a visit. Our meal was a solid winner.

*Elizabeth Large*

# California Pizza Kitchen

*Pratt Street Pavilion, Harborplace • 410-783-9339*
*Hours: Open every day for lunch and dinner*
*Prices: Appetizers, $2.95-$5.95; entrees, $7.95-$10.95*
*Live music: No • Kid's menu: Yes • Waterfront views: Yes •*
*Wheelchair access: Yes • Reservations: No*
*Other locations: Yes (national chain)*

Amidst all the theme restaurants in the harbor area, California Pizza Kitchen seems oddly adult. The attractions are decent food, good service, moderate prices and a sleek interior.

The pizza here is different from the traditional thin, crisp crust with tomato sauce, mozzarella and Italian toppings. Try not to compare it to the pizza you're used to, and you'll enjoy the soft, yeasty, slightly sweet crust, which is a good vehicle for the toppings. They range from pleasantly weird (barbecued chicken) to totally bizarro (hoisin duck portobello).

We ordered the BLT pizza the waitress recommended. That was wild and crazy enough. Think of it as fresh tomatoes and crisp bacon baked into the warm, soft, yeasty crust. Chilled chopped iceberg tossed with mayonnaise is piled on top. Cheese is not part of the equation. Somehow it works.

The chain's most popular selection is the barbecued chicken pizza. The toppings are slices of barbecued chicken, sliced red onions and smoked Gouda sparked with cilantro. Keep telling yourself, "It's not pizza," and you'll love it.

If you don't want goat cheese pizza, California Pizza Kitchen has introduced two new varieties. These innovations involve ingredients like tomatoes, mozzarella cheese, Parmesan, basil and garlic. Yes, the same kitchen that brings you tandoori chicken pizza now has two "Traditional Italian Pizzas."

You don't have to have pizza at California Pizza Kitchen, but it's a good idea. The "Original Chopped" entree salad features salami, cheese, roast turkey, tomatoes and a lot of chopped iceberg. Not bad, just not very interesting. Kung pao spaghetti with shrimp had lots of heat but not much else.

First courses, though, were as successful as our pizzas. "Tuscan hummus" might disappoint if you're expecting hummus, but why should you? The smooth puree of white beans flavored with sesame, garlic and lemon had fresh chopped tomatoes on top and warm pita bread to spread it on.

If you feel like soup, get the "Two in a Bowl." The yin and yang of the white potato leek next to a blush-pink Southwestern tomato and corn tortilla soup was beautiful. The soups tasted great together, too. Best of all our first courses, though, were fragile won ton dumplings filled with sesame ginger chicken, delicious and also beautifully presented.

California Pizza Kitchen has rich chocolate, ice cream and whipped cream desserts, plus area favorites like apple crisp with ice cream and Key lime pie with whipped cream. Management knows that people may put up with fusion cuisine in pizza, but when you're talking dessert, it better be familiar.

*Elizabeth Large*

# Candle Light Inn

*1835 Frederick Road, Catonsville • 410-788-6076*
*Hours: Open Mondays - Saturdays for lunch and dinner,*
*Sundays for dinner only*
*Prices: Appetizers, $4.25-$17.95; entrees, $17 to $25*
*Live music: Thursdays and Saturdays, spring through fall •*
*Kid's menu: No • Waterfront views: No • Wheelchair access: Yes •*
*Reservations: Suggested for large parties*

To me, the Candle Light Inn's greatest drawing card is its dining-room-size gazebo where you can have a formal dinner outside. It's surrounded by trees and plants, flowering impatiens and azaleas. Ceiling fans keep the heat and bugs away.

Indoors, you can choose from any number of pleasant, old-fashioned rooms. They're more formally set up than the deck, with cloth napery and candles. The good-natured, attentive staff is among the nicest I've run into. However, the food is too uneven to recommend without qualification.

If I went again, I'd order crab in any of its various forms. A hot seafood antipasto featured four mushroom caps piled high with lumps of crab meat in a creamy imperial sauce. I would skip the gritty clams casino first course. Luckily the sauteed scallops and shrimp were perfectly cooked, buttery and tender, so there was more than enough for a first course. We also tried the shrimp bisque. Like several of our choices it wasn't bad — hot, thick but not too thick, generous with shrimp. It's just that you might want more than not bad for the money.

With a bit more attention to detail, this could be a very good restaurant. For example, the veal Oscar. The veal was tender and white, but tasted poached rather than sauteed — which would have been OK if it hadn't been dredged in flour. The fresh asparagus on top was cooked to tender crispness, and lump crab meat had been applied lavishly. Its bearnaise sauce, however, had curdled. Fresh tuna Cajun style had the perfect balance of spices— zingy but not overpowering the fish. Alas, it was cooked to the point of dryness. Stuffed shrimp could have stolen the show. They had been generously stuffed with good crab imperial. Too bad they, too, were overcooked.

Attention is paid to the vegetables here. Broccoli was steamed tender, highly seasoned zucchini was still slightly crisp on the edges. But attention isn't paid to everything: Our inedible butter had taken on odors from elsewhere.

The desserts we had were made by Renaissance Pastries. Tiramisu comes in cake form. A triple chocolate mousse cake is the perfect remedy for massive chocolate withdrawal. The only dud: a cheesecake that was properly creamy and rich and had gorgeous strawberries, but was topped with artificial whipped cream and thick, sweet strawberry sauce.

In spite of food that sometimes faltered, we ended up having a good time. The setting is so pleasant, and the staff went out of its way to make sure we were happy. And when the owner came around at the end and asked how the meal was, you got the feeling he really cared.

*Elizabeth Large*

# Capitol City Brewing Company

*Light Street Pavilion, Harborplace • 410-539-PINT*
*Hours: Open every day for lunch and dinner*
*Prices: Appetizers, $3.50-$7.95; entrees, $12.95-$14.95*
*Live music: No • Kid's menu: Yes • Waterfront views: Yes •*
*Wheelchair access: Yes • Reservations: Accepted for large parties*
*Other locations: 1100 New York Ave., N.W., Washington • 202-628-2222*
*7735 Old Georgetown Road, Bethesda • 301-652-2282*
*1612 U St., N.W., No. 400, Washington • 202-232-6629*
*2 Massachusetts Ave N.E., Washington • 202-842-2337*
*2700 S Quincy St., Arlington • 703-578-3888*

The Capitol City Brewing Company is for serious beer drinkers. I'm not a beer drinker, so I can't give you an informed opinion about whether the Pale Rider Ale is better than the Golden Boy Kolsch. I can tell you that there are a lot of pipes, copper barrels and Escher-like stairs leading to industrial-looking spaces where serious brewing stuff seems to be going on.

Meanwhile, on the ground floor is the restaurant space, with red leather-look booths and tables with wooden chairs near a large bar. There are also 48 outdoor tables.

Capitol City has a brew-pub menu for the most part, with food that would go well with different styles of beer. This starts with the bread basket, which is filled with hot soft pretzels and a horseradish-mustard dipping sauce.

The food is imaginative for a brew pub, but not all of it works. An appetizer of smoked chicken quesadillas would have been delicious, but it was too fiery. Likewise, the Thai chicken salad had good greens, snow peas, shiitakes, red onions and peanuts, but its grilled chicken was overcooked and the dressing was too spicy for my daughter to eat.

A starter of fried chicken fingers coated with cornflake crumbs was moist, crunchy and deliciously greasy. Even better were the jalapeno poppers, the deep-fried peppers filled with hot, melting cream cheese. If you want something somewhat healthier, there's a "chef's catch." This evening it was a thick, snowy fillet of catfish pan-fried in a golden cornmeal batter. Yellow rice and a vegetable medley of broccoli, squash and cauliflower rounded out the plate.

Capitol City Brewing Company has serious brew-pub food, like a sausage platter with sauerkraut. Even this has a gourmet twist; the locally made sausages are grilled and come in three "flavors": duck, bratwurst and Thai chicken.

Still, the dish didn't taste markedly different from the classic sausage and sauerkraut. The roasted peppers are a great accompaniment; the apple chutney is just so-so.

There's no reason to expect a brewery to have great desserts, so we weren't surprised that the creme brulee was gummy and the peanut butter mousse pie was somewhat tasteless. But I was impressed by the size of the slice — it was 6 inches high and looked like a quarter of the pie.

*Elizabeth Large*

# Capriccio

*846 Fawn St., Little Italy • 410-685-2710*
*Hours: Open every day for lunch and dinner*
*Prices (on regular menu): Appetizers, $5.95-$10.50; entrees, $14.95-$22.95*
*Live music: No • Kid's menu: No • Waterfront views: No •*
*Wheelchair access: No • Reservations: Suggested*

Just to warn you up front: Capriccio's daily specials, recited in loving detail by your waiter except for the prices, will cost you almost double what most of the regular menu does.

So be sure that you ask how much that special seafood ravioli appetizer is ($10.95), or the swordfish ($30) or the veal tenderloin ($31). And as for desserts, also not on the regular menu, strawberries zabaglione will set you back $7.50 and cherries jubilee for one, $6.50.

If you do stick to the regular menu, you can eat well and happily for about what it costs at other Little Italy restaurants. And as long as you know what you're paying for the specials, you can eat well and happily with them, too.

This is a nice, cozy little restaurant with decent food, not quite the chic eatery it would like to be. Chic eateries don't, for instance, put the olive oil for dipping bread in a sherbet glass with a spoon. And a restaurant that serves sides of red-sauced spaghetti with entrees shouldn't also be offering champagne sorbet between courses.

But forget such minor details and focus on the complimentary and tasty hors d'oeuvre of green beans and potatoes marinated in vinaigrette and decorated with fragrant basil leaves. Enjoy the straciatella soup made with fresh spinach and an incredibly rich homemade chicken broth.

True, a first course of carpaccio was mighty skimpy on raw beef and overloaded with caponata (eggplant salad) and pecorino Romano cheese. But what there was was delicious. And if you get past the price of the seafood ravioli, you'll love the fresh shellfish, tender pasta and pink cream sauce.

The enormous piece of veal tenderloin with portobello mushrooms in a dark and fragrant wine sauce was a fine dish, although I could have done without the couple of pieces of boiled turnip that accompanied it.

But no one could fault the baby asparagus with hollandaise that came with the swordfish. And the swordfish itself was spectacular: fresh as could be, moist and tender. Too bad it was dressed with chopped raw onion as well as capers.

Capriccio's house salad is an extravagant concoction of Boston lettuce, radicchio, carrots, tomatoes, olives and pepperoncini — a meal-in-itself sort of salad. For something simpler, you might try the arugula and sliced mushrooms.

But simple is simply not an option for dessert. How often do you get table-side cooking these days, with a tuxedoed waiter preparing cherries jubilee or peach flambe while you watch? Done with flames and flourishes, dessert alone is worth the price of admission.

*Elizabeth Large*

# Carney Crab House

*2014 E. Joppa Road, Parkville • 410-665-5000*
*Hours: Open daily for lunch and dinner*
*Prices: Appetizers, $3.95-$9.95; entrees, $3.95-$35.95*
*Live music: No • Kid's menu: Yes • Waterfront views: No •*
*Wheelchair access: Yes • Reservations: Accepted*

The Carney Crab House has been serving steamed crabs and seafood since 1961. Longevity counts for a lot in this business, but our experience was disappointing.

The decor didn't look as if it had changed in the three decades Carney's has been open, which isn't necessarily a bad thing in a crab house. It's done in the Baltimore-basement style, with mint green walls, lots of paneling and kitschy knickknacks.

Looking around the large upstairs dining room, we found most patrons were busily snapping claws, tapping away with wooden mallets and happily extracting one of the pleasures of summer in Baltimore. Downstairs, there were two more rooms devoted to cracking crabs.

We tried the large crabs, doused in a coating of hot spice. The mixture was a blend of cayenne, black pepper and salt more than anything resembling Old Bay. It was a nice change — extra hot and not too salty. Compared to the rest of our meal, they were standouts, even though they were brought to our table lukewarm.

That might have been the fault of our waitress, though, and not the kitchen. In fairness, it was her first week on the job, and she seemed a bit nervous. Food arrived before silverware, and dessert arrived while dirty dishes were still on the table.

She did go to bat for us over an order of baked clams, though. When the chef told her the restaurant didn't serve them, she showed him the menu. "He told me these were baked," she said as she presented us with six large, slightly rubbery clams. They were unlike any baked clams we had ever seen. They came with no breading or topping, just some butter-flavored oil on the side.

It set the tone for the rest of our meal. Shrimp bisque was thick with too much flour and had bits of crab cartilage. The Buffalo wings were limp and covered in a thick puddle of sweet barbecue sauce. The Caesar salad would have been fine if there was about a head more romaine, it was so drenched in dressing. Carney's "famous" all-lump crab cakes had a glue-like consistency and hadn't been broiled enough. The strip steak was underdone, a bit gristly and essentially flavorless.

One surprise was a basket of hot, fresh rolls, all golden and tasting homemade. Did they come from the same kitchen?

If it sounds like I'm being too hard on Carney's, consider its prices. When you charge $22.95 for gluey crab cakes, or $14.95 for shrimp Creole and it tastes like a can of whole stewed tomatoes that has been heated over rice, you deserve all the criticism you get.

*Kathryn Higham*

# Carrabba's Italian Grill

*Long Gate Shopping Center, Ellicott City • 410-461-5200*
*Hours: Open every day for dinner, brunch Sunday*
*Prices: Appetizers, $4.95-$7.95; entrees, $8.95-$18.95*
*Live music: No • Kid's menu: Yes • Waterfront views: No •*
*Wheelchair access: Yes • Reservations: No*
*Other locations: Yes (national chain)*

Carrabba's happens to be the companion chain to the Outback Steak House, probably the most popular steak house in America, maybe the world. But in spite of that, Carrabba's seems to be doing very well indeed.

And there's a reason that's so. Carrabba's has an almost perfect balance of decent food and decent prices. The large but somehow cozy dining room, with its ceiling fans and open kitchen, has a pleasant Mediterranean feel to it — not particularly memorable, but tastefully done in warm, earthy colors.

It's a place to bring kids, and if you're here for a birthday — as several tables usually are — the staff sings "Happy Birthday" in Italian. It's not the most restful place for a meal. Also, the kitchen is churning out a lot of food in a hurry, so the chicken, say, might be a bit overcooked and the ravioli may not be arranged on the plate with much style.

Having said all that, the food at Carrabba's is still very good for the price. The fish of the day was a large piece of fresh salmon with a delicate, lemony sauce. The Italian salad has fresh romaine, summer tomatoes and a four-star vinaigrette.

The calamari looked a little pallid, but the squid was tender and its batter light, crisp and grease-free. The dipping sauce is a fresh-tasting, chunky marinara. Soft, fresh fried mozzarella is also a winner.

The boneless chicken breast was a bit dry, but it had the benefit of a brightly flavored Marsala sauce studded with mushrooms and prosciutto. The fettuccine Alfredo looked like noodles in a heavy sauce, which it is, but tastes pretty good.

Tender half-moon ravioli, called mezzaluna, are stuffed with minced chicken, ricotta and spinach, and served with a creamy, tomato-pink sauce. A plate of these gets a bit monotonous; you'd do better to share with someone.

What doesn't work here? A shrimp appetizer has a thick, almost bitter lemon-garlic sauce and more pieces of garlic bread than shrimp. Bruschetta are too much like melted cheese sandwiches with tomato or mushroom toppings and not enough like an appetizer.

A dessert of ice cream with caramel sauce and "roasted cinnamon rum pecans" was oddly tasteless. But other desserts will make you happy, like a butter cake with fruit and whipped cream and a soft tiramisu with hot fudge sauce (overkill, yes, but good).

As moderately priced chain restaurants go, Carrabba's is top of the line. Unless you want small and personal, I can't suggest any better place to take the kids and have a decent, traditional Italian meal.

*Elizabeth Large*

# Carrol's Creek

*410 Severn Ave., Annapolis • 410-263-8102*
*Hours: Open every day for lunch and dinner, brunch Sunday*
*Prices: Appetizers, $3.95-$8.95; entrees, $13.95-$23.95*
*Live music: No • Kid's menu: No • Waterfront views: Yes •*
*Wheelchair access: Yes • Reservations: No*

Carrol's Creek has the potential to be that Holy Grail for visitors to a waterfront town, a great seafood restaurant.

It's got all the ingredients, starting with a fine location right on the water. Every seat in the main dining room has a scenic view of Spa Creek. The menu isn't long, but it has a good balance of local seafood dishes and more exotic ones. The fish is beautifully fresh, the kitchen's New American creations imaginative without crossing the line into strange. A thoughtful wine list complements the mostly seafood menu.

The dining room is casual. At night the lights are romantically low, fresh flowers grace each polished wood table, the wineglasses gleam. The setting feels pleasantly formal, without any of the stuffiness of formality.

Alas, our meal subtly missed the mark. Take the Maryland cream of crab soup. It had a wonderful flavor and lumps of crab, but was so thick it was like eating a bowl of cream gravy.

We ordered three different fish prepared three different ways — rockfish, swordfish and red snapper. All were straight-from-the-water fresh, but so overcooked they were dry. Sad, because each was potentially so good. The red snapper had a lovely red pepper coulis and delicious couscous. The swordfish's olive, mushroom and artichoke salad contrasted pleasingly with basmati rice. Perfectly cooked julienne vegetables and a delicate butter sauce complemented the rockfish.

A crab cake platter was disappointing as well. The two small, perfectly seasoned crab cakes rested on fried polenta, crisp on the outside, hot and soft inside. Excellent. But for $23.95, you expect lumps of crab in your crab cakes.

Only with the house specialty, Texas barbecued shrimp, did the kitchen really strut its stuff. One side of the plate was painted in a curve with a dark, intense barbecue sauce. Fat pink shrimp wrapped in char-grilled bacon were placed on top. The other side was filled in with pale green cucumber salad. The tangy sweetness of the barbecue shrimp was heightened by the vinegariness of the sliced cucumbers.

Salads, too, pleased us. Our waitress tossed a classic Caesar salad for two at the table. Yes, they use pasteurized eggs here, along with all the traditional ingredients like fresh garlic, anchovies, lots of Parmesan cheese, lemon juice and a bit of anchovy mashed in. The house salad is a trendy combination of mixed greens, walnuts, blue cheese and dried cranberries.

Desserts aren't made on the premises, but there's plenty on the dessert cart to appeal to your sweet tooth, most notably an old-fashioned, moist carrot cake with luscious cream cheese frosting and juicy bits of pineapple. A fruit and cheese platter and a bowl of fresh fruit are also available.

*Elizabeth Large*

# Charleston

*1000 Lancaster St., Inner Harbor East • 410-332-7373*
*Hours: Open every night for dinner*
*Prices: Appetizers, $5-$10; entrees, $14-$24*
*Live music: No • Kid's menu: No • Waterfront views: No •*
*Wheelchair access: Yes • Reservations: Suggested*

After two visits, I'd say the expanded Charleston is fairly glitch-free. My lunch there failed to enchant, even though nothing much went wrong. It's simply that many of the lunch dishes work better as dinner first courses. Take the crab and corn salad with its lemony, tarragon-scented sauce. As lunch, you would expect it to have more in the way of greens than a little feathery frisee.

And then there's the setting. At lunchtime, our view outside the expanse of windows was a parking lot and a chain-link fence. The rooms seemed large and somewhat impersonal — there wasn't even a flower or a candle on the table.

But at night the restaurant was romantic, its soft peaches and greens glowing in the indirect lighting. A charming palm motif repeats in the carpeting, and there are elegant sconces and latticework by the open kitchen. The kitchen itself becomes a stage where clever cooks work their magic.

I loved the death-by-cream Charleston she-crab soup; the slithery, hot, cornmeal-crusted oysters; the delicate little jade-green haricots verts; the hot puff of an individual spoon bread. I loved the wild boar chop, meaty, flavorful and tender, with a parsnip flan and baby spinach leaves.

Sushi-grade tuna, served medium rare, was set off with the refreshing bite of a tapenade-like relish made with black and green olives. Enormous shrimp were sauteed with fiery andouille sausage and bits of Cajun ham, then served over grits that tasted as if they had been cooked in pure cream.

Plump boneless duck breast with a citrusy glaze had an elegant accompaniment of poached pears and shiitake mushrooms. A superb creme brulee and bread pudding tasted unexpectedly like a hot chocolate-banana souffle. All these good things are complemented by the restaurant's impressive wine cellar, which has more than 250 selections.

Still, as good as our meal was, it could have been better. The pastry of the crawfish and lobster napoleon was undercooked and doughy. While the combination sounded good, its heavy, cream-laden sauce wasn't wonderful. The shell of a lemony tart with a crisp bit of meringue was also undercooked. Maybe the pastry chef was simply having a bad day.

Our waitress was excellent — friendly without being too friendly, getting the food on the table with flawless timing. But she had been instructed to give us more information than we needed to know. (Example: The fat from the heads of the heads-on shrimp is rendered for added flavor.)

Still, the restaurant seems to have become reinvigorated after its move to new and larger quarters. Charleston is a plus for all who love imaginative food and Southern cooking.

*Elizabeth Large*

# Charred Rib

*Yorkridge Shopping Center, Lutherville • 410-561-0060*
*Hours: Open every day for lunch and dinner*
*Prices: Appetizers, $2.95-$8.75; entrees, $8.95-$19.95;*
*Live music: Thursday, Friday, and Saturday nights • Kid's menu: Yes •*
*Waterfront views: No • Wheelchair access: Yes • Reservations: Accepted*

Our dinner at the Charred Rib didn't start off well. We had had reservations for a week, so we weren't happy about being put in the Outer Siberia room behind the bar — a brown box of a room with no pictures on the walls. Of course, not everyone can sit in the two pretty main dining rooms when the restaurant is this busy. But we wanted to.

Not only was our dining room ugly, it was noisy. All the families with young kids seemed to be in this room. When the hostess led us to a table next to the door that led to the bathrooms and kitchen, I dug in my heels.

Eventually, we got a better table — but not in the main part of the restaurant. Eventually, the families with young children left, so the noise level dropped. But next time I would request a table in one of the main dining rooms.

At first glance, the menu looks as if a bunch of fraternity guys planned it. Potato skins, buffalo wings, ribs and the like are a mainstay. But you'll also find plenty to appeal to almost any taste. The special of the day was blackened mahi-mahi. The fillets, fresh and flavorful, were topped with delicious backfin crab meat. It was a very appealing dish, one that you wouldn't expect from the same kitchen that produced the onion loaf, a spectacularly greasy mass of fried onions.

A big drawing card is the rib combos: ribs with chicken, ribs with crab cake, ribs with fried oysters, ribs with shrimp tempura — you get the idea. The ribs, generously meaty, aren't charred at all. In fact, ours had a sort of steamed softness. The sauces we tried, the original and Cajun, were quite good, smoky sweet and homemade-tasting.

Still, I would order the Charred Rib's filet mignon over its ribs, much as I love barbecue. Two delicious 4-ounce filets, cooked rosy pink, were wrapped with bacon and perfectly grilled. They were certainly better than the crab imperial, which contained little in the way of crab.

The Charred Rib has good buffalo wings, fat little morsels with a spicy-vinegary sauce that grows hotter as you keep eating, and lots of celery and blue cheese dressing to cool you off. They and other starters are standards, except for the coffee salad. It's made of lettuce, tomatoes, egg and onion chopped together and tossed with a homemade coffee dressing.

Our meal had its ups and downs. Typical was dessert: an array of fabulous not-made-in-house cheesecakes, and then a homemade rice pudding so thick and gummy you could stick your spoon in it and pick it up by the spoon. But if you factor in the reasonable prices, and the excellent service; if you know what to order; and if you sit in the main dining room, you could have a great time at the Charred Rib.

*Elizabeth Large*

# Chiapparelli's

*Where: 237 S. High St., Little Italy • 410-837-0309*
*Hours: Sundays through Thursdays 11 a.m. to 11 p.m., Fridays and Saturdays 11 a.m. to midnight*
*Prices: Appetizers, $3-$7; entrees, $10-$22*
*Live music: No • Kid's menu: Yes • Waterfront views: No •*
*Wheelchair access: Yes • Reservations: Suggested*

When I first moved to Baltimore, Little Italy was the place to go if you wanted to eat downtown. And Chiapparelli's was probably *the* restaurant in Little Italy. The amazing thing is that it hasn't changed that much in all these years.

Case in point: the salad. Perhaps the most famous house salad in Baltimore. But it no longer seems out of the ordinary, maybe because the night before I had eaten a house salad at another restaurant made of baby mixed greens and radicchio with a fresh pear-basil vinaigrette. Sound too upscale for you? Even the salad bar at the Giant gives you a variety of greens and vegetables.

But the waitresses at Chiapparelli's still ladle out huge platefuls of chopped iceberg and mix them with oil and vinegar and lots of cheese, and add a cherry tomato and a pepperoncini. It's OK, but I wouldn't say it's the best house salad in Baltimore, or even in Little Italy.

One thing has changed: Little Italy, and specifically Chiapparelli's, is no longer a cheap place to eat. The shocker for me was a first course, shrimp Nicola. There were four large shrimp in a pool of lemon butter for $10. Nicely cooked shrimp, but still . . .

A better bet for a starter would be a half order of Mom Chiapparelli's ravioli ($10.95 as a main course). The homemade pasta pillows are soft and huge, plump with ricotta and spinach. (Less salt in the filling and less red sauce on top, and they'd be even better.)

Less salt in the Alfredo sauce, and grilled chicken with fettuccine Alfredo ($13.95) would have been the dish of the evening. The pasta in its rich cheese, cream and butter sauce sparked with prosciutto would satisfy your most wicked cravings; and the boneless chicken breast was perfectly charbroiled. No such care had been taken with the pescatore ($17.95). Mussels, clams, calamari and shrimp were all overcooked. These along with whole stewed tomatoes were served on a bed of linguine.

Bread? Not up to the standards of Little Italy's best restaurants. Cappuccino? It's made from a mix. Desserts? The made-on-the-premises filling of a cannoli had the texture of mashed potatoes. Try instead an ice cream concoction of chocolate and vanilla with cherries in a hard chocolate shell.

The best thing about Little Italy's restaurants, though, is that you can come away from a pretty ordinary meal fairly happy — as we did. Chiapparelli's dining room is homey and cozy, and the waitresses are so pleasant. It's a nice place to be.

*Elizabeth Large*

# Chris' Charcoal Pit

*1946 West St., Annapolis • 410-266-5200*
*Hours: Open Tuesday through Saturday for lunch and dinner*
*Prices: Appetizers, $2.50-$4.25; entrees, $4.95-$12.95*
*Live music: No • Kid's menu: Yes • Waterfront views: No •*
*Wheelchair access: Yes • Reservations: No*
*Credit cards: None accepted*

Some say gyro. Others yee-roh. Whichever way you pronounce it, the Greek sandwich of thinly sliced meat wrapped in a pita is one of the specialties at Chris' Charcoal Pit.

There's nothing fancy about Chris' Charcoal Pit, as its name suggests. Grecian columns and a brass chandelier try to dress up the simple blue and white space. But the walls are cinder block, the plates are molded plastic and the napkin holders are affixed with table numbers, diner-style.

Who wants fancy china for an overstuffed sandwich dripping with good stuff? All that's needed are plenty of napkins and a healthy appetite. Start with a glass of wine, and Greek appetizers. Our favorites were a plate of feta, sliced tomatoes and cucumbers, and savory kalamata olives; and soft pita triangles to spread with Chris' wonderful taramasalata, a fluffy pink pate with the salty punch of fish roe.

The chicken gyro was huge, filled with the thinnest slices of moist chicken breast, lettuce, tomato, feta and honey-mustard dressing instead of the traditional yogurt-garlic sauce. It was hard to tell that the chicken fillets had been breaded and sauteed because they were sliced so thin. This unorthodox rendition was served with long, golden fries. A lamb gyro and pork souvlaki sandwich also are available.

We tried the latter on the Greek sampler platter. The meat was not nearly as tender as we had expected. It seemed a little overcooked. The rest of the platter was a success: dolmades, grape leaves with a moist filling of rice and meat; moussaka, layers of eggplant, creamy custard and ground beef; and pastitsio, the Greek version of lasagna, made with ziti-like noodles. All three were light-tasting, covered in tomato sauce with a hint of cinnamon. There was a small Greek salad on our plate, as well.

Our waitress suggested the Korinthian, a chicken breast filled with feta and spinach, bathed in a mushroom creme sauce on saffron rice. It wasn't bad, but it wasn't very memorable, either. Those who rate dinners for quantity as much as quality won't be disappointed, however.

There also are Italian dishes, from spaghetti and meatballs to manicotti. We also tried a small cheese pizza. It had a lovely homemade crust — golden and chewy.

We finished with a sweet Greek coffee, which our waitress made especially for us, and a sampling of the desserts that the restaurant makes in-house. The creme caramel was delicate enough, but fairly tasteless, and the rice pudding, looking as wan as oatmeal, was studded with al dente rice. Crisp, nut-filled baklava served in a foil cup was a better choice.

*Kathryn Higham*

# Ciao

*51 West St., Annapolis • 410-267-7912*
*Hours: Open for dinner only Tuesday through Saturday*
*Prices: Appetizers, $3.25-$9.95; entrees, $11.95-$20.95*
*Live music: No • Kid's menu: No • Waterfront views: No •*
*Wheelchair access: Yes • Reservations: Accepted*

Ciao has a good location, in a storefront in the historic district — particularly convenient for visitors to Annapolis. The dining room is charming, with soft blue walls, tile floors, decorative pottery and fresh white cloths on the tables. A handsome, cherry-stained bar runs along one wall, but be warned that customers are allowed to smoke there.

The menu is a hodgepodge, but an appealing one. Shrimp and corn quesadillas share space with Moroccan chicken, steak au poivre, Mediterranean meatloaf and almond-crusted trout. This is imaginative and beautifully presented food — but not, it must be admitted, always the most successful food.

Take a first course of yellow and red tomatoes layered with fresh mozzarella, drizzled with basil-flavored oil and sprinkled with pine nuts. It shouldn't have been a surprise that in mid-June the tomatoes had very little flavor. You would do better with the Prince Edward Island mussels and their pleasant Italian plum tomato sauce, or the quesadillas filled with shrimp and corn. Their citrus aioli had plenty of zing.

That same garlicky, lemony mayonnaise enlivened the trout crusted with ground almonds. But hearty chunks of spicy sausage didn't complement the fish as well as the delicately bitter flavor of the braised broccoli raab.

Mediterranean meatloaf — made of ground lamb and beef — is Ciao's signature dish, our waiter told us. We loved its rich brown gravy with wild mushrooms, the pretty new potatoes and the sauteed green beans on the side; but the meatloaf itself tasted a bit too much like leftovers.

Still, the only real disappointment was a dish that sounded so promising: fresh egg bucatini (a kind of pasta) with spinach, grilled chicken and roasted eggplant. It arrived piled in a too-small bowl, which meant it wasn't attractive, and the combination was oddly tasteless. I picked at it and filled up on the delicious warm focaccia that came with our dinners.

That evening a fruit soup was offered as either an appetizer or dessert. Pureed berries were swirled with cream and a bit of Chambord liqueur. Very nice, but a whole bowl of it was a bit much. It worked better as a sauce for the chocolate mousse cake. As an appetizer it wouldn't have worked at all; it was simply too sweet.

Best of all our desserts was the restaurant's tiramisu: moist and full of rich espresso flavor.

To sum up, I'd say that this was an uneven meal that ended well. The setting is so pretty and the staff so friendly you probably won't be unhappy with your meal, even if things aren't quite perfect.

*Elizabeth Large*

# Ciao Bella

*236 S. High St., Little Italy • 410-685-7733*
*Hours: Open daily for lunch and dinner*
*Prices: Appetizers, $3.50-$21.95; entrees, $10.95-$24.95*
*Live music: No • Kid's menu: No • Waterfront views: No •*
*Wheelchair access: No • Reservations: Suggested*

Not to make too much out of a bowl of soup, but Ciao Bella's is no ordinary minestrone. It's a summer stew of vegetables at their peak of freshness. Instead of beans, pasta and tired cubes of frozen vegetables, there are hand-cut chunks of celery, carrots, plum tomatoes, zucchini, corn and chopped greens. They have been seasoned with herbs and simmered just long enough for their flavors to merge.

Owner Anthony Gambino is running a tight operation here. The kitchen, for the most part, pays attention to details, as does the wait staff, which showered us with fastidious service.

We liked the atmosphere in the dining room. The place is done in cream and wine, with dark green curtains cascading through gold hoops, and prints of Renaissance women hanging on the walls.

In some respects, Ciao Bella is a typical Little Italy restaurant. Its house dressing, a creamy vinaigrette with bits of cheese and a touch of sweetness, tastes a lot like the house dressing at some of the restaurants up the street. Prices are mostly moderate, but specials and market-priced dishes can be high, a common problem in Little Italy.

The market price for our crab toast appetizer, essentially two pieces of garlic bread topped with crab imperial, is $17.95. It's hard for any appetizer to live up to that price, and this one, though rich tasting, doesn't quite make the grade.

The menu at Ciao Bella, like at most restaurants in the neighborhood, is filled with Italian classics, from parmigiana and cacciatore to Marsala and piccata. Under signature entrees, there are dishes that sound more unusual, like the shrimp Ricardo with a sherry-orange cream sauce. Unfortunately, the sauce is so startlingly sweet — with pieces of orange segments tossed in — that it's barely edible.

The shrimp was served over linguine, cooked as nicely al dente as our penne primavera. The sauce on the penne reminded us of the minestrone, with freshly cooked carrots, celery and greens in a chunky tomato sauce scented with white wine. It's simple, satisfying and low-fat to boot.

That's not how we'd describe our broccolini di pollo, a breaded chicken cutlet topped with broccoli spears, sliced mushrooms, melted provolone cheese and a full ladle of butter sauce. The portion was enormous, with the two tender chicken breast fillets nearly covering the plate. But the rich sauce was a problem. The dish would be better without it.

Desserts included a classic spumoni and cannoli, and tortoni with a twist — dipped in white chocolate and filled with raspberry preserves and vanilla ice cream.

*Kathryn Higham*

# City Cafe

*1001 Cathedral St., Mount Vernon • 410-539-4252*
*Hours: Counter service daily for breakfast, lunch and dinner; full service daily for lunch and dinner; brunch on weekends*
*Prices: Appetizers, $3.50-$7.95; entrees, $5.50-$16.95*
*Live music: No • Kid's menu: No • Waterfront views: No • Wheelchair access: Yes • Reservations: Suggested on weekends*

Our timing was a little off when we visited the City Cafe recently. As we left, we learned that this Mount Vernon eatery was about to change part of its menu, as it does each season. We enjoyed our meal so much, my guess is that City Cafe will be serving food that is every bit as interesting and well executed as what we sampled.

There's a confidence to the menu, the same kind of confidence that shows in the hip, New York-style personality of this spare black and white eatery. Walls are hung with rotating exhibitions of art, but the real show stopper is the wide expanse of windows looking out on the street.

Up front, tables always seemed to be jammed with people who have ordered sandwiches or lattes at the counter. A full menu is served at a small section in the back, where we sat.

One appetizer we hope makes it through the menu changes is the whole portobello mushroom cap filled with wilted spinach and crab. Served on baby greens, the mushroom was finished with a canopy of melted provolone, and a slightly sweet, light cream sauce. Other starters included a buttery spinach and corn strudel, ringed with hot pepper oil, and a small house salad made with mesclun lettuces, sprouts and cucumber slices. If you're not a ginger fan, choose a subdued vinaigrette over the zippy ginger-orange dressing.

For dinner, the Southwestern chicken is a good pick, one that most likely will be on the spring menu, the manager told us. This is a layered affair: a ring of luscious creamed corn with chopped bell pepper and onion, a mound of chipolte mashed potatoes and, on top, two grilled chicken breasts glazed with roasted red pepper jam. It was as rich and comforting as striking Texas oil.

Our polished, low-key waiter told us that the chef was experimenting with making his own pizza dough. We liked our cheese-striated, crispy crust, even if it was pre-baked. We crowned it with artichokes, roasted red peppers, mozzarella and a pesto that was full of flavor but not too oily.

The only entree that missed was a skimpy serving of sun-dried tomato ravioli. The portion wasn't really the problem. It was the flavor of the tomato sauce, which didn't have a hint of the sherry or basil the menu promised. The simple, chunky tomato sauce masked the delicate tang of the sun-dried tomatoes in the ravioli filling.

My only quibble is if the menu changes seasonally, why does the kitchen use ingredients out of season? We prefer our fresh tomatoes and silver queen corn at their summer peak.

Timing is everything.

*Kathryn Higham*

# Cockey's Tavern

*216 E. Main St., Westminster • 410-840-2134*
*Hours: Open Monday to Friday for lunch and dinner,*
  *Saturday for dinner*
*Prices: Appetizers, $6.95-$10.95; entrees, $15.95-$23.95*
*Live music: Some weekends, call ahead • Kid's menu: No •*
*Waterfront views: No • Wheelchair access: No • Reservations: Suggested*

Cockey's Tavern is authentically historic — it was built in 1782. No treaties were signed here, no famous presidents ate in the main dining room. Still, you can almost feel the ghostly presence of all the customers who have come before you. These rooms have a patina to them, a faded not-quite-glory.

These days, the beautiful original woodwork and elegant light fixtures share space with a layer of Victoriana and masses of silk flower arrangements that have been added to give the restaurant a more current appeal.

Cockey's Tavern is no longer quite the special-occasion restaurant it used to be. Some meals-in-themselves salads have been added to the dinner menu, and food from the lunch menu is available any time on the weekends. But most of the dinner menu is quite serious, old-fashioned, upscale American food: steak, fancy veal dishes, stuffed shrimp and lobster tail.

Oddly enough, the wine list doesn't match up to the menu. If it's champagne-taste food, it's a beer-budget wine list, headlined by a Georges Duboeuf Pouilly-Fuisse.

Think of eating here as a step back into the past, when customers weren't that interested in the perfect wine to go with their crab imperial. They wanted big portions, which you certainly get here.

Remember when people wanted their seafood bisque made with lots of seafood and lots of cream? That's how Cockey's Tavern makes it. They wanted their mashed potatoes done by hand with lots of butter and a touch of garlic. Check. Old-fashioned salads with tomatoes and cucumbers and red-onion rings on top. Check. Large hunks of filet. Check.

The crab cake that came with the filet was salty, but it had nice crab lumps and not much filler. The filet came overcooked, but it was whisked away and replaced by a pinker one.

Shrimp over toast with a wash of silky cream sauce made another decadent first course. My advice for the pina colada chicken: Push off the pineapple bits, peel away the coconut tempura batter, and enjoy the moist white meat inside.

Cockey's Tavern does have less elaborate offerings, like swordfish with a caper-butter sauce. The fish was fresh and not overcooked, but only the capers had much flavor.

The restaurant features its own dessert specialties like bananas Foster. The buttery brown sugar and rum sauce with chunks of ripe banana and good ice cream would have been wonderful without the tasteless crepe. You can also get bakery imports, sundaes and banana splits. Start your meal with shrimp on toast in cream sauce, end with an old-fashioned banana split and die happy.

*Elizabeth Large*

# Coho Grill

*11130 Willow Bottom Drive, Columbia • 410-740-2096*
*Hours: Open daily for lunch, Tuesday through Sunday for dinner*
*Prices: Appetizers, $2.75-$8; entrees, $5.50-$16.50*
*Live music: No • Kid's menu: Yes • Waterfront views: No •*
*Wheelchair access: Yes • Reservations: No*

The Coho Grill is hidden from view, tucked away inside the Hobbits Glen Golf Course. We missed our turn as we drove through the residential neighborhood where the golf course is located. No one else seemed to have trouble finding the restaurant, though. We waited 40 minutes before getting a table, and the crowd had hardly dwindled by the time we left. Reservations are not accepted.

Good food and a warm, comfortable atmosphere are what draw people here. Done in warm peach tones to contrast with a pitched ceiling of exposed dark wood, the restaurant features tables and booths on two levels. Strategically placed plants provide privacy, and curiosities like microscopes and globes on a high bookshelf add visual interest.

We had a long time to soak in the atmosphere, waiting for our appetizers. Once they arrived, though, we were happy: skewers of moist chicken with a light and spicy peanut sauce; a cup of mushroom soup, with finely minced mushrooms in a delicate cream base; and silky crab dip with the surprise of artichoke hearts.

A woodland salad was an appealing combination of tastes and textures, with baby greens, walnuts and portobello mushrooms slivers, served with an herb vinaigrette.

We also liked crisp-edged Angus beef in an onion-wine sauce, and the Southwest cassoulet. This rich mix of white beans, grilled chicken, sausage and potatoes had a note of mellow sweetness, an interesting take on a French classic.

There were a few minor problems. A fillet of salmon was cooked to perfection, but the distinctive flavor of the fish was mismatched with tropical mango salsa. While the pasta was slightly overcooked in the shrimp and basil fettuccine, the shrimp were done just right — plump and succulent. What's the point of making this dish with dried basil, though?

Moist chocolate bread pudding and cakelike tiramisu with intensely flavored chocolate sauce were good choices for dessert. We weren't as thrilled with the sweet potato cheesecake. It didn't taste like either cheesecake or sweet potato pie, but more like a bland combination of both.

After our meal at Coho Grill, we learned that the owners were planning some changes to the menu, but won't be too radical. Popular dishes like the cassoulet will remain. Others will switch on a weekly basis.

We hope the service staff will get a retooling as well. We sat in our booth for almost a half-hour before anyone came over to us. Granted, the restaurant was very busy, but a few extra people busing tables, taking drink orders or simply offering apologies would have gone a long way.

*Kathryn Higham*

# Corks

*1026 S. Charles St., Federal Hill • 410-752-3810*
*Hours: Open for dinner only Tuesday through Sunday*
*Prices: Appetizers, $5-$8; entrees, $14-$23*
*Live music: No • Kid's menu: No • Waterfront views: No •*
*Wheelchair access: Call ahead • Reservations: Suggested*

Corks' wine list isn't a wine list. It's a major literary work. It has a table of contents. An introduction. Maps. A glossary. By the time you actually read it all, dinner is over. But if the list's sheer size doesn't put you in a panic, you'll find it's actually user-friendly, with a breezy and non-jargony text.

In contrast, the food seems to have been given short shrift. Instead of a bound volume like the wine list, the menu consists of one page — three appetizers, a couple of soups, nine entrees. Each entree, of course, has a wine suggestion with it. But happily, the small open kitchen in front of the restaurant produces some superb meals.

In back of that kitchen, the dining rooms have a chic neutral color scheme, classical motifs, and sponge-painted walls. It's an elegant room, but people don't hesitate to dress casually anyway.

You might start your meal with a plump, crisply fried soft crab. Equally good are the meltingly tender, rosy slices of duck breast played against a salad of baby greens dressed with a delicate mango vinaigrette. Chilled gazpacho is also commendable, although the soup's assertive flavors overwhelm the dainty lump crab meat at its center.

The boneless flesh of a thick cut of pork loin, pearl-white shading to pink, was extraordinarily tender and delicately flavored. It was napped with a bit of cream sauce and edged with not-too-sweet whipped sweet potatoes and fresh asparagus.

If the rockfish fillet was any indication, the kitchen is adept with seafood; and I loved the fish's accompaniment of couscous and fresh corn off the cob, gently imbued with the flavors of the Southwest. The kitchen's take on chicken Veronique, a boneless chicken breast with a seductive balsamic-vinegar sauce and red grapes, had a wonderful roast-chicken flavor but was a bit overcooked. The mashed potatoes were, well, ordinary.

All in all, the meal held up to the very end, with a fine bread pudding, a poached pear with a silky creme anglaise, and strawberries with whipped cream encased in puff pastry.

My only real complaint about Corks had to do with the wine. To illustrate that half bottles are a great way to sample smaller quantities of good wines, Corks stocks four and recommends that you try them throughout your meal.

A 1993 Staglin Family Vineyards Cabernet Sauvignon should have been served with the main course, but turned out to be a 1994 Alexander Valley Cabernet. I was relieved that our check would reflect the substitution, but the waiter should have told us about the switch in advance.

*Elizabeth Large*

# Da Mimmo

*217 S. High St., Little Italy • 410- 727-6876*
*Hours: Open Mondays to Fridays for lunch and dinner, Saturdays and Sundays for dinner only*
*Prices: Appetizers, $8-$18; entrees, $11-$38*
*Live music: Every night • Kid's menu: No • Waterfront views: No • Wheelchair access: No • Reservations: Accepted*

Da Mimmo's doesn't serve wine by the glass. At a restaurant where we spent $275, I think it would be nice if we could order a white wine instead of a vodka gimlet.

But as in the NBA, you can be arrogant if you're good. But is Da Mimmo the Charles Barkley of Baltimore restaurants?

At first glance, you wouldn't think so. Its dining rooms look like many other beloved dining rooms in Little Italy: small, intimate, cozy and slightly kitschy.

The menu, too, didn't seem like anything special. The familiar pasta, seafood and veal dishes we know and love were there. But then the waiter arrived at our table and announced there were 17 specials that night. He proceeded to recite them and their ingredients, each sounding better than the last. We ended up ordering almost exclusively from the recited list. We forgot to ask what they cost, so we were surprised to find that the appetizers were $15- $18 and the entrees were $35- $38.

If you had asked my guests if the dishes were worth it, the answer would be a resounding yes. The tender homemade ravioli were plump with lobster, scallops and shrimp; and they had a creamy, fragile sauce that set them off perfectly. Da Mimmo's signature dish, a grilled veal chop, was sweetly flavorful with an edge of crisp fat. It was seasoned with olive oil and herbs, and those were all it needed.

The enormous grilled swordfish with onion and capers was almost as good, fresh and perfectly cooked, though a bit salty. Even the modest shrimp marinara was a cut above the usual — the marinara was bright and fresh, the shrimp tender and fat. But the lobster tetrazzini was a disappointment. The lobster had been so overcooked it should have been sent it back.

A large portobello mushroom extraordinaire, mounded high with lump crab meat, was almost the best first course, second only to tissue-thin slices of raw filet mignon that were topped with a little onion and capers and arranged around luscious caponata and slender triangles of Parmigiano-Reggiano cheese. The "Beverly Hills" salad, an ugly concoction of radicchio, red pepper, tomato, peppers, homemade mozzarella, one artichoke heart, one shrimp and a very good vinaigrette, struck out, though.

Deserts were fairly standard: a soft, wet tiramisu; spumoni ice cream and the like. But the cannoli was the best I've had in years.

Was it worth it? If you're willing to spend that kind of money for food alone, yes. But I don't expect the menu in an expensive restaurant to tell me "no substitutions" or "one check per table."

*Elizabeth Large*

# Della Notte

*Address: 801 Eastern Ave., Little Italy • 410-837-5500*
*Hours: Open daily for lunch and dinner*
*Prices: Appetizers, $5.95-$8.95; entrees, $9.95-$16.95*
*Live music: No • Kid's menu: Yes • Waterfront views: No •*
*Wheelchair access: Yes • Reservations: Suggested*

A tree grows in Little Italy, or so it seems inside the main dining room at Della Notte. Surrounded by decorative street lamps and a glitter-washed mural of an Italian waterfront, the faux dogwood stands at the center of the room, shading a ring of tables under its canopy.

Dining al fresco is what the designers had in mind, an effect that's helped along by street views through soaring windows. But with the columns and cascading roses, we couldn't help thinking that we were at the Italian pavilion at Epcot Center.

Don't misunderstand, we liked the fun atmosphere at this bustling restaurant and bakery. But like a tour through Epcot, there were highs and lows to our experience. Some of the food we sampled was so good it rivaled the best Italian restaurants in the city. Other dishes were mediocre.

Consider the appetizers we tried. Of four bruschetta slices, half worked (garlicky red pepper and rich olivata); half didn't (pale tomato and chicken liver). Mesclun salad with portobello mushrooms and cheese was at its summer freshest, but polenta triangles needed a better partner than the ground veal and tomato sauce that covered them.

Our favorite appetizer was the minestrone, with chunks of cauliflower, squash and carrots in a light tomato broth.

The hit of the evening was the vitello portobello entree. Scallops of tender veal were paired with meaty slivers of mushroom in a flavorful Marsala wine sauce. Bits of chopped tomatoes, powerful black olives and pesto gave the dish extra pizazz. It tasted much more updated than the typical veal Marsala. We also loved the long-roasted red potatoes, and the fresh green beans simmered in marinara, served alongside.

Among the other entrees, fettuccine Mona Lisa was tossed in a pink cream sauce with quarter-size pieces of sausage, mushroom slices and fresh spinach. The pasta was cooked perfectly al dente, and the sauce was surprisingly light.

Potato gnocchi were less successful. Their texture was too soft and gummy. Cioppino seemed more like paella, with baby clams, squid, mussels and shrimp ladled around saffron rice in marinara sauce with peas. We missed the delicate seafood flavor of the traditional Italian stew.

For dessert, feather-light chocolate cake and gooey apple cake covered in crumbs were OK. They took a definite second to the knockout tiramisu gelato. The creamy, homemade scoop was ice cream and cake swirled into one, with all the wonderful coffee and liqueur flavors of the original. We only wished we had tried one of Della Notte's gelato sundaes. Three big scoops would have suited the four of us just fine.

*Kathryn Higham*

# Doc's Eastside

*2522 Fait Ave., Canton • 410-563-3621*
*Hours: Open daily for dinner*
*Prices: Appetizers, $3.75-$8; entrees, $5.75-$16.50*
*Live music: No • Kid's menu: No • Waterfront views: No •*
*Wheelchair access: Yes • Reservations: Accepted*

There's a hideaway bistro in Canton called Doc's Eastside. The place belongs to Steve Cochran, for years the Rock and Roll Doctor on WQSR radio. Now, he's spinning a mix of Cajun, Italian and American comfort fare.

There's nothing trendy about the decor at Doc's, and that feels just right. At first, Doc's seems like a friendly neighborhood pub that serves its share of casual food, from sandwiches and burgers to pizza and po-boys. Few bars, though, could turn out a Southern-fried pork chop this good.

All sizzled brown on the outside, the thick chop was tender inside, enhanced with a ladle of subtle sage pan gravy. To make it even better, the chop was paired with incredible garlic mashed potatoes that were infused with, but not overpowered by, the essence of rosemary. Wow.

Our other entrees were almost as good. Coated with a heavy pastry crust, the homey chicken pot pie was full of chunks of chicken and finely diced vegetables, in a sauce that tasted as if it had been flavored with thyme and citrus.

The Eastside chicken, pan-fried cutlets topped with melted mozzarella, prosciutto, wild mushrooms and basil, is one of the most popular dishes on the menu, our waiter told us. When it didn't arrive with the rest of our dinners, he came over to say it was his error and not the kitchen's. His honesty and his skilled service impressed us. The chicken wasn't bad, either.

It took us a while to figure out what added the bright, tangy note to our shrimp fra diavolo. The sauce was so balanced it was hard to tell. Our best guess: a dash of balsamic vinegar.

That sauce would have gone well with the fried mozzarella, greasy-but-good parcels of fresh cheese coated with bread crumbs, and with tender calamari, barely kissed with flour for the lightest of fried coatings. Both were served with a chunky marinara sauce that seemed more like stewed tomatoes.

We preferred those appetizers to the crawfish pie, Doc's signature appetizer. The puff pastry rings filled with spicy Creole sauce and crawfish left us cold, in part because the sauce was lukewarm and overwhelmingly tangy.

These are minor quibbles, though, for a moderately priced, white-tablecloth bistro that manages to do so much right. Doc's is the perfect antidote to the cookie-cutter food turned out by chain restaurants. From homemade garlic croutons to house-blended herb butter tucked into breadbaskets, the food here starts from scratch and adds a sense of individuality to the restaurant.

Where else will you find a Canton fried banana, rolled in phyllo and oozing luscious chocolate?

*Kathryn Higham*

# Donna's Coffee Bar

*3101 St. Paul St., Charles Village • 410-889-3410*
*Hours: Open daily for lunch and dinner*
*Prices: Appetizers, $2.50-$7.95; entrees, $4.95-$11.95*
*Live music: No • Kid's menu: No • Waterfront views: No •*
*Wheelchair access: No • Reservations: No*
*Other locations: 1819 Reisterstown Road, Baltimore • 410-653-6939*
*200 E. Pratt St., Baltimore • 410-752-9040*
*2400 Boston St., Baltimore • 410-276-9212*
*2 W. Madison St., Baltimore • 410-385-0180*
*22 S. Greene St., Baltimore • 410-328-1962*
*618 Boulton St., Bel Air • 410-803-9058*
*2080 York Road, Lutherville • 410-308-2041*
*22 W. Allegheny Ave., Towson • 410-828-6655*

The Donna's in Charles Village is tiny and welcoming. There's a friendly staff, an extended menu and a loose-tea service in addition to coffee drinks.

The arty decor could be called industrial chic. Grommeted canvas, corrugated steel and exposed pipes are the yang. Fresh flowers, oak veneers and aged brick are the yin. A few of the restaurant's two dozen tables are situated outside, in a heated tent that can be removed in warm weather.

The menu is not much different from that at other locations. Prices are the same, with plenty of dinner choices under $10, but there are more dishes on the menu here.

Donna's style is updated Italian — a cross between Californian and Mediterranean. Most dishes have been given an interesting twist, or a surprise ingredient or two.

The spicy paella had more of an Italian personality than the traditional Spanish version because of a few substitutions: orzo pasta instead of rice; giant capers instead of green peas; crunchy bits of snow peas instead of bell peppers, and Italian sausage instead of chorizo. It was the hit of the night.

A tuna fish sandwich got zing from olives and capers. Plump raisins were an unexpected addition to pungent caponata, the cold Sicilian eggplant salad. We devoured it on slices of toasted crostini. For dinner, linguine tossed in tarragon cream was luscious and rich, but the meaty flavor of portobello mushrooms and the sun-dried tomatoes added verve.

My friends loved the portobello rotolo appetizer, a tortilla filled with herbed goat cheese, mushroom slices, baby greens and sun-dried tomatoes. It was rolled up and cut into pieces that could be dipped in the accompanying thick balsamic dressing. I couldn't taste the goat cheese in my piece, and preferred a dish of spicy hummus because the creamy chickpea spread had intense garlic flavor all the way through.

Our only true complaint of the night regarded the pale crust on the roasted eggplant and Gorgonzola pizza. It was too soft and white. We should have sent it back to be crisped.

For dessert, an icy mixed-fruit sorbetto and firm-layered tiramisu were OK, but the warm chocolate brownie sundae tasted like pure mother's comfort. We predict Donna's will be selling a lot of them to homesick Hopkins students.

*Kathryn Higham*

# Dooby's Bar & Grill

*3123 Elliott St., Canton • 410-534-0556*
*Hours: Open daily for lunch and dinner*
*Prices: Appetizers, $2.95-$7.50; entrees, $4.95-$14.75*
*Live music: No • Kid's menu: Yes • Waterfront views: No •*
*Wheelchair access: No • Reservations: No*

Dooby's Bar & Grill is a narrow stretch of a place, with booths up front, next to a bar illuminated by hanging lava lamps, and tables in back overlooking the steel expanse of an open kitchen. We liked the purple ceiling and the beaded curtains hanging like iridescent arrowheads over the windows. The menu, featuring California cooking, is casual and fun, but also includes some sophisticated specials.

Appetizers were a hit. Marinated and roasted asparagus, eggplant and other vegetables were sandwiched with cheese between two crisp flour tortillas for a delicious quesadilla that was dotted with sour cream, guacamole and two salsas. Fried calamari was perfectly cooked in a light batter. The squid was drizzled artistically with garlicky aioli, a great combination.

We split a Dooby's salad, which was full of mixed greens, sun-dried tomatoes, roasted peppers, marinated artichokes and sliced portobello mushrooms. The slight sweetness of the sherry vinaigrette offset the fresh bitterness of greens.

There's a whole section of grilled pizza, harking back to the California craze. Start with a great crust — not so thick that the topping is lost, but with enough bite to satisfy. Top with interesting concoctions (we went for the wild mushroom, but barbecue chicken and smoked Gouda, pesto and shrimp, and basil and tomato are other options). Grill to add a note of smoky pizazz. This pizza is hard to beat.

Entrees leaned toward Italian-inspired dishes, from the traditional veal saltimbocca to lobster and crab ravioli in tomato cream sauce. One of us thought the latter was the highlight of the meal. The sauce was delicious, a creamy pink cloud that stopped just this side of being overly rich. The black- and red-striped ravioli looked quite chic, but to my mind tasted more of cheese than seafood.

Chicken scaloppine was served on capellini in a lemon-butter sauce with tricolor peppers. The sauteed chicken was moist and velvety. This may not have been the most exciting dish in the world, but it was well-executed and satisfying.

On another visit, we'll try the grilled salmon BLT with dill havarti and red pepper remoulade, or the seafood salad with lump crab, lobster, shrimp and smoked salmon.

With so many interesting choices on the menu, it was surprising to find only two desserts. The tiramisu reminded us of cheesecake, with a ribbon of chocolate at its base and thick, cheesy layers. It was quite good, but a carrot cake was undistinguished, and had pasty frosting.

Dooby's is a welcome addition to the restaurant scene in Canton. In fact, it makes me wish there was one near me.

*Kathryn Higham*

# Due

*25 Crossroads Drive, Owings Mills • 410-356-4147*
*Hours: Open daily for dinner*
*Prices: Appetizers, $5.95-$10.95; entrees, $10.95-$28.95*
*Live music: No • Kid's menu: No • Waterfront views: No •*
*Wheelchair access: Yes • Reservations: Suggested*

Due is decorated in a scheme of brown and white — warm wood paneling and chairs contrasting with white tablecloths, scalloped curtains and an exuberant display of cooking utensils spray-painted white and arranged like flowers on long wooden stems. At the center of things is the copper-accented exhibition kitchen, where three chefs turn out everything from simple brick-oven pizzas to grilled fish and meats.

The expensive, garlic-studded veal chop, several inches thick, buttery tender, is worth every penny. Glazed in a rich, brown sauce, it was served with caramelized onions, gently sauteed spinach and herb-roasted baby new potatoes.

On the other side of the culinary and budgetary spectrum, the pizza scampi was equally well done, made on the thinnest of cornmeal crusts and topped with garlic oil, jumbo shrimp and robust cheeses. Fried garlic slices dotted the top, a pungent alternative to pepperoni.

Those crispy garlic slices also were scattered over our crab and corn risotto appetizer, giving a deeper note to what was a deliciously light take on this rice classic. The lumps of crab remained intact, and fresh kernels of corn burst with sweet flavor in each bite. We sampled risotto again with our grilled tuna. It was spread with an assertive olive tapenade and came atop a bright-green spinach risotto that was mild-tasting and creamy-textured.

The hit of the night was the polenta-stuffed portobello appetizer, a savory layer cake that sandwiched cornmeal and ricotta between roasted mushroom caps — with the best portobellos I've had in Baltimore. As for our salad of thinly sliced rare lamb, arugula and white bean salad, we liked the mix of flavors and the way cracked black peppercorns intensified the peppery flavor of the bitter greens.

Skip the bruschetta with goat cheese and diced vegetables. There are more interesting appetizers, and you're bound to have enough bread. Our server kept our bread basket filled with tempting slices of soft focaccia and crusty loaves.

Only the fettuccine with charred vegetables, Gorgonzola and beef tenderloin got a lukewarm reception. The flavors were lackluster, the cheese was undetectable and the fan-sliced beef on top was underdone for an order of medium.

But one miss is not bad for a dinner that started with delicious salt-rubbed focaccia and finished with four-star desserts. Rich creme brulee with chunks of chocolate. A tower of cornmeal pound cake filled with strawberry cream. A blueberry tart wrapped in a flat pentagon of buttery pastry and drizzled with creme anglaise. Splendido.

*Kathryn Higham*

# Edo Sushi

*53 E. Padonia Road, Timonium • 410-667-9200*
*Hours: Open every day for lunch and dinner*
*Prices: Appetizers, $4.25-$7.95; entrees, $8.95-$17.95*
*Live music: No • Kid's menu: No • Waterfront views: No •*
*Wheelchair access: Yes • Reservations: Accepted for large parties*

Don't let the name fool you. Edo Sushi, the new Japanese restaurant in Timonium, offers much more than raw fish on seasoned rice. Traditional casseroles, teriyaki, tempura and noodle dishes are all on the menu. About the only thing you can't get here is a Japanese beer; the restaurant doesn't have a liquor license but is happy for you to bring your own alcohol.

This is a sunny, cheerful dining room with lots of blond wood. Kimono-clad waitresses carrying the sushi chef's pretty creations glide from table to table. Fragrant tea is kept steaming hot in thermos carafes. Voices are low. The only thing that disturbs the feeling of peace is the drum near the door. Customers are supposed to strike it for good luck when they leave. And they do.

You can make a dinner of sushi here, with a choice of soup or salad and rice. The soft fish against sticky rice, counterpointed by the pungent horseradish-like wasabi and fiery-sweet slices of ginger, is not to be missed. But you could also begin with a piece or two of sushi and then follow them with one of the other Japanese dinners.

If raw fish isn't to your taste, the Maryland roll with crisp fried soft crab, rice and a tangy sauce is delectable. Or start with gyozo, little moon-shaped dumplings filled with ground pork and shrimp, made to be dipped in a vinegary sauce.

Edo soup arrives at the table in a mini-teapot. Pour the fish broth into the tiny bowl provided and drink it, then lift the teapot lid and pull the seafood out with your chopsticks.

The restaurant has fine tempura — each jumbo shrimp and fresh vegetable surrounded with a thin, crisp batter that's remarkably grease-free. Or you can get one of the casserole dishes, like shabu-shabu. The waitress brings a hot plate and a pot of broth to the table. When the broth comes to a boil, the cook adds napa cabbage, tofu, mushrooms, noodles, spinach and translucently thin slices of raw beef. It's eaten in soup bowls with spoons, but you also use your chopsticks to dip the ingredients into a lemon and soy sauce.

Those interested in a more straightforward meal will be happy with the tender boneless breast of chicken in a gingery, not-too-sweet teriyaki sauce. It comes with broccoli, steamed rice and a knife and fork.

Japanese restaurants have little interest in desserts and Edo Sushi is no exception. There are only two on the menu, so we tried them both. After Edo Sushi's fine tempura, the tempura ice cream seems like a travesty — a scoop of vanilla ice cream with a topping of fried tempura batter. The green-tea ice cream is a lovely celadon, but shut your eyes and I defy you to tell the difference between it and the vanilla ice cream.

*Elizabeth Large*

# El Azteca

*12210 Route 108, Clarksville • 410-531-3001*
*Hours: Open daily for lunch and dinner*
*Prices: Appetizers, $2.95-$5.95; entrees, $6.75-$13.95*
*Live music: Sunday night • Kid's menu: Yes • Waterfront views: No •*
*Wheelchair access: Yes • Reservations: Accepted for large parties*

El Azteca dishes out nuance and surprise alongside the ubiquitous rice and beans.

Papier-mache parrots perch amid hanging plants at this small storefront (stuck unceremoniously between a High's and a liquor store), above tables covered in rose vinyl. On Sunday nights, strolling musicians serenade the tables. Food, not atmosphere, is the reason to come to El Azteca, though.

The menu includes the standard combination platters of tacos, burritos and enchiladas, but try something a little different. For us, it was the albondigas, a special the night we visited. They're wonderful meatballs spiked with rice and mint, simmered until they almost fall apart in a thick tomato-onion sauce, and topped with crumbly cotija cheese.

We felt as if we were trying chicken mole for the first time, because the thick mahogany sauce was so complex and intriguing. The owners import chocolate, chilies and seeds from Mexico to give it an authentic taste. The dish was an enormous portion, a mound of moist chicken breast meat cut into strips and arranged next to sides of mildly seasoned rice and creamy refried beans. Fresh vegetables or salad can be substituted for the beans, the rice or both.

I've eaten my fill of fajitas, so even the flourish of steam coming off the cast-iron pan hardly catches my attention. But not all have been as well-executed as the shrimp fajitas at El Azteca. The jumbo shrimp, glazed with the smoky essence of the pan, were seared with green peppers and onions and cooked not a moment too long. We rolled them up in tortillas with guacamole, lettuce and pico de gallo.

In addition to the complimentary basket of tortilla chips, try the taquitos for a starter. They're tightly rolled, quickly fried tortillas, filled with a faintly sweet mixture of shredded beef and soft corn masa. They struck me as a crisp, flavorful alternative to tamales.

There's nothing unusual about the quesadilla, but nothing disappointing either. Pieces of long-cooked chicken and a mix of cheeses are sandwiched between crisp tortillas.

The cup of chili tastes anything but ordinary. It could be the texture created by using both chunks of steak and ground beef, the from-scratch kidney beans, or the flavor of ground chilies unmasked by spices. And the corn bread served with the chili is as dense, moist and buttery as a cookie.

As for dessert, the flan is acceptable, and so is a sundae of vanilla ice cream and strawberries, despite its topping of fried tortilla strips. But go with the sopaipillas, fried puffs of dough drizzled with honey. They are as authentic and appealing as the restaurant itself.

*Kathryn Higham*

# Ellicott Mills Brewing Company

*8308 Main St., Ellicott City • 410-313-8141*
*Hours: Open daily for lunch and dinner*
*Prices: Appetizers, $3-$8.95; entrees, $6.95-$19.95*
*Live music: No • Kid's menu: Yes • Waterfront views: No •*
*Wheelchair access: Yes • Reservations: Accepted*

The easiest way to try the restaurant's four German-style beers is to order a sampler. Our waiter, full of fermentation facts, delivered four very small beer mugs holding a few ounces each of the black Alpenhof Dunkel, the amber Alpenhof Maerzen, the golden Alpenhof Pils and the pale Alpenhof Hell.

The dark lager Dunkel was our favorite, but all were remarkably good. Braumeister Martin Virga, who learned the art of brewing beer in Munich, isn't content with these early "test batches," though. He wants to perfect a full-bodied, complex beer that "makes your tongue come alive."

To complement the beers, an interesting menu serves the casual nature of the microbrewery well. Burgers share space with wild boar and buffalo steak.

We started on an adventurous note, with venison sausage, dark and bursting with flavor, paired with more mellow veal bratwurst and red cabbage. Meaty fried turkey wings, cooked golden and greaseless, put chicken wings to shame. But what really made them work was the spicy Thai peanut sauce on the side — a great combination. Our favorite starter was the most elegant of all: slivers of juicy smoked duck breast on raspberry sauce with green peppercorns.

Dinners came with large house salads made with crisp romaine, cucumbers, tomatoes and sprouts. Ginger-sesame and cabernet vinaigrette dressings were knockouts.

From the lighter side of the menu, we tried a grilled salmon sandwich, which featured a lovely fillet and lots of long, crisp, coated fries. Seafood fettuccine was on the other side of the dining spectrum, with salmon, shrimp and a few pieces of lobster tossed in a delicate cream sauce.

We liked the wild boar in beer sauce, which had sweet and sour flavor with a hint of cumin. The meat looked like pork, but was milder. Still, stew is stew. It's hard to rhapsodize over one, even if it's served, as this was, with a scoop of creamy, butter-soaked mashed potatoes. One disappointment was the grilled buffalo steak. It was too thin and marbled with gristle, although it had nice beefy flavor.

Overall, we loved this place, with its carved honey-pine wood, its roomy upstairs dining room and its stone-walled smoking bar in the basement. Be warned, though: It's very loud. A few discreetly placed sound baffles wouldn't hurt.

Neither would a distinctive dessert. With such a deft kitchen, it was surprising that no desserts are made in-house. Not that the almond-crusted Linzer torte, sweet chocolate oblivion or dark chocolate silk cake were bad. But historic Ellicott City is a one-of-a-kind place, and Ellicott Mills Brewing Company deserves a one-of-a-kind signature dessert.

*Kathryn Higham*

# ESPN Zone

*601 E. Pratt St., The Power Plant • 410-685-3776*
*Hours: Open every day for lunch and dinner*
*Prices: Appetizers, $4.95-$8.95; entrees, $7.50-$19.95*
*Live music: No • Kid's menu: Yes • Waterfront views: Yes •*
*Wheelchair access: Yes • Reservations: No*

In my household, "SportsCenter" is a daily morning ritual, and Kenny Mayne is a god. So when we headed for ESPN Zone, the restaurant and entertainment complex based on the world's hippest sports channel, we were ready to like it.

Inside, we found that the dining room is designed for sensory overload. The one thing you don't have to do is make conversation, especially if you're seated four abreast in the anchor chairs. (The room is a working studio and can be used to broadcast shows in front of a live audience.)

Place mats are covered with up-to-date sports news and scores, trivia questions and the day's specials. Music pulses. TV screens are everywhere. A closed ESPN Zone channel with sports quotes and blooper tapes runs continuously on several screens. Periodically "SportsCenter" anchors appear on the closed channel to welcome diners. If the kids get antsy, they can go upstairs and play high-tech arcade games or shoot a few baskets until the food arrives.

Food, you might think, comes in a distant second to all the entertainment. But not so. As bar food and theme restaurants go, it does what it sets out to do very well.

We started off with nachos and cheese fries, the restaurant's two signature appetizers. One dish starts with steak fries and the other with tri-colored tortilla chips. Both were smothered in melted cheeses and bits of crisp bacon, with chopped green onion and tomato added for color. The nachos came with salsa, sour cream and guacamole; the fries with barbecue sauce and ranch dressing.

We moved straight to the star of the show, the ESPN Zone burger. A half-pound of ground chuck had pride of place on a fresh, soft, lightly grilled onion roll. It was covered with melted Cheddar and grilled red peppers, mushrooms and onions. Steak fries and slaw came on the side.

The signature pizza is a cheeseburger pizza with crumbled hamburger, Cheddar and mozzarella but no tomato sauce. It's garnished with chopped tomatoes, lettuce and bacon. ESPN Zone makes its own herbed whole-wheat cheese crust; but with all these toppings, who can tell?

The angel hair pasta with chicken, chopped fresh tomato, tiny broccoli florets and a lemony broth, which could have been an elegant dish, was grievously oversalted. A better choice, if you don't want the excellent burger, is the tender baby back ribs, with lots of flavor and a smoky barbecue sauce.

As for dessert, ESPN Zone features its own homemade ice cream and real whipped cream in various combinations with huge warm chocolate chip cookies, huge chocolate cake, "ultimate" berry cobbler and the like.

*Elizabeth Large*

# Ethel & Ramone's

*1615 Sulgrave Ave., Mount Washington • 410-664-2971*
*Hours: Open for lunch and dinner Tuesday through Sunday*
*Prices: Appetizers, $5.25-$7.95; entrees, $10.95-$20.95; no liquor license*
*Live music: No • Kid's menu: No • Waterfront views: No •*
*Wheelchair access: No • Reservations: Suggested*
*Credit cards: MasterCard, Visa only*

At Ethel & Ramone's in Mount Washington, five varieties of soup are made daily. We tried a fresh-tasting tomato with sauteed curls of fennel, a smooth pumpkin made with butter and cream, and a souplike vegetarian chili with three kinds of beans. We were warmed and happy, especially when we discovered our bread basket contained perfect crusty slices, some with sunflower seeds, some with olives.

It was a good thing we like soup, because it was the only appetizer on the menu the night we visited — a hectic evening at the restaurant, with all three partners unavoidably absent. It's a testament to the restaurant that we had a fine meal.

The menu features terrific salads, a few chicken and vegetarian entrees, and a lot of pasta, from shrimp scampi to fettuccine portobella with an herbed wine and goat cheese sauce.

If the food has a Californian-Italian personality, the decor is more old-fashioned Baltimore-British. Sitting at one of the three downstairs tables is like eating in someone's front parlor, an effect heightened by the floral wallpaper, lace curtains and antique wedding portrait of a fictitious Ethel and Ramone hanging on the wall. Upstairs, the painted paneling and industrial carpet is not nearly as warm.

Since the same specials were served for lunch and dinner, many of them were sold out. One appetizer special that was still available was the bruschetta, made with salsa, mozzarella, Parmesan and olive tapenade for a pungent twist.

For dinner, a delicate, layered torta nova came with a side salad of mesclun and romaine lettuce, cucumber, tomato and slivered zucchini. Inside the torta were bits of Yukon gold potatoes and leeks, ricotta and Gouda cheeses and flakes of smoked salmon. It was rich but not at all heavy.

Everyone at the table agreed that the Mickey salad was a winner: the freshest baby greens, creamy lumps of snow-white goat cheese, whole sun-dried tomatoes, a smattering of pine nuts and, over top, moist, shredded chicken and fresh balsamic vinaigrette. Fabulous. The tangy vegetarian lasagna was not quite as elegant, served in a massive, toppled portion next to a side salad. It tasted healthy — good for the heart, but just a bit shy of satisfying the soul. Next time I'll try scampi rosso or linguine carbonara.

After this relatively light meal, we had no problem devouring three incredible desserts made by Patisserie Poupon: creamy white chocolate cheesecake with a dark chocolate crumb crust; dense pecan bourbon pie drizzled with chocolate; and a marbleized sponge cake pyramid filled with hazelnut and chocolate mousses. Ethel & Ramone's may know salads, but it also knows decadence.

*Kathryn Higham*

# G & M

*804 N. Hammonds Ferry Road, Linthicum • 410-636-1777*
*Hours: Open daily for lunch and dinner; breakfast on weekends*
*Prices: Appetizers, $1.95-$8.95; entrees, $7.50-$27.95*
*Live music: No • Kid's menu: Yes • Waterfront views: No*
*Wheelchair access: Yes • Reservations: Accepted for large parties*

To say G & M is famous for its crab cakes is a bit of an understatement. That much was clear when we walked into this Linthicum restaurant and spotted them on almost every table. They were hard to miss.

There's nothing petite about these crab cakes, folks. Order a double platter, and you'll find yourself facing the Grand Tetons of crab, two colossal mounds studded with jumbo lumps, broiled to golden perfection.

There's more filler holding the crab together than some purists may like, but it's not thick breading. Moist and eggy-tasting, these crab cakes are light and airy, with the faintest hint of crab spice. They're not gourmet, but they are certainly the biggest I've ever had, and among the best.

The restaurant makes a stab at being polished, with white tablecloths and a display of gold-framed "art." But service is closer to what you'd expect in a diner. Plastic soda bottles are plunked down unopened, and dishes stack up too long.

That said, G & M certainly is worth a drive for its crab cakes. If you're in the neighborhood, you might want to try one of the reasonably priced specials, too. For $7.95, we sampled the fettuccine primavera in a light cream sauce, with broccoli and ribbons of carrots, zucchini and onion. It rivaled similar dishes I've had, and only needed a sprinkling of Parmesan.

Our waitress recommended the prime rib. The smallest portion at $12.95 was enough of a behemoth — a slab of juicy, tender beef that barely fit on the plate. We sent the overcooked first plate back, but were happy with the second.

Dinners come with softball-sized rolls, glossy with egg on the outside, and a simple house salad. Homemade whipped blue cheese dressing turns the salad into something special.

For side orders, stick with slightly sweet, barely dressed coleslaw and potato salad tossed with green pepper and carrot, both freshly made. Soggy frozen vegetables and instant mashed potatoes are no match.

Appetizers are not the highlight of a meal at G & M, and neither are desserts. Skip the Maryland crab soup and the baked clams casino, topped with sauteed vegetables and bacon. The combined flavors don't work together.

The best starter is a pan of stuffed mushrooms blanketed thick with rich crab imperial, and served with cocktail sauce, of all things. But it's probably not the best choice if you plan to order crab cakes for dinner.

Of the three desserts made in-house, a firm square of bread pudding was the hands-down favorite. Spiked with raisins, apple slices and a healthy splash of vanilla, it would have been even better warmed.

*Kathryn Higham*

# Gampy's

*904 N. Charles St., Mount Vernon • 410-837-9797*
*Hours: Sundays through Tuesday, 11:30 a.m. to 1 a.m., Wednesday and Thursday, 11:30 a.m. to 2 a.m., Fridays and Saturdays, 11:30 a.m. to 3 a.m.*
*Prices: Entrees, $4.50-$12.95*
*Live music: No • Kid's menu: No • Waterfront views: No • Wheelchair access: No • Reservations: Accepted*

Gampy's must be the granddaddy of fun restaurants in the area, part singles bar and part trendy eatery. The name stands for Great American Melting Pot, with a "y" thrown in.

What makes Gampy's and places like it enduringly popular is that they offer a good selection of interesting dishes for people who want a few more choices than just hamburgers and pizza. Gampy's does have hamburgers and pizza, but the pizza, for instance, is an individual one with toppings like Boursin and bacon. The thick, 8-inch crust is slathered with rich, herb-flavored cream cheese. Not exactly a heart-healthy selection, but Gampy's offers some of those, too.

You might have teriyaki vegetables, steamed but still nicely crisp with a light, faintly sweet teriyaki sauce and rice on the side. Or you could try some of the best chicken fajitas around (the high point of our meal), made with blackened chicken and soft, warm tortillas. Ignore the sour cream and guacamole on the side if you're worried about your calories.

If you're not calorie-counting, try one of the three fondues. The choices are Tex-Mex cheese, a chocolate dessert fondue or beef. For the last, raw cubes of filet mignon come with a fondue pot of hot oil and wooden sticks to cook them on. Then you dip the cooked beef in barbecue sauce, teriyaki, a peppercorn sauce or mayonnaise mixed with mustard.

We could have skipped the limited first courses. Black bean soup had an odd, indefinable flavor, and something called fried jalapeno poppers gets my vote as the strangest dish I've tried this year. Maybe ever. The peppers are stuffed with cream cheese, deep-fried and served with melba sauce.

Desserts, however, aren't limited. If the chocolate peanut butter pie and so on aren't rich enough for you, the kitchen is happy to add a scoop of ice cream and hot fudge sauce.

Gampy's isn't exactly a family restaurant, although kids would love the jazzy decor, starting with the red and blue neon zigzags on the ceiling. But it is a place with its own little quirks. Like the hot-oil call. Whoever is holding the fondue pot of hot oil yells out "hot oil, hot oil" as he carries it from the kitchen — a little bizarre if you don't know about the fondue.

Or take our waitress. She was nice as she could be until she misunderstood and brought us our check before we had ordered dessert. When we told her we weren't finished and the check would have to be redone, she muttered the f-word under her breath. It did make me a little unsure about how best to ask for the check when we really were finished. But by that time she had cheered up again.

*Elizabeth Large*

# Geckos Bar & Grille

*2318 Fleet St., Canton • 410-732-1961*
*Hours: Open daily for lunch and dinner*
*Prices: Appetizers, $2.50-$11.95; entrees, $4.95-$17*
*Live music: No • Kid's menu: No • Waterfront views: No •*
*Wheelchair access: Yes • Reservations: Suggested on weekends*

With baby cacti on the tables and a giant papier-mache lizard guarding the bar, Geckos has brought the desert to Canton. The walls are painted in Santa Fe colors and the atmosphere is Jimmy Buffett-style — laid back and friendly.

The menu is laid back, too. It's moderately priced and full of casual fare like sandwiches, quesadillas and enchiladas. That doesn't mean the staff isn't serious about food, though. The salsas are fresh, the shrimp smoked in-house, the mashed potatoes real, the giant tortilla chips homemade.

Unfortunately, those complimentary chips were some of the thickest and greasiest we've tried. Send them away and try a cup of roasted corn and crab soup. Flavored with fresh corn, the soup combines lumps of crab and potatoes in a creamy base that's not too thick.

The Southwestern wings are also a good starter choice. Rubbed with spices and roasted, they're served with a creamy dip flavored with Cheddar cheese and bits of jalapeno.

We were in the mood for a shrimp appetizer, and could have tried them fried in coconut batter, but the smoked shrimp quesadilla caught our attention. It's big enough for four to share. Bright-red tomato tortillas are filled with tender mesquite-smoked shrimp, onions, peppers and melted cheese. Cut into four huge wedges, the quesadilla is paired with a chunky mango and melon salsa, which provides just the right sweetness to offset the smokiness of the shrimp.

Our first course was so good, our waitress so friendly and, frankly, our margaritas so tall, we hardly noticed the wait for our entrees. But as the clock kept ticking, we got increasingly annoyed, especially since the restaurant wasn't busy.

When our food did arrive, it was not without problems. We couldn't wait to set a knife to the huge fist of Black Angus sirloin, but it was swamped in a tangy house steak sauce that completely overwhelmed the meat. Grilled tequila shrimp had a disappointingly flat flavor and needed some punch. The crab cake sandwich was impressive for the amount of unadulterated crab that it used, but the filler that held the lumps together was mushy and undercooked.

These dishes were rescued by fabulous go-alongs: horseradish mashed potatoes and grilled zucchini with the steak; corn-studded pancakes, cilantro pesto and mango salsa with the shrimp; and creamy four-alarm jalapeno potato salad with the crab cake sandwich. Our entrees may have needed tinkering, but there's no disputing the talent of the kitchen.

Desserts are a strong suit at Geckos, from the light coconut flan accented with toasted coconut to the pecan-filled slices of rich Mexican chocolate pate.

*Kathryn Higham*

# Germano's

*300 S. High St., Little Italy • 410-752-4515*
*Hours: Open every day for lunch and dinner*
*Prices: Appetizers, $1.95-$6.75; entrees, $12.25-$22*
*Live music: No • Kid's menu: Yes • Waterfront views: No •*
*Wheelchair access: Yes • Reservations: Suggested*

Germano's is one of those rare restaurants that has gotten better and better over time. Looking back at my review when it first opened in the '70s, I see nothing about the place that differentiated it from other restaurants in Little Italy at the time.

Through the '80s, though, owner Germano Fabiani gradually changed the menu to reflect more of the food of his native Tuscany. What I like about the menu now is the balance: regional dishes for the more adventuresome, plenty of old favorites when you just feel like fried calamari followed by lasagna. A thoughtful wine list complements either.

I also like the dining room. It's a warm, comfortable setting with exposed brick walls, a cream and brown color scheme and art nouveau posters. A charming, attentive waitress added to our enjoyment of the evening.

This food is comfort food, not haute cuisine. The bread is chewy, flavorful and fresh — just right for dipping in marinara sauce. Luckily the small, tender mussels we started with were bathed in just what we needed: an admirably fresh-tasting marinara. It was quite spicy, but the flavor of the tomatoes burst through.

You could start with a piping hot puff of a spinach souffle, baked to order and surrounded with heavy bechamel sauce. Follow it with Germano's signature dish, osso buco. The generous portion of tender veal shanks in an intricately seasoned white wine and tomato sauce comes with oven-roasted potatoes. My friend substituted a heavenly swirl of mashed potatoes seasoned with a little garlic and Parmesan cheese.

Germano's has a fine selection of grappas (a dry, colorless brandy), and grappa adds zest to the sauce of another signature dish, gigantic pink shrimp in their shells. They are superb, played off against gently charred, grilled zucchini, onions, peppers and other vegetables.

A special of clams in white sauce over linguine sounded too ordinary to bother with. But the friend who ordered it had the last laugh: The tiny clams were wonderfully tender. Perfectly seasoned, the pasta was so hot that the cheese our waitress sprinkled on it at the table melted deliciously. The dish was decorated with a few small clams in their shells and spangled with a confetti of parsley — very pretty.

On the dessert front, things weren't quite so flawless. The thick coffee sauce smothering a panna cotta (a delicate egg custard) was flavorful but unappetizing-looking. Zabaglione was mousse-like in texture rather than a light froth. But all was forgiven because of the Amaretto sponge cake, light as a cloud, studded with strawberries and sauced with the warm froth I expected when I ordered the zabaglione.

*Elizabeth Large*

# Golden Gate Noodle House

*6-8 Allegheny Ave., Towson • 410-337-2557*
*Hours: Open daily for lunch and dinner*
*Prices: Appetizers, $1.25-$4.95; entrees, $4.50-$11.95*
*Live music: No • Kid's menu: No • Waterfront views: No •*
*Wheelchair access: Yes • Reservations: Accepted*
*Credit cards: Visa, MasterCard, Discover only*

Food essayist and funnyman Calvin Trillin lamented in his book "American Fried": "I often have to sit in a Chinese restaurant helplessly while a tableful of Chinese businessmen across the room are stuffing down succulent-looking dishes that were obviously ordered off the wall."

That's kind of how we felt at the Golden Gate Noodle House, where the specials list was written in Chinese. We watched as two young women shared a plate of glistening Chinese broccoli, and what looked like a country-style stew served in an iron pot. Neither was on the regular menu.

We could have asked our waitress to decipher for us, but she had a brusque, no-nonsense style. Other tables were waiting in the Towson restaurant, painted a deep magenta and adorned with crystal beads hanging from the ceiling.

We did our best to order a mix of familiar and unfamiliar dishes. Some, such as the Sichuan pickles soup, a too-salty broth with bits of pickled vegetables, I wouldn't order again. But I'd recommend the shrimp and squid with spicy salt, coated in tempuralike batter with bits of scallion and chilies.

In a place with a name like Golden Gate Noodle House, we figured noodle dishes would be worth sampling. A lunchtime plate of chicken and square-edged lo mein noodles picked up the dark, smoky flavor of the wok. That smoky flavor was exactly what we missed in the beef and broccoli chow fun. Tender slices of beef in mild brown sauce were simply ladled on top of the wide, milky-white noodles.

The Hunan chicken represents what this restaurant does best. Velvety pieces of chicken were stir-fried with tender-crisp bites of broccoli, snow peas and Chinese cabbage.

There are many dishes under $6, including Sichuan shrimp, in a fragrant, bright red sauce that's more sweet than hot, and vegetable moo shu, a tangle of shredded cabbage, black mushrooms, baby corn and broccoli served with thin pancakes and hoisin sauce. Dishes are served as they're ready, so be prepared to share a dish as you wait.

There's a whole section of Hong Kong-style noodle soups on the menu. We liked the fresh, springy egg noodles in our shredded pork and cabbage soup, but the long pieces of pork were fatty and too big for easy handling. You can order hot and sour soup with noodles or without, as we tried it. It was mild and full of mushrooms and vegetables.

Other than soup, we didn't have much luck with appetizers: heavy egg rolls made with too much dough; steamed dumplings with a mealy vegetable filling; and the combination platter with items like greasy shrimp toast. But stout pork dumplings, called "pan-fried buns," are worth a try.

*Kathryn Higham*

# Hamilton's

*888 S. Broadway, Fells Point • 410-522-2195*
*Hours: Open every day for dinner; prearranged private lunches for parties of 15 or more*
*Prices: Appetizers, $5.75-$7.50; entrees, $16-$25*
*Live music: No • Kid's menu: Yes • Waterfront views: No • Wheelchair access: Yes • Reservations: Suggested*

Hamilton's low-key and jazzy feel may have been forced on them by circumstance. Located in the Admiral Fell hotel, the restaurant doesn't always attract guests that are dressed to the nines. But the restaurant rises to the occasion, with good and handsomely presented food — contemporary American and fun.

The seasonal menu was weighted toward meat when we visited, notably steaks, venison and pork. There are also seafood choices, like the wonderfully fresh fillet of grouper crusted with sesame seeds, surrounded by a celadon-green sauce and decorated with pomegranate seeds. The grouper comes with a fennel-wheatberry pilaf and spaghetti squash.

I'd be hard pressed to choose between the grilled pork loin and the braised lamb shank. The pork is pearly white, juicy and tender. A balsamic vinegar glaze gives it sweetness; and carrots, sugar snap peas and portobello mushrooms add lively color. The lamb , on a bed of risotto and a minty wine sauce, explodes with flavor. Fried onion rings hang jauntily from the shank bone.

Even the most mundane-sounding dishes surprise and delight. The "seasonal garnishes" with a trio of smoked fish turn out to be a bit of superb, sharply seasoned potato salad, caviar wrapped in tissue-thin slices of cucumber and chopped papaya. The fish itself is excellent — the salmon, tuna and trout retaining their individuality through their smoky flavor.

Pumpkin soup garnished with rock shrimp is surprisingly delicate for something so rich with cream, and the flavor of pumpkin is subtle. A flavorful veal and venison pate is one of the best I've tasted in recent memory, and having pear compote as a counterpoint is a stroke of genius.

Even the light, crisp-crusted rolls served with sweet butter are noteworthy. The engaging wine list is seasonal, so it can mirror the changing menu. And "engaging" describes the warm and professional servers who wait on us as well.

So is there anything not to like? I'm reduced to nitpicking.

The kitchen turns out several fabulous and complicated dinners, but something as simple as the fried onion rings on the lamb shank are soggy. My first cup of coffee is strong and bitter. I try again and the second is wonderful.

Desserts are fascinating but flawed. Banana bread pudding tastes much like banana bread with homemade ice cream and praline sauce. A wonderful butter cake with dried cranberry compote could use a bit less Grand Marnier.

Oh, well. These are all quibbles. Overall, I'd say our evening at Hamilton's was a success.

*Elizabeth Large*

# Hampton's

*Harbor Court Hotel, 550 Light St., Inner Harbor • 410-234-0550*
*Hours: Open Tuesdays to Sundays for dinner, Sundays for brunch*
*Prices: Appetizers, $11-$16; entrees, $25-$38; prix-fixe dinners, $45 and $55*
*Live music: No • Kid's menu: No • Waterfront views: No •*
*Wheelchair access: Yes • Reservations: Required*

At Hampton's, the food is almost incidental to the whole experience. A meal here is the epitome of the good life, with plush surroundings, exquisite service, a wine list with many choices by the glass and Beethoven for background music.

Even the flowers on the tables are the same as the last time I visited — a single gardenia floating in a glass bowl. In fact, the salmon-colored dining room has changed so little over the years that it's beginning to have a faded grandeur rather than its earlier nouveau-riche showiness.

I suppose if I had to generalize about how this meal differed from my last at Hampton's, I would say there's less in the way of caloric luxury. If you've come to equate heavy cream with happiness, you're out of luck. The new menu is also going to be less appealing to the masses.

Dinner began with an exquisite hors d'oeuvre, a bit of buttery-smooth fois gras with flecks of raisins and walnuts, one perfect miniature asparagus, two pencil-thin bread sticks and a little pinot noir sauce. As far as I was concerned, it was the high point of the meal.

A marvelous lobster bisque was ladled into a cold soup bowl at the table, lowering it to room temperature.

Slices of duck in a salad with wilted spinach and forest mushrooms were cooked well-done and so were quite tough.

Sauteed oysters dusted with curry arrived warm, but they were nestled in a cold cucumber coulis — somehow the contrast didn't work.

Speckled trout and crab saltimbocca wrapped with Parma ham was a bit dry because the fish had been overcooked.

A warm chocolate hazelnut cake sounded moister and richer than the reality turned out to be.

On the other hand, a first course of raw tuna, lusciously ripe avocado and ruby summer tomatoes, built into a little tower, was one of the best things I've ever eaten. It was decorated with a summery little sauce reminiscent of gazpacho.

Rack of lamb chops vibrated with flavor, and were so lusciously tender you could cut them with the proverbial fork. They were served with crisp, fried ravioli, a clever accompaniment, smoky-flavored grilled eggplant and smooth polenta.

Breast of pheasant offered more subtle pleasures, the meat firm and white with a zingy sauteed spinach and an elegant bit of wild-rice sauce.

For a light for dessert, try the delicate peach soup with a spoonful of homemade Key lime ice cream floating at its center. Or throw caution to the winds and order the dessert trio. Mousse encased in chocolate lace, a miniature creme brulee and a nut tartlet were pure bliss.

*Elizabeth Large*

# Han Sung

*3570 St. John's Lane, Ellicott City • 410-750-3836*
*Hours: Open Tuesday through Sunday for lunch and dinner*
*Prices: Appetizers, $1.50-$7.95; entrees, $7.95-$24.95*
*Live music: No • Kid's menu: No • Waterfront views: No •*
*Wheelchair access: Yes • Reservations: Accepted*

My politically astute friend pointed out that while relations between the countries of Japan and Korea are strained at best, relations between their cuisines are booming. You'll find Japanese sushi and sweet Korean barbecue on the same menu at Han Sung in Ellicott City.

This spare, bright restaurant has the feeling of a luncheonette, with tables topped in wood-grain Formica and cartons stacked in the hallway. There's little ornamentation outside of a few paper lanterns, sushi posters and a small sushi bar.

Despite the toned-down atmosphere, service is gracious and efficient. Our waitress, who kept our cups filled with green tea, suggested the Japanese sunomono as an appetizer. It was a delicious cold salad of vinegar-dressed cucumber, sea vegetable, octopus, squid and, unfortunately, fake crab. The mandu gook soup, the Korean version of won ton soup, was wonderful, with delicate ginger-spiked dumplings and slivered threads of cooked egg, seaweed and cellophane noodles.

Another Korean dish, the nokdu bean pancake, was pleasantly chewy, with a golden, greasy crust. It was cut into bite-sized pieces to dunk into a soy-based sauce. Our favorite was the deep-fried soft-shell crab, wrapped in a tempuralike batter and served with a zingy ginger dipping sauce.

From the sushi bar, we tried the rainbow maki, a giant roll swirled with different colors, flavors and textures. Each roll was wrapped on the outside with a piece of tuna, salmon or yellowtail, and filled inside with cucumber, roe and cooked eel. Our only problem was figuring out how to eat it without it falling apart. Fingers were the best option. A spicy yellowtail roll was just as fresh and appealing.

While there are no Korean barbecue tables at Han Sung, they do prepare barbecue skillfully in the kitchen. Our sizzling platter of jae-yuk guey, thinly sliced pork, arrived with a flourish. The meat was tender and lean, tossed with onions and scallions in a sweet and spicy sauce.

Our waitress brought curly lettuce leaves and bean paste so we could roll up the meat "taco-style."

Another Korean dish, a whole corvina fish, was not as easy to appreciate. Our waitress compared it to rockfish, but it was so heavily salted, it tasted more like salt cod. A thick, salty dipping sauce didn't help matters, but we liked the tiny salads of kimchee, bean sprouts and other vegetables that accompanied the fish and the pork barbecue.

Desserts, as in most Asian restaurants, are limited to ice cream. Skip the green-tea flavor, and order the tempura instead. They take a scoop of vanilla, dip it in tempura batter and fry it so quickly, the ice cream doesn't melt.

*Kathryn Higham*

# Hard Rock Cafe Baltimore

*Power Plant, Inner Harbor • 410-347-7625*
*Hours: Open every day for lunch and dinner*
*Prices: Appetizers, $3.59-$6.99; sandwiches, salads and entrees, $5.99-$15.99*
*Live music: No • Kid's menu: Yes • Waterfront views: Yes •*
*Wheelchair access: Yes • Reservations: No*
*Other locations: Yes (international chain)*

Go to see more rock and roll memorabilia collected in one place than you ever dreamed possible. Gawk at the blue Cadillac hanging over the guitar-shaped bar. Go to drink thick chocolate malts in Hard Rock Baltimore souvenir glasses and eat fat bacon cheeseburgers and superb french fries. Go to hear the loudest music you've ever heard.

One of our 18-year-olds guests covered her ears and said, "I wish they'd turn down the music." We didn't try to talk over the music. We wanted to save our voices for the important stuff, ordering dinner.

Ah yes, the food. It seems a bit beside the point, doesn't it? To generalize, this is what good chain-restaurant food should be. Not too ambitious, generous portions, consistent quality from restaurant to restaurant.

The menu is divided between nostalgic diner fare (shakes, burgers, a blue-plate special) and trendy casual food (nachos, Caesar chicken salad, grilled-vegetable sandwich) — with a little Memphis thrown in (barbecue chicken, ribs).

The Hard Rock's pig sandwich falls under this last category. The menu says it's the restaurant's most popular sandwich. This is a sanitized but pleasant enough version of barbecue, with thick slices of pork shoulder and a vinegar-tinged sauce on a fresh bun. Nothing messy about it — a plus or a minus, depending on your attitude about barbecue.

You could make a meal of the Hard Rock's appetizers, like "Tupelo style chicken" — juicy morsels of crisply fried boneless breast with apricot and mustard dipping sauces. Two could make a meal of the nachos, piled high with pinto beans, sour cream, salsa, melted cheese and peppers.

If you're watching your calories, this probably isn't the best place to eat; but you can try the grilled Chinese chicken salad with fresh greens, vegetables, Mandarin oranges, fried noodles and a good peanut and honey-lime dressing.

Fajitas with all the fixings, including guacamole, are another reasonably healthful and good choice. There's a vegetarian version available if you're so inclined.

The Hard Rock Cafe has all the usual decadent desserts, like chocolate chip cookie pie and hot fudge brownies. A slice of strawberry rhubarb pie sounded good to me, but judging from the soggy crust — not the freshest I've ever had — the Hard Rock isn't moving many slices. Instead have a cold, thick, chocolate milkshake; they're great.

Not a bad meal, all things considered. And when you consider that visitors will be likely to drag us locals down there, we should all be very grateful the food is decent.

*Elizabeth Large*

# Hard Times

*8865 Stanford Blvd., Columbia • 410-312-0700*
*Hours: Open daily for lunch and dinner*
*Prices: Appetizers, $1.95-$5.95; entrees, $3.95-$6.50*
*Live music: No • Kid's menu: Yes • Waterfront views: No •*
*Wheelchair access: Yes • Reservations: Accepted for large parties*
*Other locations: Yes (national chain)*

Hard Times tries hard to appeal to the varied tastes of American chili lovers. That includes the Texas purists who want all meat and no beans, the spaghetti-loving nonconformists of Cincinnati, and healthy eaters from all parts who prefer a meatless variety.

Decorated with lassos, horseshoes and other cowboy paraphernalia, the restaurant has the look of an old sepia photo.

At Hard Times, you can decide for yourself which chili you like, without shelling out a dime. Just ask for a sampler dish of the four chili variations: Texas, Cincinnati, vegetarian and turkey. Spoon some on saltines and then order your favorite.

One taste might be enough, though. That's the way we felt about the herb-stricken turkey chili, which had so much sage and thyme that it almost tasted dirty. The Texas-style chili was wet with meat juices, mildly seasoned and full of coarsely ground beef that is sure to win fans.

My friend preferred the taste of the chunky vegetarian chili made with peanuts, green bell peppers and jalapenos. Unfortunately, he ordered it "five-ways." Translation: 1) chili, 2) spaghetti, 3) beans, 4) Cheddar cheese, and 5) onions. It arrived looking like an unappealing plate of pasta with watery sauce.

Spaghetti is Cincinnati's contribution to the world of chili, along with a sweet dose of cinnamon. It's an unusual combination, and it's prepared expertly at Hard Times.

While chili dominates the menu at Hard Times, it doesn't quite hit the culinary bull's-eye. That honor belongs to a perfectly cooked, hand-formed burger with fabulous flavor. It's made with the same beef that goes into the Cincinnati chili. The roll was stale, but the accompanying coleslaw was freshly made, and thin, skin-on fries were fantastic.

Beef isn't the only meat on the menu, however. Chicken is available on sandwiches, pasta and as a topping for a salad of romaine and iceberg lettuce.

At the bar, all the finger foods are worth a try — crisp Texas wings with tangy hot sauce; greaseless, crunchy jalapeno poppers dripping cheese; and pale, batter-dipped onion rings, so sweet they must be Vidalias.

To go with them, there are 10 microbrews on tap. Our waiter demonstrated impressive first-hand knowledge of the beers, giving each enthusiastic endorsement.

Another kind of beer makes a perfect dessert at this chili parlor: mahogany-colored, honey-sweetened root beer with a scoop of vanilla ice cream. The frozen peanut butter pie, fudgy Oreo pie and sophisticated lemon-blueberry shortbread are all suitable as well.

*Kathryn Higham*

# Harryman House

*340 Main St., Reisterstown • 410-833-8850*
*Hours: Open every day for lunch and dinner*
*Prices: Appetizers, $5.75-$10; sandwiches, $6.25- $10.75; entrees, $14-$24.*
*Live music: No • Kid's menu: No • Waterfront views: No •*
*Wheelchair access: Yes • Reservations: Suggested*

You could call the Harryman House old-fashioned. After all, the log cabin that forms part of the restaurant is 200 years old. And the kitchen has never had a reputation for producing cutting-edge food. Good but traditional. Dependable but not exciting. That's the Harryman House.

Only it's not.

Avoid the dining rooms near the popular and noisy bar, and make your way back to the original log cabin room or the enclosed porch surrounding it. Here, for a complete change of pace, families and serious eaters are conversing quietly. It's a pleasant room, with a sense of history, but it's not fancy except for the white linen and candles on the tables.

But what makes the Harryman House seem really up to date is the menu. Not that there's a lot of over-the-top food on it, but the concepts are Now.

Trendy menu concept No. 1: Appetizers that are expensive compared to the entrees but that really function as small meals in themselves. Take the slices of grilled duck breast, with undertones of honey and orange. They are placed while still warm on a bed of mixed greens, while fresh raspberries point up the raspberry vinaigrette of the greens. This was my favorite of the more-than-appetizers we tried, but I also enjoyed the smoky flavor of the trout cake, which comes with a green salad on the side, where you might expect a sprig of parsley. Less successful was a goat cheese and Vidalia onion tart, warm and puffy but too sweet for a first course.

Trendy menu concept No. 2: As many salads, sandwiches and such as haute cuisine dinners. (Who woulda thunk it — nachos deluxe on the same menu as glazed salmon with a thyme-honey infusion?) I was tempted by a filet mignon sandwich smothered in mushrooms and onions; but the yellow corn salmon burger with pineapple-tomatillo chutney and sweet potato fries sounded more intriguing. The fries were great, but the salmon burger was pretty forgettable.

Not so the gorgeous shrimp chartreuse, the perfectly cooked crustaceans piled high with grilled eggplant, zucchini and tomatoes, with a lovely buttery sauce and sprigs of fresh rosemary. It's an example of trendy menu concept No. 3: Food that is at once elegant, fresh, light and not over-fussed with.

But for dessert, forget trends. Forget fresh and light and indulge in ripe bananas sauteed in butter and brown sugar over ice cream. Or the dainty individual chocolate bundt cake, which has a healthy slug of molten chocolate at its center. But if you must have something light, it's hard to beat the cloudlike chiffon Key lime pie.

*Elizabeth Large*

# Haussner's

*3242 Eastern Ave., Highlandtown • 410-327-8365*
*Hours: Open Tuesdays to Saturdays for lunch and dinner*
*Prices: Appetizers, $4.10-$10.35; entrees, $7.60-$25.95*
*Live music: No • Kid's menu: No • Waterfront views: No •*
*Wheelchair access: Yes • Reservations: Accepted for lunch*

If you've never been to Haussner's before, picture a restaurant like no other. It has a European feel to it, with its dark paneled walls, white tablecloths and amazing art collection of over 700 works. Every spare inch of wall space is covered with original oil paintings, watercolors, bas-reliefs, vases, statuary, figurines and I don't know what all.

According to the menu, artists like Durer, Rembrandt and Whistler are represented.

Haussner's has its own bakery; its spectacular dessert cases decorate the front of the restaurant. It has a stag bar, complete with nudes (objets d'art, that is). And a museum that contains the overflow art from the spacious dining rooms.

Like the art, there is a gem or two on the menu if you know where to look. The fried eggplant is a Rembrandt among vegetables, with its hot, soft interior and crisp, deliciously greasy exterior. Great dumplings, if you like heavy, flavorful dumplings. Order one of each, Tyrolean and potato, swimming in a good, thick gravy. I could make a meal on the potato pancakes alone — thin, crunchy-edged slices of pure bliss.

Haussner's Wiener schnitzel a la Holstein is the Cadillac of Wiener schnitzels. The veal cutlet is tender, flavorful and not too heavily breaded. Its fried egg is perfectly done, and anchovies and capers lend a little pizazz.

But then the baked clams taste like chopped rubber bands tossed with garlic butter and arranged in clam shells. Fried calamari would be just about perfect except that the kitchen has over-doused the crisp rings with lemon juice. The gorgeous rolls, pumpernickel sticks and muffins are cold and tasteless. The famous strawberry pie is awash in blood-red glaze and the crust is too soggy to eat.

Somewhere between these highs and lows falls the rest of our meal. Maryland crab soup has the usual vegetables, bits of crab and seasonings. It's a perfectly respectable version, but if this was the only crab soup you'd ever had, you'd wonder what all the fuss was about.

Crab Clinton involves white lumps of crab, bits of Smithfield ham and spinach over green and white fettuccine in a rich cream sauce. Not bad, but a little goes a long way. A "Frenched" pork loin chop is pleasant enough, but the horseradish-mustard glaze is surprisingly sweet. A chocolate mousse cake looks gorgeous, and a mile-high slice of coconut cake is lovely and fresh. Both are fairly tasteless.

We've sampled so much food, our nice waitress has had to bring it on a trolley. Amazingly, she doesn't seem to notice. My impression is that everyone orders like a pig here, not just restaurant critics. Haussner's menu is just too tempting.

*Elizabeth Large*

# The Helmand

*806 N. Charles St., Mount Vernon • 410-752-0311*
*Hours: Open daily for dinner only*
*Prices: Appetizers, $2.95; entrees, $8.50-$14.95*
*Live music: No • Kid's menu: No • Waterfront views: No •*
*Wheelchair access: Yes • Reservations: Accepted*

The Helmand is that rarity, a restaurant that does what it sets out to do superbly. But if Afghan food with its emphasis on vegetables and stews and flavors of yogurt, mint, cardamom and garlic doesn't appeal to you, then read no further.

Although it's not haute cuisine, the quality of the Helmand's food remains at a consistently high level. No eating place in Baltimore gives you better value for your dining-out dollar. All first courses on the regular menu are $2.95, while main courses are kept under $10. (Only one dish on the list of daily specials goes up as high as $14.95.)

You don't expect an inexpensive ethnic restaurant to have a decent wine list, but the Helmand does. Short but decent. And you might not expect such an appealing setting.

The two dining rooms are comfortable and romantic, with Afghan textiles decorating the walls, fresh white napery and flickering candles on each table. (The tables are, I admit, a bit too close together; but that's only a problem when the restaurant is very full. Then it can be quite noisy.)

You should start with tender aushak, delicate pasta pillows filled with chopped leeks. Two sauces complement them: ground beef and yogurt infused with mint. Also outstanding are ethereally crisp, golden pastries filled with ground beef or leeks and covered with flavorful sauces. Sauteed pumpkin with yogurt-garlic sauce is the signature appetizer; it's delicious but sweet enough to end a meal rather than begin it.

I never get quite as excited about the main courses as the appetizers; but that's only because I've eaten so much by that point, including too much of the warm flat bread with butter melting softly on it.

The char-grilled rack of lamb is available only on Friday and Saturday nights. But I'm perfectly happy with dishes like baby eggplant stuffed with spinach in a sun-dried tomato sauce, or tender boneless chicken, tomatoes and button mushrooms in a sauce made of yogurt and sour cream. This last is served with fiery spinach and highly seasoned rice.

As good as these are, the most satisfying of our main courses was a moist and flaky sea bass, arranged in a sort of stew with slices of fresh ginger, tomatoes, raisins and red-skinned potatoes.

According to our waitress, some customers come just for the ice cream, which is served with dates, figs and mango. Other pleasing dessert choices are an unassuming custard with fresh cut-up fruit and berries, and a pretty plate of pastries. If you haven't left room for dessert, at least have a cup of the strong and satisfying Afghan tea brewed with cardamom.

*Elizabeth Large*

# Hunt Valley Szechuan

*9 Schilling Road, Hunt Valley • 410-527-1818*
*Hours: Open Monday through Saturday for lunch and dinner, Sunday for dinner*
*Prices: Appetizers, $2-$6.95; entrees, $7.45-$24.95*
*Live music: No • Kid's menu: No • Waterfront views: No • Wheelchair access: Yes • Reservations: Accepted*

There are many things to like about the Hunt Valley Szechuan, a restaurant recommended to me by readers:

The microwaveable takeout containers. You don't have to order the Peking duck in advance. The Asian sweet and sour cabbage slaw that arrives at the table when you sit down.

The miso soup. I know, I know, miso soup is Japanese. But the Hunt Valley Szechuan advertises itself as specializing in Chinese and Japanese cuisine. It also has a sushi bar.

The variety of lamb dishes on the menu. The service, as speedy as if everything had been prepared in advance. (Maybe that's not a good sign.) The free orange sherbet at the end of the meal.

You may have noticed that I'm skirting the central issue — how the food tastes. That's because the Hunt Valley Szechuan is a pleasant enough place, one that I don't want to be negative about. But the fact is that it's no better and no worse than others of its kind: the contemporary decor, which once must have seemed quite daring but now looks a bit dated; the chef's specialties, which are much the same as every other Sichuan restaurant's (General Tso's chicken, orange beef); the heavily sauced dishes designed to appeal to American tastes.

The Peking duck, a house specialty, had a fine crisp skin and no fat, but the meat was dry. The pancakes, which you spread with hoisin sauce and fill with bits of duck meat, skin and scallions, were thicker than they should have been.

The cold noodle appetizer in a peanut butter and sesame oil sauce was too sweet and had none of the promised cucumber. Lamb in black pepper was wonderfully tender, but its sauce had so much canned ground pepper we couldn't eat it. The tea was so strong and black it was almost undrinkable.

I can be more positive about some of our dishes. Subgum soft won ton soup for two was made with a fresh-tasting, not-too-salty chicken broth, lots of fresh vegetables and a good amount of shrimp, chicken and pork.

From the Japanese side of the menu, vegetable tempura was lightly battered and crisply fried and not too greasy.

The kitchen produces respectable versions of fresh scallops with mixed vegetables in a mildly seasoned sauce and a "Two Flavors" dish (shrimp in a sweet and sour sauce on one side of the plate, and a spicy pork on the other, separated by a line of broccoli). But neither was better than you could get at almost any neighborhood Chinese restaurant.

Afterward, when I asked my friends what they thought the best part of the meal was, one of them said, "When we played charades with the fortunes in the fortune cookies."

*Elizabeth Large*

# Hunters Lodge

*9445 Baltimore National Pike, Ellicott City • 410-461-4990*
*Hours: Open Monday through Friday for lunch, every night for dinner, Sunday brunch*
*Prices: Appetizers, $5.50-$9.95; entrees, $9.95-23.95*
*Live music: Friday and Saturday nights • Kid's menu: Yes •*
*Waterfront views: No • Wheelchair access: Yes • Reservations: Accepted*

You have to wonder why the Hunters Lodge parking lot is full every night.

Here's a former Chinese restaurant that's been converted into a log cabin. It sits smack dab on Baltimore National Pike among the strip malls — not the most scenic location.

The rustic interior is warm and cozy in a country fried steak kind of way. The tables are close together, with white tablecloths over cheerful red ones. A baby cries fretfully in one corner. There are hundreds of places just like the Hunters Lodge. So why is every table filled?

The answer, of course, lies with the food. It's a most amazing combination — given the setting — of homey Greek dishes and haute contemporary American.

On the menu you have spanakopita and duck confit. Moussaka and rack of lamb with port demi-glace and a potato and garlic napoleon. Stuffed grape leaves and garlic prawns over creamy polenta with a vegetable ragout.

The food presentation is almost a work of art. A fat chunk of braised salmon, fresh and moist, is arranged with barley-studded risotto and a melange of fall vegetables. Tender white medallions of veal have a pretty, buttery sauce and a mash of carrots, turnips and celery root. A dusting of chopped parsley around the edge of the plate, little dots of caviar, sprigs of rosemary or thyme finish it off.

And don't write off the homey Greek dishes. The tyropita — hot pillows of flaky phyllo dough with a soft filling of feta, fontina and Parmesan — were superb. They were paired with a salad of baby greens and chopped tomatoes and onions.

And to finish: a fabulous creme brulee with cold, quivery custard under a hot, crisp caramelized topping. True, one could argue that surrounding it with creme anglaise was overkill, but what a way to go.

I can't say everything is perfect. Serve white fluff bread if you must, but then don't give us trendy herbed olive oil to dip it in. The soup of the day, asparagus, was a flavorful, thick, rich puree; but it's an odd option out of season. Crispy shrimp (coated with Greek "shredded wheat" and then deep fried) were wonderful, but the sauce they were placed on contained too much mustard. A beautiful chocolate pate dessert was simply too bittersweet.

Still, these are quibbles when you think about having a place like this in the neighborhood, where you can go in jeans and take the kids. They'll be happy with the pasta marinara while you indulge in the strip steak with a Gorgonzola sauce, sun-dried tomato polenta and wild mushroom duxelles.

*Elizabeth Large*

# Ikaros

*4805 Eastern Ave., Highlandtown • 410-633-3750*
*Hours: Open for lunch and dinner every day except Tuesday*
*Prices: Appetizers, $1.95-$4.95; entrees, $7.85-$14.95*
*Live music: No • Kid's menu: No • Waterfront views: No •*
*Wheelchair access: Yes • Reservations: Accepted*

Ikaros, the granddaddy of Greek restaurants in Baltimore, is alive and well in Highlandtown.

Opened in 1969, the restaurant is still going strong. The rooms sport crisp stuccoed walls, dark wood ceilings, oversized photos of life in Greece, white tablecloths and enough touches of blue to call to mind the Aegean. The menu has remained relatively untouched.

Ikaros is, after all, a place of tradition, not cutting-edge innovation. Portions are large, and the dishes served are likely to show up on Sunday-dinner tables in Greek homes.

The lamb braised in wine and tomato sauce is a perfect example. The meat was tender and flavorful, falling from the bone after hours of slow cooking. It was served on an enormous platter, the meaty shank pieces nestled against overcooked crescent-shaped pasta in an uncomplicated sauce. The dish had a certain homey appeal, but not the kind of dazzle that would make us want to order it again.

We'd rather recommend the moussaka, made with lots of sharp cheese. Layered as usual on a bed of eggplant slices, this vegetarian version was so richly seasoned we didn't miss the meat.

Crab-topped fish wrapped in phyllo sheets looked spectacular. But the enormous strudel-like roll was filled with a pasty crab imperial that overwhelmed fresh flounder fillets inside. It was served with green beans, simmered to softness in a tomato sauce, much like the one we had with the lamb.

Appetizers pleased us more. Plump grape leaves stuffed with a loose filling of beef and rice were moist and delicious, topped with a creamy lemon sauce. The cucumber and sour cream-based tzatziki was full of garlic punch and spread on soft Italian bread. Pureed eggplant salad, flavored with garlic and the sweet pungency of something that tasted like pickled relish, was terrific, too.

If you're looking for interesting ethnic flavors, skip the entrees altogether. Make a meal of a few appetizers and a large Greek salad with tomatoes, green peppers, olives and feta. Follow up with a tiny cup of Greek coffee and Ikaros' wonderful custard cake. This thick square of delicate pudding was the highlight of our meal. A dense rolled baklava and a kataifi, a pastry made with nuts, syrup and what looks like shredded wheat, tasted overly sweet in comparison.

For many people, the appeal of eating ethnic food comes from discovering something new. That's part of why we loved the eggplant salad and custard cake so much. They may be classics in Highlandtown, but before we tried them at Ikaros, they were Greek to us.

*Kathryn Higham*

# J. Paul's

*Light Street Pavilion, Harborplace • 410-659-1889*
*Hours: Open Monday through Sunday for lunch and dinner;*
  *weekend brunch*
*Prices: Appetizers, $4.95-$8.95; entrees, $10.95-$19.95*
*Live music: No • Kid's menu: Yes • Waterfront views: Yes •*
*Wheelchair access: Yes • Reservations: Suggested*
*Other locations: Yes (regional chain)*

J. Paul's features an antique bar, fireplace, exposed brick, wooden booths and period fixtures, attempting to turn the glass and metal exoskeleton of Harborplace into an old-fashioned saloon. It works well enough, but would have worked even better in a wonderful old rowhouse.

J. Paul's, a mini-chain restaurant, became known for its crab cakes, hamburgers and house brew. But there's more — like a duckling salad with spiced pecans and a molasses and fig vinaigrette. Or seared breast of chicken with a creamy apple and leek compote. Or the 16-spice pork chop.

Still, J. Paul's is a saloon at heart; and being a saloon is what it does best. The beer drinkers loved J. Paul's smooth amber ale, but the wine drinkers weren't so happy. Our waitress told us, "If you want a Chardonnay, I recommend the Riesling." And when we ordered something different, she brought the Riesling anyway.

You can enjoy the house brew in J. Paul's signature amber ale and Cheddar soup, a creamy concoction that's silky smooth with twice the flavor of most cheese soups. Or share the enticing chipotle chicken quesadilla with goat cheese and Cheddar, spiced with the chili it's named after.

Part of the saloon dining experience is certainly scarfing down raw oysters; and J. Paul's offers several varieties, all of them plump, briny-sweet and fresh-tasting. J. Paul's crab cakes are as good as advertised, although I was skeptical when our waitress said, "They are 99 percent lump crab meat and 1 percent Japanese bread crumbs." But you can't argue with snowy lumps of backfin, the barest amount of filler, perfectly seasoned and finished off with a golden crust.

J. Paul's ribs are a specialty. It's an enormous portion of back ribs, tender but a bit drier than you may be used to. The barbecue sauce is spicy, and adds flavor without overpowering the meat. Unfortunately, the kitchen slopped the accompanying baked beans half in a bowl and half on the plate and the french fries were heavily over-salted.

The mango and rum-glazed rotisseried duckling sounded appealing. The reality was a soggy half duck with a lot of bottled chutney on top. Sides of spinach with blue cheese and golden-crusted grits cakes helped to make up for it.

Desserts are homemade. Chocolate fanciers will be enthralled with a giant brownie covered in chocolate ice cream, whipped cream and chocolate sauce; but I fell in love with the apple pie, made with fresh apples and a good crust, with J. Paul's fine vanilla ice cream nestling close.

*Elizabeth Large*

# Joung Kak

*18 W. 20 St., Baltimore • 410-837-5231*
*Hours: Open daily for lunch and dinner*
*Prices: Appetizers, $1.50-$9.95; entrees, $7.95-$29.95*
*Live music: No • Kid's menu: Yes • Waterfront views: No • Wheelchair access: Yes • Reservations: Accepted*

If you're a fan of barbecue, you owe it to yourself to try it Korean-style at Joung Kak, where the meat is cooked on a smoldering caldron set smack into the center of your table.

Joung Kak stays open until the early-morning hours serving Korean, Japanese and Chinese dishes. Its forte, though, is Korean barbecue. Half the restaurant is set up for tabletop grilling, with individual steel exhaust hoods overhead.

Ask for one of those barbecue tables, and enjoy the show. Soon after we ordered, a delicate-looking waitress amazed us by carrying an iron pot full of burning wood coals to our table. The pot looked heavy. Plunk it went into the round cavity in our table and was quickly topped by a brass grill cover.

While the grill was heating, our waitress brought us lots of bowls: rice, salads, sauces and vegetables — a dozen tiny accompaniments to the two barbecue dishes we had ordered. Then came the marinated meat: raw sirloin, sliced exquisitely thin, and two racks of short ribs. The waitress cut the meat off the bones in front of us with a pair of jumbo shears.

Half the sirloin was cooked first, followed by the rib meat and then the rest of the sirloin. We wrapped slivers of cooked beef in curly lettuce leaves, layered with soybean sauce, raw garlic, shredded scallions and sliced jalapenos. The meat was fabulous. Tender. We even liked the robust flavors of the accompanying raw garlic and chili.

This communal meal was a fun way to eat. We took turns lifting meat off the grill with chopsticks and passing around bowls of spicy pickled kimchi, young spinach leaves with red chili dressing, sweet and sour radish, stir-fried seaweed, bean sprouts in sesame oil and fried tofu.

Our two barbecue dishes were enough for four to share, but we also sampled a gigantic seafood pancake (chewy squid, shrimp and whole scallions encased in a battered disk), and a spicy "hot pot" soup (made with fresh codfish steaks, cabbage, zucchini and chunks of creamy tofu).

We liked the tempura coating on a fried squid appetizer, but the pieces were tough. Fried dumplings, filled with seasoned pork and bean threads, and a dumpling soup, in a broth with sliced beef and egg, were both better starters.

The menu at Joung Kak can be dizzying. There's a full page of sushi, loads of lunch specials, Chinese and Japanese dishes, plus dozens of Korean specialties. Some, like the cabbage-wrapped oyster and pork, sounded intriguing. Others, cold pigs' feet and barbecued beef heart in particular, might appeal to more adventurous palates.

We'll definitely be back for another group barbecue, though. It was the most fun we've had eating in a long time.

*Kathryn Higham*

# Joy America Cafe

*800 Key Highway, Federal Hill • 410-244-6500*
*Hours: Open Tuesday through Sunday for lunch and dinner,*
  *Sunday for brunch*
*Prices: Appetizers, $5.25-$9.95; entrees, $17.95-$28.95*
*Live music: No • Kid's menu: Yes • Waterfront views: Yes •*
*Wheelchair access: Yes • Reservations: Requested*

If the thought of one more chain steakhouse opening up in Baltimore makes you want to move to another state, run — don't walk — to the Joy America Cafe in the American Visionary Art Museum. Its strange but poetic menu is an antidote for every ordinary restaurant meal you've ever had.

At lunchtime the staff will try to get you in and out in under an hour (unless you want to linger). And there are some choices for conservative eaters, like the chicken breast on focaccia sandwich. At dinner, however, our meal was surprisingly uneven and the service erratic. At these prices, you expect things to be close to perfection.

The setting almost made up for the flaws. Dinner is the time to eat outside on Joy America's balcony, as the day slowly fades and the city's lights start to wink on. The large, curvy balcony has a panoramic view of the harbor on one side and an engaging view of Federal Hill on the other.

The dinner menu is a dazzling combination of Southwestern and Pacific Rim. Each plate is a dramatic work of art, decorated with squiggles of colorful coulis, spangled with herbs and garnished with everything from a slice of fresh fig to a curlicue of caramelized sugar.

The combinations are surprising, to say the least. Delicious rack-of-lamb chops, tender and pink and charred at the edges, were paired with polenta flavored with coconut and dried cherries. Unfortunately, we got three enormous slabs of this sweet polenta, which would have worked in moderation, and only a decorative scattering of slender haricots verts.

As complicated as this food is, the slip-ups were simple, like salmon cooked to the point of dryness. Luckily, the green-lipped mussels alongside the fish were as plump and flavorful as they were beautiful in their green shells. And Asian noodles with a rhubarb sauce had lots of fruity pizazz.

Appetizers had their ups and downs. Ahi tuna and salmon rolls were very fine, their delicate flavors accented with fiery wasabi and Asian oil. Scallops and bite-sized pieces of tender beef were skewered with pearl onions and kumquats — marred only by overcooked tenderloins. Corn chowder with smoked chicken and julienned zucchini tasted like the essence of fresh corn and cream but had too much hot pepper.

Desserts sounded wonderful but only one was flawless — something called "Spoons of Joy," three Japanese soup spoons filled with three different flavors of creme brulee.

There's so much potential here, and the view alone is worth a visit. But sometimes the simplest things — like not overcooking the fish — are overlooked.

*Elizabeth Large*

# La Tavola

*248 Albemarle St., Little Italy • 410-685-1859*
*Hours: Open Friday, Saturday, Sunday for lunch, dinner every day*
*Prices: Appetizers, $5-$7; entrees, $12-$24*
*Live music: No • Kid's menu: No • Waterfront views: No •*
*Wheelchair access: Yes • Reservations: Suggested*

You've heard the complaints about Little Italy: The restaurants are clones of one another. Nobody's doing any original cooking. It's turned into a tourist trap. It's not the bargain it used to be. Like most generalizations, they aren't true, except maybe the last. But if you have any doubts, try La Tavola.

Start with the decor. The entrance is a screaming yellow, except for the purple door. The ceiling is intensely blue. The potted palms add a nice tropical touch. The windows are draped in gauzy purple stuff. No matter what you think of the effect, it doesn't look like any other restaurant in Little Italy.

We started with wonderful bread and three superb first courses. The kitchen successfully pairs fresh mozzarella with roasted sweet peppers instead of the traditional tomatoes.

Equally good was insalata di mare. Tender scallops, mussels, calamari and chunks of shrimp tossed with vinaigrette and green olives were nestled in a radicchio leaf.

Carpaccio tartufato turned out to be a salad, too. The shavings of raw beef and Parmesan were bedded on arugula and dressed with vinaigrette; the flavors and textures mingled beautifully.

Each pasta on the menu sounds better than the last. The mafalde alla fiorentina, a potentially chancy combination, pleased us. The curly-edged noodles were cooked perfectly and tossed with spinach scented with nutmeg, ricotta that melted into a creamy sauce, pine nuts and raisins.

La Tavola offers various grilled fish — from monkfish to swordfish. We settled on the marinated salmon with mushrooms and roast potatoes. The buttery sauteed mushrooms were a high point of the evening. But while the salmon steak was beautifully fresh, the much-touted marinade didn't flavor it as much as we expected. And the fish would have been moister if it had been grilled a shorter time.

Still, the only dud of the evening was cotoletta alla milanese. This was breaded and fried veal scaloppine, covered with chopped radicchio, red onion and tomato. It was an interesting idea, but the reality didn't have a great deal of flavor.

On to dessert. Tiramisu is featured, but you can get tiramisu everywhere. Instead have the chocolate "salami," thin slices of dried-fruit-and-nut-studded chocolate roll that look exactly like salami slices. They were prettily arranged with fruit on a pool of zabaglione. Thin slices of pear poached in red wine on more of that creamy custard made a fine light dessert. Or go for an old favorite, cannoli, with the restaurant's own filling sparked with ground nuts and chocolate.

*Elizabeth Large*

# Ladew Topiary Gardens Cafe

*3535 Jarrettsville Pike, Monkton • 410-557-9570*
*Hours: Seasonal; open for lunch every day, dinner Thursdays only*
*Prices: Appetizers, $4.75-$6.75, entrees, $9.75-$12.25*
*Live music: No • Kid's menu: No • Waterfront views: No •*
*Wheelchair access: Yes • Reservations: Accepted for dinner*

One hot summer evening, we drove to Monkton to have supper in the lush greenness of Ladew Topiary Gardens.

In spite of the heat, it was pleasant on the cafe's brick patio, what with the fragrant gardenia plant at its center, the perennials around the stone wall, the deep woods as backdrop. (Eat outdoors because the cafe isn't air-conditioned.)

Not a breeze was stirring, but with a nice cold supper we would have been perfectly comfortable. We thought we'd start with the soup of the day, a spectacular cream of asparagus, silky against the tongue and a perfect pale green. The only catch: It was served hot. Then what about an entree salad? Sorry, it's available only at lunch.

We ordered the salmon, but, unfortunately, it comes with two vegetables that not only were hot but looked hot on the plate: a timbale of bright yellow rice and highly seasoned chunks of zucchini cooked with tomatoes.

Portions are small here, which is fine — they are priced accordingly. Too bad the kitchen overcooked the thin fillet of salmon. Its raspberry sauce, a bit sweet for my taste, turned up again on both the baked Brie and our dessert plates; but at least the kitchen didn't drown the fish in it.

A crab cake was chock-full of lump crab meat and nicely seasoned, except that it was too salty. It had an excellent remoulade sauce, but the waitress had to be reminded to bring it. Saffron rice and zucchini wouldn't be my first choice to have with the crab cake. Much more appealing-sounding was what comes with it at lunchtime, a vegetable pasta salad.

The dinner menu is limited. If you don't want soup or salad, the only first course is warm Brie with caramelized almonds and raspberry sauce, which we liked. You could order a salad of baby lettuces with raspberry vinaigrette. But I recommend the classic Caesar salad, with good, fresh romaine, lots of cheese, whole anchovies and a zingy dressing.

Follow it with farfalle pasta tossed with shiitakes, chevre, sun-dried tomatoes, kalamata olives and pine nuts, and you've got yourself a meal.

Save room for dessert, because it's the best part. There are only three: strawberries on a warm, sweet biscuit covered with whipped cream; a suave chocolate mousse bombe; a cheesecake with a fresh berry sauce. We also ordered two coffees and an ice tea; but the waitress couldn't remember what we had wanted, she said, so she just brought an extra coffee.

On paper the service sounds dreadful. But they were nice kids who seemed to be trying hard. The setting was casual and we were having a good time, so it was hard to get too upset that our water glasses weren't refilled.

*Elizabeth Large*

# Lennys Chop House

*Harbor Inn Pier 5, 711 Eastern Ave., Inner Harbor • 410-843-5555*
*Hours: Open Monday through Saturday for dinner*
*Prices: Appetizers, $7.50-$16.95; entrees, $16.95-$59.90*
*Live music: Wednesday, Thursday, and Saturday nights •*
*Kid's menu: No • Waterfront views: Yes • Wheelchair access: Yes •*
*Reservations: Suggested*

If you're tired of exotic ingredients, clever pairings and over-elaborate presentations, you will love Lennys' simple and nostalgic menu of comfort foods: steaks and chops and a wedge of iceberg lettuce with blue-cheese dressing.

But there's simple and then there's simple Lennys-style. This is one handsome restaurant, with its high ceilings, clean lines, dark, rich woods, muted colors and splendid chandeliers. There's a swanky bar, a wine room and a private dining room. The service is superb. The food is outrageously indulgent. Who could mind simplicity when you're talking about triple-cut lamb chops, full of flavor, with edges of crisp, sizzling fat? Or icy-cold, meaty oysters on the half shell?

Steaks are superb — cuts like a large porterhouse are grilled to rosy perfection. Of course, you pay for perfection, up to $59.90 for a 32-ounce double sirloin.

You can get a Brobdingnagian pork chop, the snowy white flesh just tinged with pink so it retains its juicy flavor. Order the old-fashioned, yummy, creamed spinach and perhaps the well-seasoned mashed potatoes with it.

Seafood is as good as the steaks and chops. Lennys' tuna is sushi grade and has the texture of filet mignon when ordered rare. Beautifully cleaned, fat mussels are steamed in an engaging sauce of wine and tomatoes. A lobster cocktail consists of half a chicken lobster out of its shell, arranged artistically on the plate and served with a fiery remoulade.

Most of the first courses are seafood, but you could also get a warm duck salad. The duck is shredded, then tossed with baby greens, goat cheese, spiced pecans and large, strong-tasting canned hearts of palm.

The kitchen is best when it's preparing the superb ingredients in as simple a way as possible. I'm not sure why the porterhouse steak, for instance, comes with one fried onion ring and a teaspoonful of sweet shallot marmalade on it. I simply scraped the marmalade off the steak. The fried onion ring didn't make much sense with the pork chop, which was accompanied by a sophisticated fruit and nut compote.

With the rest of our meal being larger than life-size, we weren't surprised to find that the desserts were, too. We contented ourselves with a fine bread pudding, a large but delicate slice of coconut cream pie, a deadly, flourless chocolate cake and profiteroles, cream-puff shells filled with ice cream and hot fudge.

If I could change anything at Lennys Chop House, I'd put pepper grinders on the tables instead of pepper shakers. I like to season my own food if the chef doesn't.

*Elizabeth Large*

# Linwood's

*25 Crossroads Drive, Owings Mills • 410-356-3030.*
*Hours: Open for lunch Monday through Saturday, dinner every day*
*Prices: Appetizers, $5.95-$11.95; entrees, $13.95-$29*
*Live music: No • Kid's menu: No • Waterfront views: No •*
*Wheelchair access: Yes • Reservations: Suggested*

The hostess leads us into Linwood's handsome dining room, all dark wood and sleek curves. When we reach our table, I look down and spend a moment admiring it. This is a roomy table set for serious eating. The linen is good quality, white and spotless, the napkins folded simply. The silverware, a plain pattern, looks pleasingly heavy. The china is classic white; the glassware, clean-lined.

I like this table so much it almost makes up for the fact that we've been seated as close as possible to the kitchen door. But when you realize that this was my most serious complaint about our evening at Linwood's, you'll have a good idea why this self-styled cafe-grill, where you can spend $50 a person without half trying, remains such a favorite with so many people.

Oh, there are things I could nit-pick about. But food like Linwood's signature veal chop with broccoli and a sweet-onion-stuffed potato is as close to perfection as it gets. The magnificent chop is bathed in a rich demi-glace; an elegant hollandaise graces the broccoli. The earthy flavor of the potato is all the better for the sweetness of its onion stuffing. And one fine fried onion ring leans jauntily against the broccoli.

Linwood's menu changes weekly, but there's usually a veal chop on it. And pastas, salads and sandwiches like grilled chicken on sourdough share equal billing with the pricer grilled venison and rack of lamb.

You could even make a light supper of an appetizer like the rich potato torta layered with smoked salmon, with mesclun greens draped with more smoked salmon next to it. Or the sweet-sour barbecued shrimp over a salad of chayote and slivered red peppers strewn with dry-roasted peanuts.

Linwood's New American cuisine is interspersed with comfort food: homey dishes like roast chicken with whipped potatoes and calf's liver with onions and bacon. There are also a few classics like sole meuniere — gently sauteed fish in a buttery sauce with lemon juice and parsley. Or for some adventure, you could try the robust, tender grilled venison loin and wild rice studded with pecans and dried cherries.

The same combination of sophistication and comfort that ran through the whole meal was found among the desserts. There's the Jackie O of ice cream sandwiches, made with quality ice cream, cut in sections and arranged with a couple of different dessert sauces. But for pure homey comfort, wait the required 20 minutes and enjoy the hot, fragrant apple tart. And for pure sophistication, luxuriate in Linwood's classic creme brulee with its custard of heavy cream and egg yolks and its crackling caramelized sugar topping.

*Elizabeth Large*

# Little Havana

*1325A Key Highway, Federal Hill • 410-837-9903*
*Hours: Open for lunch and dinner every day, Sunday brunch*
*Prices: Appetizers, $3.25-$7.95; entrees, $9.95-$17.95.*
*Live music: No • Kid's menu: Yes • Waterfront views: Yes •*
*Wheelchair access: Yes • Reservations: Suggested*

No one is going to walk unsuspecting into Little Havana and not think, "This is a bar." First of all, there's the bar. Huge. Dominating. Ornate. Then there's the bar atmosphere. Dim. Smoky. A pool table to one side.

But you could argue that this shabby-chic interior is a sort of Disney-esque re-creation of a pre-Castro cantina. Instead, as at any other theme eatery, all this is just window dressing for a restaurant that offers a menu of authentic Cuban and Cuban-accented dishes.

In the summer, when the magnificent deck is filled with tables, Little Havana looks a lot more like a place to eat than a place to drink. In the winter, it looks like a place to drink. And for all the talk of upscale Cuban cuisine, the best part of the menu is the bar food.

Start your meal with salpicon de mariscos, a medley of small shrimp, scallops and pieces of fish over French bread. The subtle bit of chopped-tomato sauce sparked with capers was addictively good. Fried and surprisingly light black-bean cakes with sour cream and guacamole also pleased us, although the guacamole had all the flavor and texture of baby food. Marinated baked chicken wings came with a fiery tomato dipping sauce, but the wings' spicy marinade gave them enough flavor to stand alone.

We tried three entrees. Ropa vieja, which means "old clothes," has one of those unfortunate names that invite jokes unless the dish is really flavorful. Alas, the shredded beef and vegetables in a grayish-brown sauce over a pile of rice was completely tasteless. Better was a thin fillet of grilled swordfish topped with a mix of blueberries, mango and finely chopped red sweet pepper. What it lacked in excitement it made up for by not having a grayish-brown sauce. Slices of flavorful pork tenderloin with an appealing 10-bean salsa would have been excellent if the pork hadn't been tough.

As for dessert, butterscotch flan and Key lime pie had an authentic denseness to them; the surprise was a fudgy devil's-food cake with coconut icing that would please the most hardened chocoholic. But what pleased us most was the exceptional Cuban coffee that ended our meal.

There are small pleasures here besides the appetizers and coffee — mostly involving the impossibly funky decor. The menus are stored in what looks like an authentic Cuban newspaper box. Tea bags, sugar, bread, even the check are presented in tin or wooden cigar boxes.

And the restrooms are a must-see: The stalls are constructed of corrugated iron and galvanized pipes. Noisy when you open and close the doors, but wildly inventive.

*Elizabeth Large*

# Lord Baltimore Grill

*Hilton Baltimore, 20 W. Baltimore St., downtown • 410-539-8400*
*Hours: Open every day for breakfast, lunch and dinner*
*Prices: Appetizers, $5.50-$8.35; entrees, $15.95-$27.95*
*Live music: No • Kid's menu: Yes • Waterfront views: No •*
*Wheelchair access: Yes • Reservations: Accepted*

The new Lord Baltimore Grill in the Hilton downtown is the kind of restaurant that gives hotel dining a bad name. It's never a good sign when you walk into a dining room at a reasonable hour and just about every table is empty. After all, to a certain degree hotels have a captive audience.

The Grill's dining room itself is pleasant enough. It's a handsome room done in soft neutrals, designed to relax and soothe. As for the menu of American foods, it's short but well-conceived. It was the execution we had problems with.

Take the house specialty, carrot chips with a Gorgonzola dipping sauce. If you are going to take long shavings of carrot and deep fry them so they look like an enormous plate of overdone bacon, you don't do it in advance. (Why else would the carrot chips be cold and tough?)

Nor can I recommend the Clipper City ale-battered onion rings. "Try these as a terrific appetizer," says the menu. Try these as a terrific appetizer only if you want what looks like a dinner plate of greasy doughnuts put down in front of you.

Nothing else was quite so dreadful as those two, but there were enough minor annoyances to make us cranky. Beautifully pan-seared rock fish, for instance, was supposed to be served on roasted Silver Queen corn and sweet red onions. What we got looked and tasted like canned creamed corn.

The sun-dried tomato risotto was made with regular tomatoes. Crab cakes — good crab cakes — were ordered broiled and arrived fried. Steak that was supposed to come to the table sizzling in butter actually arrived with two pats of herbed butter on top, no sizzle.

A la carte gratineed asparagus tasted good, but were unpleasantly shriveled from being left too long under the broiler. A char-grilled pork loin was fine but overpowered by a gloppy, chutney-like sauce. Creamed spinach was swimming in liquid. Heavy desserts went untouched after a few bites.

On the positive side, an appetizer of mussels in a fine tomato sauce with cheese was the highlight of the meal. Our food in general was beautifully plated, with the grilled items garnished interestingly with whole garlic and shallot bulbs and herbs, and spangled with parsley.

What surprised us most at this expensive restaurant was the slipshod service. The waiter and busboy couldn't have been nicer or more attentive; I blame poor training. One example: Our waiter hadn't been taught how to open a bottle of wine or to let the person who ordered the wine taste it. He poured me more than a taste (although not a full glass) and immediately filled everyone else's glass before I could say anything.

*Elizabeth Large*

# Louie's the Bookstore Cafe

*518 N. Charles St., Mount Vernon • 410-962-1224*
*Hours: Open daily for lunch and dinner; Sunday brunch*
*Prices: Appetizers, $4-$8; entrees, $9-$17*
*Live music: Every night • Kid's menu: No • Waterfront views: No •*
*Wheelchair access: Yes • Reservations: Accepted*

Not much has changed at Louie's the Bookstore Cafe since it opened. The cafe, a Baltimore institution, still blends Old World and urban, art and funk, to maintain its unique personality. The shelves up front are lined with books, the scarlet rag-rolled walls in back are hung with rotating exhibitions, and local musicians play classical music every night.

The menu, as eclectic as ever, recently added a few more entrees, including strip steak and grilled salmon. They join such signature dishes as curried Chestertown chicken and Louie's orange-ginger stir-fry.

A new pasta offering, penne with sun-dried and Roma tomatoes, got a boost of flavor from fresh garlic and sharp Parmesan. We tried ours with slivers of chicken, but you can order it plain or with shrimp. It was a simple dish, but one that worked.

We also liked Louie's shrimp stir-fry with zucchini and red peppers, which leans more toward Thai than Chinese. Our hard-working waiter tried to persuade us to try it over rice, but we favored the way the sweet and spicy sauce glazed our wide rice noodles.

Vegetarians have a lot of choices at Louie's. One special that often turns up is the butternut squash etouffee. Showing little resemblance to its New Orleans cousin, this aromatic stew was seasoned with nutmeg and cayenne, and served over rice that seemed fragrant with jasmine. The dish was cooked perfectly, with the soft chunks of sweet squash still firm enough to hold their shape.

There's nothing quite like biting into a soft-shell crab sandwich — hot, crisp, crunchy and velvety soft in one bite. Our cornmeal-coated crab sandwich was all of those wonderful things. But the crab was so scrawny it barely seemed legal.

If you've only been for lunch, you may have missed some of the cafe's terrific appetizers. Baby mussels were luscious in basil cream with wine and garlic. The sauce was so good we could have lapped it up like bisque. The vegetable and shrimp pancake, golden and soft, made slivered cabbage and scallions something special, and a creamy mixture of sherried crab filled a square of puff pastry for a lovely crab tart.

Only the Middle Eastern salad was a disappointment — an arrangement of under-seasoned falafel on mesclun greens with feta and a few cold grains of rice thrown in almost as an afterthought.

Crumbly chocolate-chip cheesecake and smooth chocolate mousse pie, both made with thick chocolate crumb crusts, and tart strawberry rhubarb pie enveloped in golden pastry, are just three of the many desserts baked daily by the staff. Leave room to try at least one.

*Kathryn Higham*

# M. Gettier's Orchard Inn

*1528 E. Joppa Road, Towson • 410-823-0384*
*Hours: Open every day for lunch and dinner*
*Prices: Appetizers, $6.50-$9.50; entrees, $12.95-$22.50*
*Live music: Tuesday to Saturday nights • Kid's menu: No •*
*Waterfront views: No • Wheelchair access: Yes • Reservations: Suggested*

Michael Gettier made his reputation with a French restaurant, M. Gettier in Fells Point. Those who remember M. Gettier's menu of frog legs, sweetbreads and the like may be surprised to find that crab cakes, prime rib and Maryland crab soup share equal billing with more unusual dishes here.

M. Gettier's Orchard Inn doesn't have the quaint Gallic charm of the Fells Point restaurant. There are no windows in the dining room, but lots of mirrors and draped fabric, along with big flower arrangements and low lighting. The seating at every table in our dining room was a cushiony banquette.

The place was packed on the evening we ate there. That seemed to be why the service was sluggish.

As for the food, I didn't mean to suggest you can only get crab cakes and so on at the new Orchard Inn. You might start with a splendid "tart" that's actually a decorative row of shrimp arranged with slices of grilled portobello, a flaky puff pastry and a heady cream sauce. Or have an elegant chowder loaded with cream, with the smoky flavor of grilled chicken and what tastes like fresh Silver Queen corn.

M. Gettier's carpaccio, sheer slices of seared tenderloin, is blissfully good, set off with pickled onions, capers and garlicky mayonnaise. The smoked fish plate surprises and delights: Bluefish, trout and salmon each have a different sort of smoky flavor, while the whole smoked baby squid, tangy cucumber salad and herb mayonnaise are perfect accents.

Entrees are also good, but not quite up to the perfection of the first courses. If I had to offer some constructive criticism, I'd say pay a little more attention to vegetables. We got nothing more inventive than piles of seasoned rice or mashed potatoes and a mix of yellow squash and snow peas.

But the star of each plate was very good indeed. We were impressed by slices of richly sauced rare duck breast, juicy and almost fat-free, served with a round of slightly charred grilled pineapple. Fruit showed up again in an apple-almond compote with the pink and flavorful grilled lamb fillet. Fillets of flounder were wrapped around spinach, crab meat and one fat shrimp, then bathed in a silky Nantua sauce.

Desserts? It's a tough call. Should it be homemade ice cream in several different flavors, a creamy mocha tort or an intensely lemony lemon tart? I vote for the extraordinarily creamy bread pudding studded with cranberries.

M. Gettier's coffee was excellent, but the tea drinker among us was given an herbal tea bag, which is like serving Postum to someone who has asked for coffee.

All in all, a satisfying evening. Gettier isn't blazing any culinary trails. Just serving good food that will make people happy.

*Elizabeth Large*

# Main Street Blues

*8089 Main St., Ellicott City • 410-203-2830*
*Hours: Open daily for lunch and dinner*
*Prices: Appetizers, $2.50-$7.95; entrees, $6.25-$16.95*
*Live music: Wednesday to Saturday nights • Kid's menu: No •*
*Waterfront views: No • Wheelchair access: No • Reservations: Accepted*

New Orleans is known as much for its music as its food, so it makes perfect sense for Main Street Blues to capitalize on the marriage by featuring Big Easy fare and live music.

A thin stretch of a restaurant, the tables hug the teal sponge-painted walls all the way to the mural in the back depicting blues greats B.B. King and Muddy Waters. The atmosphere is simple but fun, with alto and tenor saxophones hung on the wall, along with framed programs of jazz and blues shows. Tablecloths may be vinyl, but the ceiling is pressed tin and the floors oak.

That highbrow/lowbrow quality comes through on the menu, too. There are meaty chicken wings, done buffalo style, despite the menu's claim of a chipotle hot sauce. There are also oysters Louisiana, as good a baked oyster as a person has a right to expect. Baked on the half shell with cream, fresh spinach and chunks of smoky tasso ham, the oysters turned into hot, buttery morsels in their luscious sauce.

Similarly, dinner choices range from upscale filet mignon to a down-home catfish po' boy. Served on a toasted hoagie roll with lettuce, ripe tomato and pink Cajun dressing, the catfish was dredged in cornmeal and fried greaseless and golden. The filet mignon was fabulous, smoky and as soft as butter. The plate was pretty, too. Accompanying the beef were fried potato threads and a melange of thick-cut, roasted eggplant, zucchini and onions. But why did the kitchen set all that gorgeous food on a pile of instant mashed potatoes?

Our portion of jambalaya was huge, a mound of the tomato-based rice dish, studded with lots of shrimp and chunks of smoked and regular ham. It wasn't spicy-hot, but it was loaded with thyme, which almost overwhelmed the other flavors.

Another New Orleans classic, the seafood etouffee, was ladled over two chicken breast fillets on rice. Bits of scallop, whole shrimp and oysters were smothered in the mild brown sauce, with tender baby mussels dressing the side of the plate like groupies. We liked the delicate seafood flavor of the sauce, but etouffee neophytes may expect more fireworks.

On the job only a week, our friendly waiter struggled through the night, at one point delivering desserts and walking away with our forks still in his hand.

Fortunately, the desserts tasted almost as good as they looked — a sundae made with dense, fudgy wedges of homemade brownie, a tart blueberry-peach crisp and a cakelike strawberry shortcake, all served with vanilla ice cream. Only the banana bread pudding with bourbon sauce was served a-la-mode-less. It was as moist, decadent and tropically seductive as New Orleans itself.

*Kathryn Higham*

# Maison Marconi's

*106 W. Saratoga St., Mount Vernon • 410-727-9522*
*Hours: Open for lunch and dinner Tuesday through Saturday*
*Prices: Appetizers, $7-$12.50; entrees, $11-$23*
*Live music: No • Kid's menu: No • Waterfront views: No •*
*Wheelchair access: No • Reservations: Suggested (jackets required)*

Doug H. had lived in Baltimore for 13 years, but he had never heard of Marconi's. Doug H. got taken to the local landmark recently, ordered minestrone and shrimp Creole and pronounced the restaurant "nice but dated."

Elizabeth L., a longtime resident of Baltimore who knew Marconi's well, ordered the lobster Cardinale, the fried eggplant, the creamed spinach, the strawberry Melba. She didn't say much (she was too busy eating), but she smiled a lot.

So it goes. How to explain the appeal of this old-fashioned restaurant to those who don't have it as part of their pasts? How to justify a wine list that not only doesn't list vintages, it doesn't even list vineyards?

Everyone knows not to order the shrimp Creole at Marconi's if you're expecting anything but a mild, bland version, because, frankly, much of the restaurant's clientele isn't as young as it used to be, and its collective stomachs can't tolerate very spicy food. (At least that's my theory.)

You order the lobster Cardinale if you're in the mood for something extravagant. Lobster meat, mushrooms, lots of cream, sherry and Gruyere cheese are arranged in the lobster shell and broiled for a few minutes. It's a handsome dish. Or you have one of the oyster specials, like the plump sauteed oysters arranged on a slice of Smithfield ham.

As for first courses, have the delicious antipasto, which features fat lumps of lobster with Russian dressing, a couple of steamed shrimp with cocktail sauce, quarters of hard-boiled egg, a fine slaw, Italian cold cuts, pimentoes and anchovies.

I'm not a fan of the house salad, which is chopped lettuce, egg and tomatoes in a mayonnaisey dressing; but Marconi's clientele seems to love it. Instead, I'd have one of the a la carte vegetables, specifically the fried eggplant. It tastes like eggplant but has the texture of a cloud and a crisp gold exterior.

Doug H. had a slice of the "Dark Side of the Moon" chocolate cake for his dessert. Foolish. Everyone knows that such a trendy dessert wouldn't be a big seller at Marconi's, so chances are it wouldn't be all that fresh. And, indeed, it was a bit dry. Elizabeth L. had rich vanilla ice cream with plump strawberries and Melba sauce. Her husband and their other guest shared Marconi's signature dessert: more of that good ice cream with homemade bittersweet fudge sauce served in a bowl on the side.

Doug H. glanced around and probably wondered what he was doing sitting on an uncomfortable bentwood chair in a dining room that looks like a pale green and white wedding cake. Elizabeth L. sat back and enjoyed being waited on by a truly professional and responsive waiter.

*Elizabeth Large*

# Mangia

*81 Main St., Annapolis • 410-268-1350*
*Hours: Open daily for lunch and dinner*
*Prices: Appetizers, $3.25-8.95; entrees, $5.95-$16.95*
*Live music: No • Kid's menu: Yes • Waterfront views: No •*
*Wheelchair access: Yes • Reservations: Not accepted*

Mangia owner Pietro Priola has come up with a recipe that appeals to tourists and locals, as well as students: Serve good food at reasonable prices in a congenial atmosphere. People will come.

Mangia, which opened in May 1997, sits right in the center of the action on Main Street, opposite the City Dock. That makes it a convenient spot to grab a pizza slice from the downstairs carryout. Upstairs, there's a small bar and the main seating area, decorated with signed posters, jerseys and sports paraphernalia. But Mangia has a certain refinement that suits this historic city, from its dark green walls to its polished fireplace mantel.

Our young server recommended the ravioli Florentine as one of the restaurant's most popular dishes. We could see why. It tasted as good as it looked, and it was drop-dead gorgeous: pink tomato cream against a pillow of jewel-bright steamed spinach, the cheese ravioli tossed with peas and tiny squares of prosciutto and roasted peppers.

Just as beautiful was the Mangia salad, ringed by red radicchio leaves. We couldn't taste the flavor of the raspberry-hazelnut vinaigrette, because the arugula and Gorgonzola were so wonderfully assertive. The salad also was tossed with romaine, pine nuts and yellow and red bell peppers.

Besides calzone, sausage roll and stromboli options, there's a whole list of brick-oven gourmet pizzas to explore at Mangia. We had our pizza topped with a chunky marinara, onions, red peppers and mushrooms. The crust was thin and had a crisp bottom and a chewy texture.

Pasta e fagioli usually is served as a thick soup of cannellini beans, but we liked the thinner, tomato-based variation at Mangia. The little beads of ditalini pasta were traditional. The bits of broccoli weren't, and they added a novel vegetable flavor to the soup.

The rest of our meal was fairly mediocre: herb-battered zucchini sticks that were a little greasy; tiramisu with cream that tasted like the refrigerator; and a hot seafood appetizer that needed a better mix of shellfish. We would have gladly traded the two big chowder clams for a few littlenecks and the unappealing scungilli for more than the one shrimp we got.

Linguine with sauteed chicken breast, thin circles of Italian sausage and lemony-tasting garlic-wine broth missed, but mainly because the sausage was lackluster.

Overall, though, we were content with our meal, which ended with a particularly good cannoli, full of thick ricotta cream flavored with cinnamon and chocolate chips.

*Kathryn Higham*

# Mangia Mangia

*834 S. Luzerne Ave., Canton • 410-534-8999*
*Hours: Open every day for lunch and dinner*
*Prices: Appetizers, $4.25-$7.50; main courses, $8.50-$15.95*
*Live music: No • Kid's menu: No • Waterfront views: No •*
*Wheelchair access: Yes • Reservations: Not accepted*

When we arrived outside Mangia Mangia, a mural artist was on a ladder winding spaghetti made of hose around a giant fork. The whole front of this Italian restaurant is one glorious mural of food. Too bad there isn't outdoor seating on the other side of the street so diners can enjoy it while they eat.

The interior of the small bar-restaurant looks fabulous as well. It's funky but clever, with bold use of color, posh light fixtures, a mosaic of antique doors on the walls, mismatched chairs and tables set with tea towels for napkins. Rarely has so much decor been accomplished with so little.

The menu, which makes use of trendy ingredients like portobello mushrooms and cilantro, has an appealing, down-to-earth quality as well.

Pizzas sport thin, crisp crusts and toppings like roasted vegetables with smoked mozzarella, where the smoky cheese complements the wood-fire flavor of the crust.

Pastas start with either linguine or the pasta of the day; you pick a topping from 16 sauces such as spinach pesto and mussels pomodoro. Basic sauces like the marinara are also very good. On the minus side, a shrimp Diavolo sauce created from the marinara featured fat shrimp but too much red pepper for my taste. Marinara over linguine came with my entree, a stuffed portobello napoleon A large mushroom was layered with slices of artichoke heart, crab meat, roasted red peppers and fontina, and baked so the cheese melted appealingly into the layers.

If you want something simpler, try a satisfying sandwich like the grilled chicken with prosciutto, tomatoes, spinach, melted provolone and roasted pepper mayonnaise. Crunchy "chips" made from fried and salted pasta came with it.

The kitchen can handle more sophisticated food as well. The fresh fish of the day, Chilean sea bass, was moist and fresh, with a salsa that added vivid flavor. This was a beautiful plate. Alongside the fish were delicate sweet potato fries, thinner than a pencil, confetti bits of yellow pepper and startlingly green beans, tender-crisp and flavorful.

You could start your meal with Mangia Mangia's ambrosial mushroom ravioli. Yes, the ravioli had too much herbed cream sauce, but it's so good you'll forgive the kitchen. The delicate fried calamari is as fine as you'll get anywhere, and the fragile smoked tuna carpaccio with reggiano parmigiana and capers is out of this world.

With food this good, you hope for wonderful bread. Alas, the focaccia and rolls have little character. Oh well, all the more room for a dessert of Italian cookies and biscotti, fresh-tasting cannoli or the decadent pralines and cream cheesecake.

*Elizabeth Large*

# McCafferty's

*1501 Sulgrave Ave., Mount Washington • 410-664-2200*
*Hours: Open for lunch weekdays, dinner nightly*
*Prices: Appetizers, $6.95-$8.95; entrees, $16-$28*
*Live music: Every night • Kid's menu: No • Waterfront views: No •*
*Wheelchair access: Yes • Reservations: Accepted*

At a time when every restaurant that opens in the Baltimore area seems to be another steakhouse, McCafferty's — known for its superb beef — has broadened its repertoire.

The menu has expanded to include seafood and elaborate appetizers and entrees. Beef still has pride of place — prime rib, 1-pound New York strip, filet mignon. But customers can now also get daily specials like shrimp with shrimp-stuffed raviolis and sauteed triggerfish in lemon creme fraiche.

The comfortable, understated dining room is decorated with sports memorabilia and caricatures. At many tables you can watch ESPN and the Orioles game running concurrently on the bar's two TVs. But those same tables are set quite elegantly, and a pianist plays in the background.

We order exclusively from the daily specials menu. From past experience I know that the beef and mashed potatoes would make us happy. I'd heard that the traditional Maryland seafood dishes, such as soft shell crabs and crab cakes, are great. But how about the flashier creations?

Oddly enough, the most deeply satisfying is a modest first course, a vegetable lasagna. Squash, sweet red peppers, onions and carrots are layered delicately with softly melting Asiago cheese and just a bit of tomato sauce. It's subtle and delicious. Contrast that with the shrimp appetizer. Two fat shrimp are mounded with an elaborately seasoned crab stuffing that, unfortunately, drowns out the flavor of the crab.

Likewise the lobster salad appetizer is overly complicated. Chunks of lobster and slivered vegetables tossed with vinaigrette are so luxurious that their crisply fried herbed phyllo basket seems like overkill.

While there is no beef on this night's specials menu, the veal strip loin, two generous pieces, is sensational. Perfectly grilled, it's enhanced by the dark, winey sauce and the chewy texture of chanterelle mushrooms. Wild-rice pancakes add even more texture. (The promised crab meat, however, is almost nonexistent.)

Desserts disappoint us. Puff pastry layered with chocolate mousse, pastry cream and berries is pleasant enough (from the description we expected it to be fabulous). But a pecan pie in a heavy crust tastes of molasses and nothing else.

Raspberry mousse with a few blackberries and strawberries is very good once it sits awhile and softens, but it comes to the table frozen solid. A chunk of mousse has been scooped out and plunked down on the plate unattractively. All the more shocking when we get the bill, and see that we've been charged $7.25 for a scoop of icy mousse and a few berries.

*Elizabeth Large*

# McCormick & Schmick's

*711 Eastern Ave., Pier 5, Inner Harbor • 410-234-1300*
*Hours: Open every day for lunch and dinner*
*Prices: Appetizers, $3.95-$29.55; entrees, $8.90-$29.90*
*Live music: No • Kid's menu: Yes • Waterfront views: Yes •*
*Wheelchair access: Yes • Reservations: Suggested*
*Other locations: Yes (national chain)*

Maybe there's a reason Baltimore has never had a great seafood restaurant. Maybe Baltimoreans don't want a great seafood restaurant — if by "great seafood restaurant" you mean a place that offers 20 different kinds of fresh fish fixed in exotic ways.

Maybe to most Baltimoreans "great seafood" means crab cakes and steamed crabs, and maybe when tourists come to town that's what they want, too. No one could deny the city has great crab houses and great restaurants that serve, among other things, excellent seafood.

I hope for McCormick & Schmick's sake my theory isn't true. This pleasant restaurant has good food, a fine view of the water, a large menu that changes daily depending on what seafood is fresh, and a friendly staff.

Yes, it's a chain. But as chains go, it's a decent one. Imagine a tasteful decor that sports dark-wood paneling and period stained-glass light fixtures with a fabulous Inner Harbor view.

McCormick & Schmick's can teach us a thing or two about seafood. How often do Baltimoreans get to try six different varieties of oysters at once (from Nova Scotia, British Columbia, Washington and Virginia)? With the oyster sampler you can compare — which is briny, which is sweet, which has an almost crunchy texture and which is slippery-tender.

You won't find the Chilean sea bass on every menu in town, either. The mild, almost sweet white fish was expertly cooked, contrasting nicely with the pleasantly bitter greens, the woodsy mushrooms, the tang of the vinaigrette.

If you want something less subtle, Key West red grouper has plenty of kick. The fillets were pan-fried with a spicy cashew crust, while melted butter and rum added more flavor. They came with wild rice, broccoli and julienned carrots.

Both of these entrees were more interesting to me than the jumbo lump crab and seafood Newburg, with a rich cream and sherry sauce and more shrimp and scallops than crab. McCormick & Schmick's has a respectable fried calamari with a couple of good sauces to go with it, but I can't see starting with anything but those oysters on the half shell. We also tried the crab dip, recommended by our waitress. Lots of flavor, but with fried chips covered in melted cheese it made a heavy and greasy starter.

As for dessert, you can go light (fresh berries) or you can go artery-clogging heavy (a dense chocolate truffle cake). Or you can take the middle course, a silky creme brulee, a slightly tart mixed-berry cobbler or a warm caramelized apple pie with cinnamon ice cream.

*Elizabeth Large*

# Mediterranean Palace

*5926 York Road, Baltimore• 410-532-6677*
*Hours: Open Monday through Saturday for lunch and dinner*
*Prices: Appetizers, $1.50-$4; entrees, $3.95-$9.99; no liquor license*
*Live music: No • Kid's menu: No • Waterfront views: No •*
*Wheelchair access: Yes • Reservations: Accepted*
*Credit cards: Not accepted*

Mediterranean Palace makes a world-class falafel, a falafel that's worth a long drove to the corner of York Road and Northern Parkway.

I suspect that Maan Kanfsh knows he has a winner on his hands, and that's why he keeps handing out complimentary servings of his delicious fried chickpea patties. They're soft inside, crisp and nutty with sesame seeds outside.

Half of the menu lists things like overstuffed cold-cut submarines; the other half, the half that interested us, features Middle Eastern appetizers and entrees.

Unfortunately, nothing else we tried was quite on par with the stellar falafel. Service, though friendly, was spotty and slow, especially as the restaurant got busier. And the atmosphere was typical of a luncheonette with an open grill. Thin plastic tablecloths and a couple of fake plants are the main embellishments at Mediterranean Palace.

One of the best ways to taste a number of things is to order the popular Mediterranean sampler. It includes baba ghannouj (roasted eggplant spread), hummus (a dip of ground chickpeas), falafel, tangy rice-stuffed grape leaves and a small mixed salad. A basket of warm pita wedges is served alongside for scooping and dipping.

Both the baba ghannouj and hummus were creamier than most and had a slight bitter edge from the addition of sesame tahini — an edge we enjoyed. Another good pick is the falafel or chicken kebab sandwich. Both sandwiches are served with chopped salad in large, warmed pitas.

The falafel comes with tahini sauce, while the moist chicken pieces are tossed with spices that are ruddy-colored and mild. The sandwiches have more appeal than the bland kubbeh siniyeh platter, which features dense, dry squares of crushed wheat layered with a sparse filling of ground lamb.

Another option is to make a meal of appetizers. For $1.50, try a Syrian spinach pie, which is completely different from the Greek version. Wrapped in golden dough, this flat pastry is filled with mildly spiced spinach and onions. We especially liked foul, a strong-tasting salad of whole fava beans dressed in olive oil, tahini, chopped tomatoes and garlic.

Tabbouleh, made with bulgur wheat, chopped parsley and cucumber, was tamer than we're used to, without the assertive flavor of lemon, but it was still refreshing.

On Saturdays, a homemade sweet cheese dessert called katyaff is on the menu. If you visit during the week, try a cardamom-perfumed Turkish coffee and a store-bought sweet — a nutty roll dense with pistachios; a delicate, crumbly pastry filled with a dark paste of dates; or a flaky, crisp baklava.

*Kathryn Higham*

# Micah's

*5401 Reisterstown Road, Baltimore • 410-764-7240*
*Hours: Open daily for lunch and dinner*
*Prices: Entrees, $4.90-$9.65; no liquor license*
*Live music: No • Kid's menu: Yes • Waterfront views: No •*
*Wheelchair access: Yes • Reservations: Not accepted*
*Credit cards: Not accepted*

Micah's is a soul-food restaurant with a split personality — part cafeteria, part banquet hall. If you don't mind carrying your own food on a plastic tray to the dining room, Micah's is a good choice for a hearty, comforting meal of lake trout, ribs or smothered pork chops.

We entered the bright cafeteria on a recent weekday night, and got on line to survey the evening's choices. Most people were having their dinners boxed up for carryout, but a few, like us, were planning to eat in the dining room. Our food was put on ceramic plates, instead of into plastic foam containers, and was covered with plastic domes to keep it warm.

After we paid for our meal, we walked down a hall into a large, carpeted dining room, with a half-dozen small chandeliers and lots of tables covered in pink cloths and glass toppers. The room looked perfect for a wedding reception, right down to the raised dais and the drum set in the corner.

When we sat down, we realized we had assembled what looked like a smaller version of the Sunday dinner in the movie "Soul Food." Among our dishes: crisp-fried lake trout with string beans and candied yams. Succulent barbecued ribs with potato salad and corn bread. Peppered pork chops with collard greens and black-eyed peas. This meal could bring tears to the eyes of any displaced Southerner.

The clear favorite was the lake trout, wrapped like a bouquet of flowers in a sheet of tinfoil. Fresh from the fryer, the fish was moist and pearly under its crisp coating. Two large pan-fried pork chops would have been fine on their own, but some peppery gravy made them even better. Our other pork dish, the tender, sweet barbecue ribs, was a winner, too.

Micah's makes its fried chicken with a light coating of flour. It was cooked perfectly, but if you like the thick crispiness of the Colonel's chicken, you might be disappointed.

The only dish I wouldn't order again was the meatloaf, a small oval mound that looked skimpy compared to the portions of our other dinners. It was too moist, almost to the point of falling apart.

Of our side dishes, we loved the chopped collard greens, livened up with a touch of sweetness; the home-style macaroni and cheese; the caramelized yams. Grainy, homemade corn muffins, buttered lima beans and tangy potato salad with the crisp crunch of celery, were close seconds.

Desserts got mixed reviews. The carrot and chocolate cakes needed better frostings, but the pineapple-upside-down cake and sweet potato pie won us over with old-fashioned appeal. Neither was too sweet. Both had home-baked flavor. They were just the right finish for a country-style meal.

*Kathryn Higham*

# Michaelangelo

*2552 Riva Road, Annapolis • 410-573-0970*
*Hours: Open for lunch Monday through Friday, dinner nightly*
*Prices: Appetizers, $4.50-$8.50; entrees, $13-$22*
*Live music: No • Kid's menu: No • Waterfront views: No •*
*Wheelchair access: Yes • Reservations: Suggested*

Nothing is simple at Michaelangelo, and for the most part that's fine. From the Mediterranean decor to the food on your plate, a lot is happening here. That's not surprising, I suppose, when the cuisine is a combination of Northern Italian, French, Spanish and American.

A steak isn't just a steak. It's a charred filet mignon with herbed potato salad, bacon, scallions and "a natural sauce." But it sounds pretty good, doesn't it?

The only soup regularly on the menu is a puree of cranberry bean with "crispy" prosciutto. Ravioli are asparagus ravioli with a light white truffle mascarpone cream sauce.

The decor is heavily Mediterranean, including wrought iron, stucco, terra-cotta tiles and pillar candles. Abstract paintings contrast oddly with the rest of the room.

These days when restaurants change their menus, it's usually to add more casual food. Not so at Ristorante Michaelangelo, where the owners have upscaled the menu. The wine list reflects the new seriousness of the kitchen, including a fine selection of wines by the glass.

An appetizer of house-smoked duck breast over a bed of warm, wilted greens and dried cranberries with a garnish of crisply fried threads made from beets sounded odd, but the smoke and tang of the flavors and the contrast of textures were very appealing.

I also liked the soup of the day, a smooth, thick acorn-squash puree with pieces of duck confit at its center. Equally good were grilled portobello mushrooms, meaty and slightly charred, with Gorgonzola cheese, pine nuts and a balsamic vinegar reduction — bold flavors that worked well together.

Among the seafood entrees, Michaelangelo has a couple of traditional Spanish dishes, paella and zarzuela de mariscos; but our waiter suggested the fish of the day, an enormous fresh fillet of salmon over a potato, mushroom and tomato hash.

You could get away with a relatively inexpensive pasta dish like tortelloni (a larger version of tortellini) filled with smoked mozzarella and enhanced with a fresh tomato sauce. Or you could splurge and have four tender rack-of-lamb chops, pink and juicy, with an herb crust and a tomato and onion sauce sparked with fresh mint. Flanking them were mashed potatoes made green with the addition of fresh basil. As if there weren't enough herbs already, the plate was decorated with a sprig of rosemary.

Desserts include a good tiramisu and Michaelangelo's answer to Key lime pie, a lemon torta. But the star of the show was a frozen, crunchy-smooth concoction of chocolate mousse and hazelnut crust.

*Elizabeth Large*

# Mill Towne Tavern

*3733 Old Columbia Pike, Ellicott City • 410-480-0894*
*Hours: Open daily for lunch and dinner*
*Prices: Appetizers, $2.25-$7.25; entrees, $5.95-$18.95*
*Live music: No • Kid's menu: Yes • Waterfront views: No •*
*Wheelchair access: Yes • Reservations: Suggested for large parties*

It isn't hard to imagine horses clopping along the streets of historic Ellicott City. What is hard to imagine is that they were ever kept in what is now the handsome Mill Towne Tavern.

This former stable, once condemned, has been transformed into an inviting restaurant with warm, clubby dining rooms on two levels.

Inside, there's no sense of the building's rustic past, except for the rough granite walls, where folk-art paintings are hung in heavy gilt frames. There was no stone in the lower dining room where we were seated, but the room was just as charming, with its ceiling painted in a muted green gloss and windows draped in soft brown velvet. The setting is upscale yet casual, which is exactly the tone that the menu sets.

Light fare is given as much attention as entrees. There are almost 20 sandwiches on the dinner menu, from perennial favorites like crab cakes and burgers to the more inventive fillet bearnaise and stuffed portobello mushroom.

Our waiter, who grew a little less attentive as the night wore on, started out with a flurry of helpful suggestions. One of his recommendations was the grilled steak sandwich. Alongside crispy coated steak fries, the small New York strip was tender, though a bit overcooked. Served whole, it barely fit on its kaiser roll, underneath a pad of lettuce and tomato.

The option of a casual, inexpensive meal is perfect for people who come to this town to shop the antiques stores rather than to spend big bucks on dinner. However, most people around us seemed to be ordering more elegant dishes, like the rockfish special topped with crab meat. Surrounded by bright green snow peas and soft roasted potatoes, the golden, pan-seared fish was cooked perfectly, flaking into luscious white morsels. Lumps of crab and a light butter sauce added just the right amount of richness.

We weren't as pleased with the shrimp and andouille fra diavolo, which we ordered with fettuccine. The sauce was too loose and chunky, tasting like canned tomatoes. The only boost of flavor came from slices of spicy Cajun sausage.

Our appetizers were uneven, too. The quesadilla was satisfying — a cheesy version filled with chopped tomato, Monterey jack and Cheddar — but tender, greaseless fried calamari and Maryland crab soup both could have used more zip. Though the flavor was wonderful, the artichoke and crab dip was as thin as bisque, dripping off our French bread crostini.

We finished on a sweet note, with dense chocolate bourbon cake, moist peanut butter layer cake and chocolate-covered macadamia nut torte on a buttery crumb crust. In the race for decadence, the torte was the winner by more than a nose.

*Kathryn Higham*

# Milton Inn

*14833 York Road, Sparks • 410-771-4366*
*Hours: Open for lunch Monday through Friday, dinner every day*
*Prices: Appetizers, $6-$65 (beluga caviar); entrees, $18-$28*
*Live music: No • Kid's menu: No • Waterfront views: No •*
*Wheelchair access: Yes • Reservations: Suggested*

The Milton Inn has long been Baltimore's favorite destination restaurant. The place has had its ups and downs, but people have always been willing to drive to eat in the lovely candlelit rooms of this 18th-century fieldstone building.

But how do you fill the seats weeknight after weeknight? History, romance and elegant food have never come cheap. And there's not a ready customer base in the immediate neighborhood. In fact, there's not much of an immediate neighborhood — that's part of the Milton Inn's charm.

The most obvious answer greets you at the door. The staff is young, energetic, enthusiastic and quite glad to have you there. The dining rooms are appealing. They look fresh and inviting, but not too new. Just the period air you want with none of the inconveniences — no shabby carpets or cranky plumbing here.

And while this is a restaurant that prides itself on haute cuisine, if you aren't up for, say, aiguillette of duck, you will also find some old favorites on the menu. Maryland crab soup. Clams casino. Crab cakes. Grilled fillet of beef. Caesar salad.

We sampled several of these old favorites: crab soup with enormous lumps of crab meat; eight fat clams casino instead of the usual six; plump broiled crab cakes. They are all competently done, but my sense is the chef would rather be cooking venison noisettes.

That dish featured tender, full-flavored slices of meat luxuriating in a dark, velvety sauce, which had just a hint of sweetness. Polenta "porridge" offers a smooth contrast, while wilted mustard greens add plenty of texture and bite.

You could begin with lumps of lobster and inky black pasta in a bit of sweet vanilla sauce, a startling and luxurious interplay of flavors that somehow works. Or try the delicate lamb carpaccio, seared but still almost raw, with greens and a tangy balsamic vinegar sauce.

Specials might include a superb blackened rockfish with a shellfish etoufee as a sauce, dark and rich and spicy. A gorgeous veal chop was so fat and flavorful it didn't really need its Oscar treatment — but who can resist lump crab meat, fresh asparagus and a silky bearnaise, even if they are overkill?

The wine list isn't extensive, but it complements the menu well in both scope and price. Those who want wine by the glass will also be happy with the selection.

For dessert, we had a couple of wonderful chocolate concoctions and a less wonderful apricot almond tart with a delicate ginger ice cream. But the best dessert was the creme brulee, a model of its kind — the creamy chilled custard a seductive contrast to its crackly caramelized sugar topping.

*Elizabeth Large*

# Morton's of Chicago

*Sheraton Inner Harbor, 300 S. Charles St., Inner Harbor • 410-547-8255*
*Hours: Open every night for dinner*
*Prices: Appetizers, $5.50-$10.50; entrees, $18.95-$29.95*
*Live music: No • Kid's menu: No • Waterfront views: No •*
*Wheelchair access: Yes • Reservations: Suggested*
*Other locations: Yes (national chain)*

What makes Morton's unique is the menu presentation. After we had ordered drinks and settled into the comfortable if generic dining room, our waitress wheeled up a cart filled with raw food, including a lot of raw beef.

All of it was shrink-wrapped. Our waitress held up each plate of raw beef or seafood, from the strip sirloin to the farm-raised salmon, while she explained the virtues of the cut and the method of preparation. The beef that was shrink-wrapped without a plate, like the double filet mignon, she simply picked up and held out for leisurely perusal. A whole lobster was presented to us as you might show off a fine pet.

When she got to the beefsteak tomato, she held that out, too (the kitchen will slice it and serve it with blue cheese dressing, she told us), and the half a head of broccoli (it comes steamed with hollandaise) and the piece de resistance, a raw potato the size of Idaho. The three of us stared at it with a dazed fascination while she explained that we could get it baked or mashed or fixed a la Lyonnaise.

Morton's is on the expensive side, but who cares when you get 24 ounces of porterhouse that's this good — expertly grilled so it's pink, juicy and flavorful, charred on the outside with a crusty edge of fat? Seafood at Morton's is equally good. Pink and white shrimp with a dusting of crumbs to give a bit of texture come with a silky beurre blanc. You can have a half order of these for a first course. Scallops are fat and cooked just long enough. Fiery apricot chutney adds lots of zing.

For a different first course you could get the plate of sauteed portobello, shiitake and cremini mushrooms. It's not pretty, but the mushrooms are well-nigh irresistible: hot, buttery, garlicky and wonderfully textured. You could also have the mushrooms as a side dish with your steak, or perfectly cooked broccoli, or beautifully seasoned potatoes Lyonnaise. Only the house salad with egg and a mayonnaisey dressing was less than stellar.

While you're ordering dinner, order dessert. That way one of the delicate individual souffles will be ready when you're ready. Even better is the hot chocolate Godiva cake, baked to order with a molten chocolate center.

In other words, unlike some steakhouses, Morton's can do more than just cook great prime beef. The wine list is extensive with lots of American reds. The service is excellent.

Morton's biggest problem is the setting. It's a pleasant enough dining room; but when you're spending this kind of money, you might want a decor that's more luxurious — or at least something with a little more pizazz.

*Elizabeth Large*

# Mount Washington Tavern

*5700 Newbury St., Mount Washington • 410-367-6903*
*Hours: Open every day for lunch and dinner; Sunday brunch*
*Prices: Appetizers, $3.50-$7.95; entrees, $12.50- $21*
*Live music: No • Kid's menu: No • Waterfront views: No • Wheelchair access: No • Reservations: Accepted*

When you enter the Mount Washington Tavern, you're greeted by a swinging bar crowd, loud music and the Beer Drinkers Hall of Fame, suggesting a place that specializes in bar food. However , the Tavern servers dinners like prime rib, swordfish topped with brie and a veal du jour.

Ask to be seated in the Garden room. The hostess will lead you back to a two-story-high, light-filled room painted white where it isn't glass. Hexagonally shaped, with a deck-like level running around its perimeter and an abundance of plants, the room is quite appealing.

It's too bad the Garden allows smoking and has a television and a raucous bar crowd when there's space for that up front.

But give the Tavern credit: It's progressed far beyond the Buffalo wing and nachos stage.You can start, for instance, with tender ravioli stuffed with minced porcini, shiitake and portobello mushrooms, prettily arranged on a bright red tomato sauce. This was the best of our first courses.

A steamed seafood sampler included clams, oysters and mussels and two enormous shrimp, all cooked a bit too long for my taste. The melted butter didn't taste like real butter, and the cocktail sauce was too spicy to eat. Clams casino were nicely seasoned, with crisp curls of bacon; but the clams were minuscule. A cup of black bean soup was inedible — perhaps someone dumped too much sherry in it. All this didn't bode well for what was to come next, but the kitchen handled our main courses much better than the starters.

Prime rib cabernet was a handsome 12 ounces of full-flavored, well-trimmed beef. The sauce was a combination of the beef's natural juices cooked down a little with red wine. The meat was topped with a saute of mushrooms, artichoke hearts and onions. You'll be glad to get the vegetables, because all that comes with dinner is corn bread (it's very good) and your choice of baked potato or green beans.

A special that evening was soft-shell crabs — meaty, crunchy-skinned and juicy — sauteed with Cajun spices and served over a tangy-sweet smoked corn and papaya relish. A very fine dish. Another good seafood possibility is the tender oysters imperial piled high with lump crab meat.

I had a wonderful veal chop — flavorful and tender — so good it didn't need any sauce. (I didn't like the sauce it came with, a sweet lemon grass and coconut cream concoction.)

For dessert, how about a tuxedo cake that combines a bittersweet chocolate mousse with a sweet white chocolate mousse? Or a warm brownie topped with ice cream, chocolate sauce and whipped cream? With those and more, this would be a nice place to come for dessert and coffee after a show.

*Elizabeth Large*

# Nacho Mama's

*2907 O'Donnell St., Canton • 410-675-0898*
*Hours: 11 a.m. to 1 a.m.*
*Prices: $3.95-$13.95*
*Live music: No • Kid's menu: No • Waterfront views: No •*
*Wheelchair access: Yes • Reservations: Not accepted*

Probably the best hint I could give you about Nacho Mama's is not to ask what "Mexican cowsay" is on the menu. Order the guacamole or the nachos, but don't ask about the Mexican cowsay. Because when you do, the waitress has to say, "Moo." And that's embarrassing for both of you.

From the beginning, then, you know Nacho Mama's is going to be a fun, wacky kind of place. Luckily, though, not all the cutesiness makes you want to gag. You may puzzle over the words on the menu under the chips and salsa — "the first hubcap is free" — but then you notice the good tortilla chips and mildly hot salsa on the table are served, yes, in a hubcap.

The best thing about Nacho Mama's is that it's exactly what it bills itself as: a hangout. You have to like the looks of the place, with its shrine to Elvis surrounded by a string of red chili pepper lights, the floor painted with more chili peppers, the little shelf in your booth built to hold a variety of hot pepper sauces. You begin to get the drift here. Still, the decor isn't all Tex-Mex; there are sports memorabilia and some local artifacts, such as signs from Ocean City.

Order a beer or a glass of sangria (no harder liquor is served, so forget the margarita), enjoy the music, and have some Mexican food. Have a lot of Mexican food. Get an appetizer, a salad and a main course and the table won't hold it all.

Quantity and low price are the big draws here, but some dishes are worthy of note. The excellent chili is made with shredded beef and beer and no beans; it's packed with flavor and tongue-searing spices. The black bean soup — a soup of some sophistication, and not too heavy — is equally good.

A special that night was shrimp ranchero, with nice fat shrimp that weren't overcooked. True, the ranchero sauce tasted remarkably like the salsa we were dipping our chips in; but it tasted even better on shrimp than chips. The rice with the shrimp, subtly seasoned with cilantro, was a high point of the meal. The rest of dinner was hit-or-miss. The supposed Caesar salad was identical to the ensalada del casa — I can't believe the kitchen deliberately puts broccoli in caesar salad and just happens to leave off the croutons.

The guacamole was so smooth and so far removed from the original avocado I had to believe it wasn't made fresh. Chicken and beef fajitas were OK, but if you want guacamole or sour cream with them, you have to order them specially.

For dessert, you can have that fine Mexican specialty, cannoli with Hershey's chocolate sauce squirted on it. Or a more authentic strawberry quesadilla (which would have been better without the tortilla, leaving just the strawberries, whipped cream and Hershey's syrup.)

*Elizabeth Large*

# Needful Things

*2921 O'Donnell St., Canton • 410-675-0595*
*Hours: Open daily for breakfast and lunch*
*Prices: Appetizers, $1.25-$3.75; entrees, $1.50-$5.75*
*Live music: No • Kid's menu: No • Waterfront views: No •*
*Wheelchair access: No • Reservations: Not accepted*
*Credit cards: Not accepted*

A Canton coffee shop called Needful Things is actually in need of a few things of its own, primarily a steadier hand in the kitchen. What it does have is lots of charm, an inviting atmosphere and a simple menu for breakfast and lunch.

Needful Things was packed when we visited. We opened the screen door to the lace-curtained restaurant and waited our turn to be seated. Black-and-white tile floors, a fireplace and bookcases painted dark green, and mismatched tables and chairs gave the room a cozy personality.

But atmosphere only goes so far. Even a neighborhood coffee shop has to have reliable food. For the most part, Needful Things does, especially for breakfast. There are bagels with all kinds of spreads, waffles, French toast, eggs and pancakes. We were drawn to the design-it-yourself dishes: the build-your-own omelet and the fill-your-own pancakes.

Our omelet was as thin as a crepe, rolled around mushrooms, bacon and Cheddar. Pancakes were thin, too. We filled ours with blueberries and walnuts, and liked the combination inside the sugar-dusted cakes.

A chicken salad sandwich was the best of what we tried on the lunch side of the menu. It was made with fresh chunks of chicken breast, tossed simply with celery and Hellmann's mayo, and served with potato chips and a pickle slice. Our North Carolina expert said the beef barbecue, made with ground beef in a tangy tomato sauce, tasted as if it had come out of a can. It may not be authentic, but some people like Manwich-style sandwiches. Caesar salad featured fresh romaine with bottled dressing and giant homemade croutons.

If we had ordered only these dishes, we might have felt differently about Needful Things. But we didn't. And some of the rest of what we tried was enough to give us chills. The worst offender was the chicken and dumplings, a misnomer by any stretch of the imagination. There was no flavor, no chicken and no dumplings, unless you count the soft globules in the pasty white stew. Our waitress was surprised when she took away our seemingly untouched plate. It's one of their best sellers, she told us. That was a surprise to us.

Soups weren't much better. The Minnesota rice soup was too bland, made with regular and wild rice in a cream base. It needed salt, pepper and a shot of pizazz. The pinkish-gray shrimp bisque had more flavor but was as thick as pudding.

So, our advice is to stick to simple things, like tuna melts or a powerhouse sandwich on seven-grain bread, eggs over easy, or cinnamon-raisin French toast. Sip a cappuccino from an oversized cup, and nibble a Linzer-torte-like raspberry cookie, topped with buttery lattice. Avoid the rest.

*Kathryn Higham*

# No Way Jose Cafe

*1041-43 Marshall St., Federal Hill • 410- 752-2837*
*Hours: Monday through Thursday 3 p.m. to 2 a.m., Friday and*
*Saturday 11:30 a.m. to 2 a.m., Sunday noon to 2 a.m.*
*Prices: Appetizers, $6-$7; entrees, $9-$12.50*
*Live music: No • Kid's menu: No • Waterfront views: No •*
*Wheelchair access: No • Reservations: Accepted on weekends*
*Credit cards: MasterCard, Visa*

I have a feeling that the No Way Jose Cafe succeeds because Baltimore needs all the good Mexican restaurants it can get.

While our meal there had its ups and downs, I like the kitchen's daring — its willingness to offer customers Mexican food beyond tacos and fajitas. Even something like the brisket sandwich sounded special: it's served on jalapeno-Cheddar corn bread.

Those who are used to American-style Mexican food may not be happy with, say, a traditional taco made with minced rather than ground meat and soft whole wheat tortillas. They may be put off by the blue corn tortilla chips served with drinks. And what Mexican restaurant do you know of that serves Caesar salad and vichyssoise as the soup of the day?

Start with a guacamole salad, the smooth and perfectly seasoned avocado puree nestled in radicchio leaves, prettily garnished with peppers and lettuce. Or the ceviche of the day — whatever freshest fish or scallops are in the market (that evening it was orange roughy), marinated in lime juice and decorated with coriander, peppers and tomatoes.

A special of the day featured half a pound of fresh tuna mesquite grilled to perfect doneness. But be warned: It was on a tomato-and-leek concasse so incendiary I couldn't eat it, and topped with smoked mussels in homemade mayonnaise, which were good but seemed unconnected to the rest of the dish.

Grilled marinated shrimp may have once had a wonderful flavor, but were cooked to dryness. Try instead Pico chicken, the boneless breast meat tender and juicy, topped with a thin coating of melted cheese and a little salsa. It came on a bed of excellent Caesar salad.

Dessert might be strawberries in sour cream or double chocolate silk pie, which "hadn't set" the night we were there, according to our waitress, and had to be sent back to the woman who bakes them.

Whatever you think about the food, you have to admit the interior of the cafe-restaurant looks great. The postage-stamp dining room in back of the bar has a mezzanine and a large skylight, and a wild and wonderful mural of the Southwest desert has been painted over the walls and ceiling. The mismatched tables and chairs strike just the right note.

The No Way Jose Cafe is a hot spot to be, so be prepared to wait to get seated and to have another margarita and wait some more once you are.

*Elizabeth Large*

# North Star

*808 Westminster Pike, Reisterstown • 410-833-3994*
*Hours: Open every day for lunch and dinner*
*Prices: Appetizers, $4.95-$10.95; entrees, $8.95-$20.95*
*Live music: Spring through fall, Tuesday to Sunday nights •*
*Kid's menu: Yes • Waterfront views: No • Wheelchair access: Yes •*
*Reservations: Accepted*

The North Star is a pleasant little restaurant.

The decor is comfy-cozy knotty-pine chic, with linen tablecloths and fresh flowers adding a dressier note. But the menu is mostly classic Maryland restaurant fare: lots of beef, crab cakes, crab imperial, a surf and turf. At the same time, there's plenty of casual food — less pricey pastas and dinner salads and even a children's menu.

To succeed, though, North Star is going to have to do everything right. Here are my suggestions for some tweaks:

1) Just about every restaurant these days has good bread. You can't get away with brown-and-serve rolls, particularly if they come to the table in pasty lumps.

2) Don't overcook tuna, even if you don't want to serve it as rare as many restaurants do these days.

3) If your menu promises that fish "can be served with any one of our chef's sauces," you have to have more than one sauce to choose from.

4) And don't serve your sauces on the side in little metal cups — presentation is important.

5) Consider having a lighter soup du jour than beef stew.

Now on to the Don't Change a Thing Department:

The night we were there featured a special that's hard to beat: a handsome slice of flavorful prime rib with a salad for $9.95. A real bargain. The excellent house salad featured greens, red and yellow peppers, cucumbers, cherry tomatoes and a fine garlic and Parmesan cheese house dressing.

Chicken Chesapeake was another winner. There was just the right proportion of boneless chicken breast, fresh mushrooms and snowy lump crab meat in a delicate, creamy sauce. Two of our side dishes were standouts: buttery whipped Red Bliss potatoes with bits of skin, and artichoke hearts in a creamy dill sauce.

A heart-warming French onion soup offered fresh-tasting beef stock and a good, cheesy crust. The smoked salmon plate was too gussied up with decorative lettuce leaves and the like; but all the right ingredients were there, from the capers to the toast points. Oysters served Casino style, with bacon, garlic butter and Parmesan, were fine except that the oysters themselves were unusually small.

A banana chocolate cake tasted fresh and good; but if you want a dessert made in-house, ask for the North Star Special. This is a star-shaped chocolate box filled with chocolate and raspberry mousses and whipped cream. It's garnished with fresh strawberries and more whipped cream. But remember that this is definitely a two-fork, two-person dessert.

*Elizabeth Large*

# Obrycki's

*1727 E. Pratt St., Fells Point • 410- 732-6399*
*Hours: Open every day for lunch and dinner, March through November*
*Prices: Appetizers, $4.75-$14.95; entrees, $12.75-$27.95; crabs, $24 - $60/dozen*
*Live music: No • Kid's menu: Yes • Waterfront views: No •*
*Wheelchair access: Yes • Reservations: Early-bird policy, call for details*

Obrycki's is a cheerful restaurant, done in warm colors with lots of exposed brick. But Obrycki's is no longer pure East Baltimore, the way it was when it opened in a rowhouse on Pratt Street. You get the feeling it could start franchising any minute. You can buy Obrycki T-shirts and Obrycki souvenir glasses. You can get the mail-order menu and send crabs and crab cakes almost anywhere in the United States.

This is the place to take your out-of-town visitors who need to be eased into the Baltimore steamed-crab experience. Here they can order three different kinds of chardonnay by the glass before they have a dozen hard-shells dumped in front of them. Here they'll get bibs.

If pounding on crabs with mallets isn't your idea of a good meal, choose one of the other crab dishes: crab cakes, stuffed flounder and shrimp, crab imperial. All of it made with gorgeous lumps of snowy backfin. Obrycki's crab cakes are wonderful: The lumps of crab are lightly bound together, have just the right seasonings and are fried to crisp perfection.

But the hard-shell stuffed crab, a house specialty, was a disappointment. The crab lumps were just as beautiful, but more breading was involved and I didn't like the seasonings as much. The best part of it was the large hard-shell itself.

Obrycki's stuffs its broiled flounder with a fine crab imperial. But the fish was dreadful. It had a faint ammonia taste and the texture of fish that has sat on a steam table.

We started with an appetizer for two, a cup of clam chowder and a couple of steamed crabs. The choice of crabs was extra-large or small, so of course we ordered extra-large. Unfortunately, our nice waitress could remember nothing, and she wrote nothing down. She gave water to the person who didn't order it, a soda to the person drinking iced tea, completely forgot the beer, and brought us the wrong size crabs.

In spite of this, the crabs were superb. The combination appetizer included fine, fat steamed shrimp; crisp tidbits of tender fried clams, little deviled crab balls and clams casino overwhelmed by bread crumbs, chopped green pepper, onion and the like. The clam chowder was pretty ordinary.

For dessert, go for the chocolate chip pie, a pecan pie with chocolate chips, served very hot so the effect is like a soft chocolate chip cookie straight from the oven. It was much better than the Key lime pie that tasted of bottled lime juice, or the rubbery bread pudding.

There are two things to remember about Obrycki's. It closes in November for the season and reopens in April. And it doesn't take reservations, so be prepared for a wait. Even on a Wednesday night it was packed.

*Elizabeth Large*

# O'Learys

*310 Third St., Annapolis • 410-263-0884*
*Hours: Open for dinner every evening*
*Prices: Appetizers, $6.95-$10.95; entrees, $14.95-$36.95*
*Live music: No • Kid's menu: Yes • Waterfront views: Yes •*
*Wheelchair access: Yes • Reservations: Suggested*

What more could you want when you eat out in Maryland's historic port city than a pleasant seafood restaurant with a view of the water? You can expect to spend lavishly here, but if that isn't a problem, you should have a good time.

O'Learys' weathered exterior is deceptive. Inside are the two impeccable dining rooms, elegant in fall colors of ocher and deep red. Expanses of windows look out over the marina.

The menu is small enough to be manageable, but has something to appeal to most tastes (as long as you want seafood).

Traditionalists will be happy with crab cakes or stuffed rockfish. For the adventuresome, tandoori salmon and lesser-known fish like opah, wahoo and golden tilefish are featured. All the dishes we tried were done with flair, and missteps were forgiven because of the quality of the seafood.

What do I mean by missteps? The tandoori salmon's cucumber yogurt sauce turned out to be chopped cucumbers on the side with a tasteless yogurt dressing. The salmon, with its gently spicy coating of turmeric and cumin, could have used a bit of sauce; but it was moist and fresh.

O'Learys' bouillabaisse is a "lite" version — more broth with fresh vegetables than stew. It just wasn't as deeply flavorful as we expected it to be. But the generous pieces of lobster and red snapper, the fresh clams, scallops, mussels and shrimp made up for any deficiencies in the broth.

O'Learys has excellent fried calamari, but instead of the usual cocktail sauce, it's served with bagna cauda, an Italian olive oil sauce, butter, garlic and anchovies. Bagna cauda is a great dip for raw vegetables, but for calamari? Pretty greasy.

The rest of our meal was just about flawless. I loved the thick, firm, white fillet of halibut with a gremolata crust that sealed in the fish's moistness. And while some might feel that stuffing soft-shell crabs with crab meat, sauteing them in a Mexican-seasoned crust, and garnishing them with plantains is a bit over the top — well, I enjoyed every bite.

As for first courses, baked oysters O'Learys are a must-have. The fresh oysters were fat, the spinach a lovely green, the sauce a fragile concoction of cream and Gruyere cheese. Creamy lobster bisque was flavorful, with succulent shellfish. Huge barbecued shrimp came with a wonderful slaw.

Two of the desserts were made in-house. One was a fine sweet biscuit shortcake filled with plump blackberries, strawberries and peaches and lavished with freshly whipped cream. Just as good was the tart Key lime pie, with an elegant crumb crust and a cloud of whipped cream.

For expense-account dinners and special occasions, O'Learys is a good restaurant to keep in mind.

*Elizabeth Large*

# Olive and Sesame

*1500 Reisterstown Road, Club Centre, Pikesville • 410-484-7787*
*Hours: Open daily for lunch and dinner*
*Prices: Appetizers, $2-$6.99; entrees, $8.95-$24.95*
*Live music: No • Kid's menu: No • Waterfront views: No •*
*Wheelchair access: Yes • Reservations: Accepted*

Chef and restaurateur John Luen has opened an Asian restaurant in Pikesville that is dedicated to serving healthy Chinese and Japanese food. Luen starts each dish with a prudent amount of olive oil and finishes most with a smidgen of sesame oil. That's how his restaurant, Olive and Sesame, came to be named.

The atmosphere seems more contemporary Mediterranean than Asian, so it wasn't wholly a surprise to find a few Mediterranean dishes on the Chinese and Japanese menu. Here, you can eat sushi and salad Nicoise, served by a polished and attentive staff.

For those watching their weight, Luen offers his popular "Revolution Diet" dishes, prepared in bamboo steamer baskets with sauces served on the side. For the chicken with spicy orange sauce, the "revolution" steamer held tender pieces of white-meat chicken and a gorgeous combination of fresh vegetables, from asparagus and carrots to broccoli and mushrooms. The calorie count on the menu said 295, but that had to be without the flavorful sauce. It had a gentle heat and the fragrant sweetness of orange peel.

There's no calorie count for dishes like sesame chicken or volcano shrimp, two winners with decidedly more calories. Pieces of boneless chicken are enveloped in golden fried batter under a thick, sweet, mahogany-colored glaze. The volcano shrimp, doused with rum and ignited tableside, is a house favorite. It has lovely depth of flavor and the right amount of spiciness, along with perfectly cooked shrimp and vegetables.

All the seafood we tried at Olive and Sesame was cooked just right: fresh scallops and shrimp stir-fried with mussels, vegetables and fat udon noodles; and more scallops and shrimp grilled with tuna and salmon on mesclun greens, with cold steamed vegetables and a smooth balsamic vinaigrette.

Appetizers were a mixed bag. Mushroom-filled miso soup and vegetarian hot and sour soup were unexceptional. Wasabi gave some punch to pale, open-topped shumai dumplings cupped in horseradish-flavored wrappers.

A starter billed as grilled tofu teriyaki actually seemed fried, not that we minded the crispy golden crust, velvety interior and buttery flavor of the tofu slices.

For dessert, don't bother with the house specialty — barely grilled banana and pineapple drizzled with chocolate and vanilla sauce. It would have been much better had the fruit been allowed to caramelize. For fun, try a Japanese ice cream sandwich in a chewy wrapper called mochi, or wait for a complimentary European-style cookie, fortune not included.

*Kathryn Higham*

# Olney Ale House

*2000 Sandy Spring Road, Olney • 301-774-6708*
*Hours: Open Tuesdays through Sundays for lunch and dinner*
*Prices: Appetizers, $1.95-$6.75; entrees, $3.95-$13.50*
*Live music: No • Kid's menu: No • Waterfront views: No •*
*Wheelchair access: Yes • Reservations: Accepted on weekdays •*
*Credit cards: Discover, MasterCard, Visa*

There's a touch of hippie wholesomeness on the Olney Ale House's menu, notably in the lemon-tahini salad dressing and macrobiotic rice pudding.

The restaurant is not fancy, but there's something appealing about its scaled-down atmosphere. We were seated next to the stone fireplace in the back room, which was painted chocolate brown and decorated with oil paintings for sale. We were told the crowd can be eclectic, as can the drink selection, which runs the gamut from natural sodas and organic Chardonnay to cider and microbrews.

Some people come just for the beef stew and freshly baked oatmeal-molasses bread. Dunking a slice into the home-style stew on a rainy night was pure comfort. The stew was made with big chunks of beef and plenty of vegetables in a light gravy. But the best dish we tried was the Maryland free-range fried chicken. Almost entirely boned with the skin intact, each bite was moist and succulent under the thin, crisp coating.

Soups are a good choice here, too. A mug of Southwestern bean was seasoned with a healthy dose of cayenne, a nice contrast to smooth cannellini beans. Paired with a large Govinda salad, it could have made a meal. We liked the mix of feta, artichoke hearts, red peppers and sunflower seeds on baby greens. We liked the homemade dressings even more — nutty-tasting lemon-tahini, smooth red ranch, and chunky blue.

The appetizer platters we tried were huge. Nachos were piled with vegetarian chili, Cheddar cheese, sour cream and chunky salsa with big slices of jalapeno. Salsa was on the winter sampler, too, along with smooth hummus and hot spinach-artichoke dip, our favorite.

From the vegetarian section, we tried the portobello sandwich, topped with lettuce, onions and melted Swiss. This was one case where we would have preferred an alternative to the oatmeal-molasses bread. Even toasted, the bread turned mushy, soaked through with mushroom juices and red pepper sauce. A roll would have been better.

The only disaster was a plate of grilled shrimp cakes. These crumbly patties tasted like shrimp-flavored hush puppies — no match for a decent crab cake.

We were so full by the end of our meal we had to force ourselves to order dessert. The brown rice pudding might be a bit too Spartan for most palates. Our helpful waitress said it improves with a touch of cream. Cheesecake topped with thick cinnamon-fudge sauce, and blueberry ice cream with the hidden crunch of white chocolate needed no improvements, though. Somehow, we found room for them.

*Kathryn Higham*

# Oregon Grille

*1201 Shawan Road, Hunt Valley • 410-771-0505*
*Hours: Open every day for lunch and dinner, Sunday for brunch*
*Prices: Appetizers, $5-$45 (beluga caviar); entrees, $18-$32*
*Live music: Nightly • Kid's menu: No • Waterfront views: No •*
*Wheelchair access: Yes • Reservations: Suggested*

When the Oregon Grille opened in the renovated Oregon General Store, a 19th-century structure at the entrance to the Oregon Ridge Park, response was enthusiastic.

Handsome, conservative rooms are at once opulent and horse-country clubby. We ate in a wonderfully cozy room with just a few tables and a fire flickering in the fireplace.

Although the menu focuses on serious steaks and chops, the food is more elaborate than an average steakhouse. All the elements are here: wonderful prime meats, the freshest of seafood and other ingredients, imaginative but not too imaginative choices. Still, our meal was oddly uneven.

Here was a beautiful rack of lamb ordered "pink" and arriving well-done. But there was no sign of its promised zinfandel sauce. Here was a fine fillet of salmon roasted on a cedar plank, very fresh but without much flavor. I don't like overseasoned and oversauced food, but this needed something. Here was a spectacular sirloin strip au poivre ordered medium rare that arrived rare and coated with so much crushed black pepper it had to be scraped off. But the quality of the meat and its dark, winy sauce almost made up for everything else.

A potentially wonderful first course of smoked salmon with wild-rice waffles failed because the waffles were almost too tough to cut with a knife.

None of this was dreadful. It's just that what was good was so very, very good, you wished the whole meal lived up to, say, the grilled oysters. The hot, plump bivalves lay on the half shell in a bit of silky butter sauce spangled with chopped chives. A first course of tender grilled breast of duck with a drizzle of blueberry "ketchup," a few fresh blueberries and a golden, crusty grits cake made me want to cheer.

Side dishes and garnishes were admirable, like the crisp frizzled onions that came with the steak and the fresher-than-fresh haricots verts, broccoli florets and sugar snap peas that accompanied the lamb. I loved the crab hash with the rockfish, made with fat lumps of snowy crab meat.

Little extras like the crisp crackers with a bit of fish mousse and tapenade that came with our drinks and crusty rolls with sweet butter also made us happy.

Save room for desserts, which range from a homey, decidedly inelegant but good hot fudge sundae to a very elegant savarin, a rich yeast cake filled with lemon curd and decorated with raspberries. Oregon Grille also has a good Key lime pie, which tasted as if it was made with fresh lime juice.

Looking back on the evening, I realize we had a fine time in spite of the glitches. (Of course, if it had been my own $200 I was spending I might feel differently.)

*Elizabeth Large*

# The Owl Bar

*Belvedere Hotel, 1 E. Chase St., Mount Vernon • 410-347-0888*
*Hours: Open daily for lunch and dinner*
*Prices: Appetizers, $4.95-$8.95; entrees, $6.95-$21.95*
*Live music: No • Kid's menu: No • Waterfront views: No •*
*Wheelchair access: Yes • Reservations: Suggested*

If you haven't been to the Owl Bar recently, you may be surprised by the changes. Italian is out, American regional is in — from Maryland to the Southwest.

We enjoyed the Southwestern dishes at the Owl Bar. One reason was the absence of cumin, which overwhelms much of Tex-Mex and Southwestern cuisine these days. Instead of cumin, there was subtlety and some inventive twists.

The tamale, over which an appetizer of spicy grilled shrimp was served, was one of the best we've ever had. Usually filled with a bland cornmeal mixture, this one held a light filling of sweet corn and black beans in a whisper of custard. Pan-fried whole trout, dipped in a coating of blue corn meal, was also a winner. The delicate white flesh of the fish was moist and delicious under the simple, striking crust. We also liked the potato, corn and red pepper hash it was served with.

The creaminess of Monterey jack cheese offset the heat of barbecued chicken in the quesadilla. There was no sighting of the promised salsa or sour cream, but the chicken-cheese combination inside crisp tortillas was so good we didn't mind.

Corn soup tasted like a too-sweet bowl of cream but it got better when we tossed in the wedge of smoked corn quesadilla and grilled asparagus that came on the side.

Not everything on the menu walks the Sante Fe way. There are old-timers such as raw and steamed seafood, brick-oven pizzas, Caesar and shrimp salads, crab cakes and grilled steaks. We opted for something a little more exotic, though, as we continued our meal: coconut peanut chicken. The meat was moist on the bone under a sweet, nutty glaze. A stir-fry of long beans, julienned carrots and mushrooms went well with the chicken, but massive potato logs just didn't work.

The same potatoes pinch-hit for French fries on the burger platter. They were too big to be crisp, and too mealy to be appealing. The burger itself, made with ground Angus beef, Jack Daniel's and bits of mushroom and corn, was well-flavored and juicy. It deserved a better bun, though. We liked the texture of polenta-crusted calamari, served with a swirled mix of cocktail sauce and ranch dressing. But it bothered us that the field greens on the plate came undressed. And that our coffee was served lukewarm.

As we finished an orange-spiked chocolate torte and a creamy vanilla creme brulee, we felt sure that whatever the changes at the Owl Bar, we would return again and again.

Other people obviously feel the same way. The Owl Bar, with its brick-patterned walls, over-scaled wooden booths and crazy copper owl keeping watch over the main dining room, is one of the most beloved pubs in Baltimore.

*Kathryn Higham*

# Pecora's

*1012 Eastern Ave., Little Italy • 410-727-3437*
*Hours: Open daily for lunch and dinner*
*Prices: Appetizers, $6.95-$12.95; entrees, $8.95-$26.95*
*Live music: Friday and Saturday nights • Kid's menu: Yes •*
*Waterfront views: No • Wheelchair access: No •*
*Reservations: Suggested on weekends*

With Frank Sinatra crooning "High Hopes" in the background, we got to thinking Pecora's in Little Italy is just the kind of place Old Blue Eyes might have fancied.

It's a place where marinara reigns supreme, where tradition outranks cutting edge, where cigar smoke wafts from the bar, and the chef checks on your table during dinner.

It's tiny and dark, with black walls and a black leather couch up front. Downstairs, against a wall of smoked mirrors, about 20 tables are covered in red over white tablecloths. Cobalt-blue wine bottles serve as centerpieces. A private dining room upstairs turns public when things get busy.

The place feels like it's been around for decades. Maybe that's because the staff members seem like family, like they've been working together for years.

That family feel put us in the mood for family-style appetizers, starting with a plate of roasted red peppers. Layered with virgin olive oil, milky buffalo mozzarella and sharp black olives, the peppers were silky slivers — soft and full of flavor.

The dressing on a Caesar salad was homemade and thick, spiked with quality Parmesan and garlic, proof that the best ingredients can transform the simplest of dishes. Mussels on the half shelf, another appetizer, were fishy tasting, but the marinara they were served in was wonderfully balanced.

That marinara sauce also raised cheesy lasagna and sides of spaghetti a step above the ordinary. It was perfect — not too sweet, not too acidic. Thick, but not chunky.

The lobster and shrimp Gaetano was one of the fanciest and priciest items on the menu at $24.95. We couldn't resist. Five jumbo shrimp and sections of lobster tail meat were sauteed in a sweet, light sauce flavored with brandy and champagne. The dish was indulgent without being heavy.

The Marsala sauce served with a veal dish was also light, with lots of sauteed mushrooms. But the thin scallops of veal were overcooked and a few were tough. Penne puttanesca was assertive, as it should be.

The chef had garnished each of our dinner plates with a roasted garlic half. The buttery garlic added mellow richness when we spread it on simple, spongy Italian bread.

Of the desserts, we liked Pecora's crisp cannoli filled with soft ricotta cream. The tiramisu, which spread like a fluffy cloud, had lots of cream but little flavor. We would have lingered over our wine if there had been any left. Our waiter had given us a high-wattage pitch for the house wine. We opted for a blended merlot, though, and liked its smooth, light flavor.

As Frank might say, "Smooth as that old devil moon."

*Kathryn Higham*

# Piccolo's

*7090 Deepage Drive, Columbia • 410-381-8866*
*Hours: Open weekdays for lunch and dinner, weekends for dinner*
*Prices: Appetizers, $4-$8; entrees, $10-$20*
*Live music: Friday and Saturday nights • Kid's menu: Yes •*
*Waterfront views: No • Wheelchair access: Yes • Reservations: Suggested*

As we entered Piccolo's, jazz musicians were playing soulfully in the sunken central bar of the restaurant, and the lights were turned down low. Candles flickered behind frosted shades. We loved the sleek ambience and the admirable service we received. We loved the jazz pianist and saxophonist. We wish we could have loved the food more, because what was good was very good.

It may be hard to imagine ravioli and spaghetti, homemade and house specialties, as ethereal, cloudlike, magical. They were. The homemade pasta for the ravioli was rolled as thin as paper. Inside was a lovely cheese filling. The simple side of homemade spaghetti that came with our veal Marsala was so delicate it was a revelation.

Unfortunately, the veal Marsala itself was laden with a sauce best described as brown gravy. Too much flour had been used, both to coat the cutlets and to thicken the sauce.

The Arborio rice in the seafood risotto had just the right texture — slightly creamy but with a bit of bite. The seafood was cooked to just the right moment. There were a few jumbo sea scallops and shrimp, a half-dozen baby mussels, and a titanic-sized portion of calamari. How many squid tentacles are necessary in a dish this elegant?

I liked the unusual combination of one of the specials, fettuccine tossed with vegetables and shrimp in a tomato cream sauce — the bitterness of the rapini, the tang of the green heirloom tomatoes, the earthy muskiness of the wild mushrooms.

Our appetizers didn't evoke criticism, but not many kudos, either. Capers were the dominant flavor on the bruschetta, an uninteresting starter. Fried calamari were encased in a wonderful batter, but they had been cooked too long.

Thin, salty prosciutto and potent salami would have been better in the antipasto pinwheels than the ham and other mild meats that were rolled inside. They were sitting on a garnish of arugula and other baby greens, with balsamic dressing and olives on the side. The best of the lot was the Piccolo salad, with radicchio, endive, artichokes, radishes and red onions. It was simple, fresh and large enough to share.

Desserts, made on-site, were more successful than our appetizers. We'd rate the creamy, sugar-crusted creme brulee first, followed by moist cheesecake, airy tiramisu and a cannoli filled with cream that tasted like maraschino cherries.

Despite the flaws, I'd go back to Piccolo's in a New York minute for more of their magical pasta. Only next time, I'd go on Sunday, when pasta dishes are $9.95, or on one of the Mondays when the restaurant holds opera night. You can't beat an aria and Alfredo.

*Kathryn Higham*

# Pinebrook Chinese Restaurant

*1011 W. 36th St., Hampden • 410-467-2499*
*Hours: Open daily for dinner*
*Prices: Appetizers, $1.20-$2.50; entrees, $3.60-$5*
*Live music: No • Kid's menu: No • Waterfront views: No •*
*Wheelchair access: Yes • Reservations: Accepted*
*Credit cards: Not accepted*

When we heard that Pinebrook Chinese Restaurant didn't take credit cards, we headed to the nearest ATM. But we shouldn't have worried. Prices are so low at this Hampden restaurant that four can eat for less than $30.

The storefront decor hasn't been altered in a long time. Bright-green Formica tables have attached benches that are curved, hard and brown. The paneling is veined with aqua, a color choice we never knew existed. With the bright blue walls up front and the giant red lanterns hanging over the counter, the overall effect is one of bold color.

There's something shocking about the menu, too. Things are missing. There are no pupu platters. No shrimp toast. No sesame noodles. Imagine, a Chinese restaurant that doesn't try to be all things to all people. But no egg rolls in Hampden? What do the locals think?

They don't miss them a bit, to judge from the delicious Chinese dumplings we tried. They were the only appetizers on the menu, offered boiled and pan-fried. These little crescent pillows of homemade dough, filled with moist pork and bits of celery, were among the lightest we've tasted. We asked for a dipping sauce in lieu of prepackaged duck sauce and mustard, and a thick mixture of soy sauce, vinegar, scallions and hot spices was whipped up just for us. Here's the best part: Ten boiled dumplings will only set you back $1.50.

The bargains continued with a family-size bowl of hot and sour soup that served four of us for just $2.50. This was a thinner version than what we're used to, with lots of cabbage, mushrooms and tofu. I liked the tangy soup, though my companions preferred something called long soup, a combination of egg drop and Chinese noodles in a beef broth.

Our entree of Sichuan shrimp ($5) was extra-spicy, as ordered. Fresh ginger gave additional spark to the stir-fry of carrots, peppers, celery, peanuts and small shrimp. The vegetables were cut by hand, giving a home-style feel to the dish.

Mongolian beef ($5) was full of big cuts of scallions and slices of tender beef in a dark gravy. The moo shu pork ($4.95), served with paper-thin pancakes, was a simple combination of cabbage, egg and pork in a thin sauce that wasn't overly sweet. We chose a curry sauce for our chicken and broccoli ($4.85). The fragrant stir-fry must have included a full head of florets, although they were just slightly undercooked.

Discretion was the key to all these dishes. They weren't the heavy, oily concoctions that the food police get so fired up over. Instead, they seemed to be the kind of fresh, wholesome dishes that you might be served in a Chinese home.

That's a meal worth seeking out at any price.

*Kathryn Higham*

# Pisces

*Hyatt Regency, 300 Light St., Inner Harbor • 410-528-1234*
*Hours: Open Tuesday through Sunday for dinner*
*Prices: Appetizers, $8-$21; entrees, $15-$28*
*Live music: Thursday, Friday and Saturday night • Kid's menu: Yes •*
*Waterfront views: Yes • Wheelchair access: Yes • Reservations: Suggested*

Pisces offers a spectacular view of the harbor — so wonderful you might not even notice how uneven the food is.

I love the look of the dining room almost as much as I love the view — comfortably contemporary with lots of slate gray, sleek wood, clever table settings and charming hanging lights of jewel-bright blue glass.

The restaurant has a New Age feel, starting with the seafood. Asian ingredients are juxtaposed with French treatments. Even though it's a limited menu, there's a vegetarian selection of grilled vegetables and herbed couscous. And trendy ingredients are featured front and center, like sun-dried tomato oil, Yukon Gold potatoes, jicama and kataifi.

Best of all, each dish sounds better than the last. Take the rockfish with lump crab meat, scallions, pine nuts, charred tomatoes and a lemon-chive sauce. Surprisingly, though, the dish had little flavor. We ran into other problems. Pisces' kataifi shrimp starts with gorgeous jumbo shrimp — no problem there. But they were coated in a thick, somewhat greasy, batter-like pastry.

For some reason, the kataifi coating also turned up on the mild, delicately textured tilapia fillet. Still, with its delicious red pepper coulis, fresh spinach cooked perfectly and braised leeks, the dish won us over. But a first course of "battered claws and oysters" was mostly greasy batter and very little seafood. Steamed mussels with garlic butter pleased us more; they were small, tender and well-cleaned.

Equally successful was a spicy seafood chowder, along the lines of Maryland crab soup but with a variety of shellfish and with vegetables that hadn't been cooked to death.

The same couldn't be said of the Chesapeake paella. Shrimp, mussels, clams, rockfish fillet, chicken and andouille sausage nestled on a bed of rice with saffron. So far, so good; but they had all been overcooked to the point of dryness.

Crab cakes with silky lemon-caper remoulade were a better choice. They were made with jumbo lumps of crab, pleasantly seasoned and arranged on a julienne of carrots and zucchini.

It's hard to generalize when you get such an uneven meal. But two things gave me hope that this attractive restaurant will get its act together. First, Pisces has fabulous bread, crusty and flavorful. That's always a good sign.

And then the desserts were uniformly lovely — an apple tart on a round of puff pastry with cinnamon ice cream; a trompe l'oeil chocolate sack filled with chocolate mousse and liqueur-soaked spongecake; a dreamy slice of cheesecake. When the rest of the meal reaches these heights, Pisces will be a restaurant with food to match the view.

*Elizabeth Large*

# Planet Hollywood

*Pratt Street Pavilion, Harborplace • 410-685-7827*
*Hours: Open every day for lunch and dinner*
*Prices: Appetizers, $6.50-$9.50; sandwiches,*
  *salads and main courses, $7.95-$17.95*
*Live music: No • Kid's menu: Yes • Waterfront views: Yes •*
*Wheelchair access: Yes • Reservations: Accepted*

When I heard Planet Hollywood was opening here in Baltimore, I imagined it would be something like the Hard Rock Cafe: a dark, crowded bar-restaurant with deafeningly loud music, featuring movie, not rock, memorabilia.

Was I wrong. Am I the only person over 12 in this restaurant? No, there are parents. It's more like eating in a theme park than a trendy restaurant. Planet Hollywood is bright, light-filled and strangely innocent.

Here's a few clues: The chicken strips are coated with Cap'n Crunch. There are more virgin coolers than white wines offered. The soup of the day is chicken noodle.

After putting our name on the list, we sat at one of the tables in the bar, and ordered appetizers and drinks. We were told the wait would be an hour, but were seated in 20 minutes.

Upstairs in the dining room, the decor is a cheerful and slightly wacky mix of movie props, zebra-skin walls and leopard-skin floors, with previews and film clips featured on several movie screens. The sound system plays pop music and movie dialogue. Tables are spaced comfortably far apart, and we have a great view of the harbor.

This is all much more pleasant than I imagined it could be. Until, alas, we get to the food. After all, what can you say about a kitchen that fries its lasagna? Yes, you read that right. Pasta tubes filled with cheese and meat sauce are lightly fried to a golden brown, as they say in menu-ese.

A Shanghai salad with greens, Asian noodles and healthful vegetables is slimy with its Thai chili peanut dressing.

There's nothing wrong with our chicken dish — in fact it's the best of our entrees — except that we ordered something completely different, a Cajun chicken breast sandwich that costs $4 less. We decide to keep the marinated chicken breasts over red-skin mashed potatoes with a simple green salad — a good decision, it turns out.

A Parmesan spinach dip reminds me of boil-in-the-bag creamed spinach except it's saltier. Crisply fried tostadas topped with barbecued chicken, cheese and onions would be a great appetizer except for the too-sweet barbecue sauce.

I like the pizza with cheese, chunks of fresh tomato, fresh basil and a thin, crisp crust — but not fresh garlic. Fajitas are OK although not great. And a wonderful brownie and ice cream concoction for dessert needs real whipped cream.

Hey, look on the bright side. When we go to the ladies' room, an attendant applies liquid soap to our hands and gives us a towel; and we have a choice of what seems like dozens of perfume bottles to squirt ourselves with.

*Elizabeth Large*

# Ralphie's Diner

*9690 Deereco Road, Timonium • 410-252-3990*
*Hours: Open daily for lunch and dinner*
*Prices: Appetizers, $1.95-$8.95; entrees, $3.95-$16.95*
*Live music: No • Kid's menu: Yes • Waterfront views: No •*
*Wheelchair access: Yes • Reservations: Accepted*

Ralphie's is not a true diner. It doesn't have wisecracking veteran waitresses or specials that include everything from a cup of soup to a piece of pie. It does have a nursery upstairs for crying babies, a $2 extra-plate charge and friendly, competent service.

Face the facts: Ralphie's is a restaurant masquerading as a diner, all dressed up with stainless steel and cool neon clocks. At one of the cherry-wood booths lining the restaurant's center isle, we felt as if we were sitting in a streamlined dining car from the 1930s. Rectangular wall sconces and frosted-glass partitions gave the room a sophisticated edge. Kids might prefer the '50s feel of the counter, which is cut off from view of the main dining areas.

The menu said the split pea soup was a specialty, and it was. A smooth puree with bits of carrots still visible, it had an unexpected brightness, as if it had been flavored with lemon and vegetables instead of a smoky ham bone.

There were no surprises when it came to the potato skins, filled with melted Cheddar and crisp bacon. We thought we'd try the onion rings, another diner favorite, but our server talked us into the "bloomin' onion." Scored, breaded and fried, the onion blossoms into a flower shape. We pulled off the petals to dunk in creamy horseradish sauce. It's perfect for a large group, or if you're in the mood for lots of grease.

Blue plate specials are the stuff of which diners are made. At Ralphie's, the hot turkey special was actually an open-faced turkey sandwich on white bread with bland gravy, the palest we'd ever seen. The meat was moist and carved straight from the bird. But the mashed potatoes didn't taste as though they were made from scratch.

The presentation of the meatloaf special took the cake. Too bad it was sitting in a puddle of canned-tasting gravy. No vegetable other than potatoes came with our dinners, so we ordered some fresh green beans on the side.

French fries don't come with burgers, either, just chips and a pickle. This was a fine-tasting burger, hand-packed, grilled to order and sitting on an egg-enriched roll. Burgers go great with a chocolate milkshake. We loved ours, all thick and frothy in its steel shaker.

From the entree selections, we tried the seafood linguine, tossed in a buttery garlic sauce. The seafood was cooked perfectly, from sea scallops and shrimp to mussels on the half shell.

But what we liked best about our meal wasn't made by the staff: smooth peanut-butter pie with silky, not-too-sweet flavor; banana creme pie as light as whipped cream; and a layered mousse tart that melted on the tongue.

*Kathryn Higham*

# Red Brick Station

*600 The Avenue at White Marsh • 410-931-PUBS*
*Hours: Open daily for lunch and dinner*
*Prices: Appetizers, $2.95-$9.95; entrees, $5.95-$19.95*
*Live music: Thursday and Friday night • Kid's menu: Yes •*
*Waterfront views: No • Wheelchair access: Yes •*
*Reservations: Accepted for large parties*

With old-fashioned street lights, broad sidewalks and a crossing guard to oversee pedestrian traffic, the Avenue is an open-air shopping mall, and Red Brick Station is smack in the middle of the action.

A fire station of yesteryear is the theme of this big brew-pub, where brick columns support arches high enough to accommodate a ladder truck. There are no shiny poles to slide down, but the bar is topped with copper sheeting, and there are displays of vintage firehouse memorabilia from extinguishers and helmets to photos and fire-company patches.

Owner Bill Blocher opened his restaurant after studying microbreweries across the country. His White Marsh Brewing Company turns out some polished English-style ales, bitters and stouts. We especially liked the smooth amber Avenue Ale, and its $2 price. It went well with our appetizers, delivered by a muscle-bound plate carrier who, as he set them down, told us to enjoy our "apps."

Among those apps, the hummus was creamy smooth. It had a hint of cumin and cayenne, and was served with pita wedges for dipping. We also liked the grilled chicken quesadilla with black beans and grilled onions in a sun-dried tomato tortilla. We asked our waiter to bring us a spoon so we could taste the broth in which our mussels had been steamed. Unfortunately, by the time he returned, we had long since abandoned the mussels. They tasted like low tide. The kitchen, to its credit, took them off our bill and off the menu for the night.

There's a section of English pub fare on the menu. We spotted lots of people eating gloriously golden fish and chips, but when we tried them, the outside was crisp, but underneath was soft and pasty in places. The three-pint pasta with English-style curried cream sauce was much better. This was an enormous bowl of penne tossed with shrimp, chicken, vegetables and flavorful sausage. Though the menu says the dish is full of fire, the spicy sausage supplies most of the heat.

From another part of the British Empire, the tender Irish filet mignon was a dark beauty, in a black, malty sauce made with stout. Sweet roasted tomatoes and Yukon gold mashed potatoes were excellent foils to the smoky, caramelized flavor of the sauce and meat.

As we walked into the Red Brick Station, we realized it would be easier to put out a four-alarm fire than to ignore the gorgeous dessert tray up front. The molten-cored flourless chocolate cake lived up to the anticipation. Dry bread pudding, and banana creme brulee capped with an unmelted sugar snowball, didn't.

*Kathryn Higham*

# Red River Barbecue and Grille

*6201 Columbia Crossing, Columbia • 410-290-0091*
*Hours: Open daily for lunch and dinner*
*Prices: Appetizers, $2.95-$6.95; entrees, $5.95-$14.95*
*Live music: No • Kid's menu: Yes • Waterfront views: No •*
*Wheelchair access: Yes • Reservations: Not accepted*
*Other locations: Yes (regional chain)*

At Red River Barbecue and Grille in Columbia, hyperbole is served up as heartily as the food. Some of their "authentic," "award-winning" dishes, though, fell as flat as a city slicker off a bucking bronco.

Because reservations are not accepted, we waited for a table with a beeper in hand, next to a display of coffee mugs and sauces emblazoned with the Red River logo. Despite framed cowboy photos and Southwestern art, the restaurant looked like any other large chain.

On the menu, a lot of restaurant perennials have been dressed up cowboy-style, like the "Rockin' Wings" with jicama and cactus ranch dressing instead of blue cheese and celery. The wings were excellent — crisply fried and lightly dressed in hot sauce. Our waitress didn't ask what kind of sauce we wanted, but guessed we'd go for the spicy "Western Wild." Small details like that were often overlooked in service.

The rest of our appetizers got mixed ratings. "Texas Torpedoes," a k a jalapeno poppers, were supposed to be stuffed with Cheddar, but it tasted like Velveeta. Chipotles gave the no-beans chili smoky verve. We liked the chunks of beef and peppers in this Texas-style variation. By contrast, the bland chicken quesadilla was a dud.

Red River says its specialty and best seller is the beef brisket, slow-cooked for 16 hours. The slices were fork-tender under tangy barbecue sauce. But the plate looked strangely empty, sporting just the sliced meat and a cup of pinto beans in a sweet glaze. Our waitress rustled up the missing house potatoes. The ribs were hyped as "award-winning" and "world famous!" We found them tough. They were supposed to be rubbed with spice and slow-smoked over hickory wood for hours, but no flavor came through.

We preferred the moist pulled pork, topped with Red River's mild barbecue sauce. The pork wasn't served on corn bread, as the menu stated, but with a muffin on the side. Buttered vegetables were substituted for promised red beans and rice. And sun-dried cherries failed to liven up the coleslaw, which was served in red tortilla cups.

For something a little less traditional, we tried the grilled chicken tossed with fusilli, black beans and fried tortilla strips. It was too dry, with not much of a sauce except for a few chunks of canned plum tomatoes.

Peach cobbler and chocolate passion cake were unspectacular, although we liked that the chocolate cake was up-ended in a margarita glass of cream. But "not-too-sweet" pecan pie won us over — for once, the menu didn't tell a tall tale.

*Kathryn Higham*

# Reisters Country Inn

*1100 Westminster Pike, Reisterstown • 410-517-1100*
*Hours: Open for lunch Tuesday through Saturday,*
*   dinner every night, brunch Sunday*
*Prices: Appetizers, $3.25-$6.95; entrees, $10.50-$17.95*
*Live music: No • Kid's menu: Yes • Waterfront views: No •*
*Wheelchair access: Yes • Reservations: Accepted*

The Forest Inn wasn't exactly a legend, but it was a restaurant with history behind it and a reputation for good food.

Steve and Devon Kurzweil, who bought the property at auction, realized that. Steve Kurzweil decided to keep the Forest Inn's rustic feeling and to continue serving American food. "I'm told," he said at the time of the sale, "that in this area I have to have a jumbo lump crab cake, so I will."

The dining room is folksy and casual to the extreme, with knotty pine walls, bay windows with Tiffany-style lamps hung in them, no tablecloths or mats, and hard wooden chairs to sit on. Kids are welcome; high chairs are provided.

And, yes, there is a jumbo lump crab cake as a special. But the food otherwise has an imaginative edge to it, which is unexpected, given the looks of the place. (Some things are a little too imaginative. The sweet honey-nut butter with the flavorful sour rye bread just didn't work. And I don't even want to *read* about a chocolate martini before dinner.)

Quite elegant dishes such as duck with glazed cherries and spiced pecans share menu space with more casual fare like crab quesadillas. Those quesadillas may not have been haute cuisine, but they were satisfying, with an unusual creamy ancho chili sauce. Bacon-wrapped shrimp in a tangy sauce and a zingy black bean salad were right on target. Sesame chicken strips over Thai noodles pleased us as well. The only problem is that these are small meals, not really appetizers.

The night we were there, mahi mahi was a special. Moist and fresh-tasting, the thick fillet was glazed with a saffron-scented sauce and served with really good vegetables — red and yellow peppers sauteed with snow peas. A New York strip steak was impressive, flavorful and cooked as ordered and sporting a little mound of chili-flavored butter. Crisply fried onion rings came with it.

Of our main courses, only my stuffed breast of chicken (recommended by the waiter) wasn't quite up to snuff. I liked the stuffing of chopped artichoke hearts, spinach and feta; but there wasn't enough of it in proportion to the chicken, and its tomato sauce was indifferent.

Desserts were a letdown. The warm peach and blackberry cobbler could have been a show stopper, but cinnamon overshadowed the fruit flavors. A fine lemon tart was so overdecorated with swirls of whipped cream and lines of raspberry sauce on the plate it looked silly. And the "Tin Roof Sundae" with two large and not very good chocolate-chip cookies, ice cream, a thin caramel sauce and finely chopped peanuts was a pedestrian ending for a meal that was anything but.

*Elizabeth Large*

# Restaurant Columbia

*28 S. Washington St., Easton • 410-770-5172*
*Hours: Open Tuesday through Sunday for dinner*
*Prices: Appetizers, $5-$8; entrees, $18-$26*
*Live music: No • Kid's menu: Yes • Waterfront views: No •*
*Wheelchair access: No • Reservations: Required on weekends*

If you're going to travel all the way to Easton to eat, it's nice to have four-star food at the end of your trip.

The restaurant is the Restaurant Columbia, a renovated, late-18th-century house that seats 28 and serves "innovative American cuisine," paired with an all-American wine list.

The two dining rooms are a handsome, though minimalist, setting for wonderful food. The freshly painted walls are off-white, the polished wood floors almost bare. One enormous gold-framed painting dominates the front dining room. The chairs are comfortable; the tables sparkle with white napery, gleaming flatware, glassware and candles in hurricane lamps.

The decoration for Restaurant Columbia's white and silver tables is the beautifully presented food. Grilled salmon, for instance, was sauced with blush pink mayonnaise, the plate strewn with a confetti of red and yellow pepper and a sprinkling of lentils. A delicious first course of crab and lobster cakes was decorated with a delicate, bright red leg or two.

The limited menu (six entrees) changes regularly. The restaurant's signature dish is a fabulous rack of lamb, pink and juicy and edged with crisp fat. A dusting of chopped pistachios added a bit of crunch, and a pool of raspberry sauce brought a pleasant tart-sweetness to the dish. Tiny swirls of nutmeg-scented potatoes dauphine were irresistible. If beef is more to your taste, Columbia's thick, rosy fillet is very fine. Attention is also paid to the go-withs, not just the centerpieces. In this case, the beef was arranged next to a sauce of creamed leeks. Potatoes mashed with pumpkin added color and flavor.

Columbia's quail were juicy little morsels, semi-boned and stuffed with wild rice and pecans. Luscious, although I could have done with less cranberry sauce.

As for first courses, a comforting down-home soup like chicken and vegetables in a hot, flavorful broth is fragrant with herbs. Equally heartwarming were the plump oysters and fresh spinach in a garlic-scented broth — not quite an oyster dish, not quite a soup, but somewhere in between.

There's also a baby pizza with a thin, almost crunchy crust and a topping of Gorgonzola, fresh figs and prosciutto.

There is a desert here for everyone. For the daring, homemade ginger ice cream in a spiky shell of crisp lemon phyllo. For the conservative, a classic chocolate mousse, suave and creamy. Other choices include a traditional French napoleon, an apple tart or one of several other homemade ice creams.

One of the charms of Restaurant Columbia is that everything is made on the premises, including the hot-from-the-oven, feather-light dinner rolls that arrived with our drinks.

*Elizabeth Large*

# Ricciuti's Brick Oven Pizza

*6420 Freetown Road, Columbia • 410-531-0250*
*Hours: Open every night for dinner, Monday through Saturday for lunch*
*Prices: Appetizers, $2.25-$6.95; entrees, $5.25-$10.50*
*Live music: No • Kid's menu: Yes • Waterfront views: No •*
*Wheelchair access: Yes • Reservations: Not accepted*
*Other locations: 3308 Sandy Spring Road, Olney • 301-570-3388*

Gourmet brick-oven pizza may be the headliner at Ricciuti's, but this Columbia restaurant also features a strong supporting cast: focaccia sandwiches, fresh salads and Italian staples from Stromboli to eggplant Parmesan.

Dressed in a green and white scheme, the restaurant features a friendly, young staff to create a cheerful atmosphere.

The brick pizza oven glows fiery hot at eye level behind the front counter. If the door is open, you can look straight in and see pizzas baking next to wood logs at temperatures up to 900 degrees, or so the menu says. We had no reason to doubt it, after taking a bite of our pizza Bianca, made with fontina, mozzarella, Romano and creamy spoonfuls of ricotta cheese. The thin crust was cooked to a golden brown underneath and had just the right amount of chewiness.

Our giant vegetable Stromboli may have been in the oven a few minutes too long, but we liked it anyway. The chewy crust of this foot-long envelope of pizza dough was dark brown, but the broccoli, zucchini, mushrooms and onions inside retained their crispness. We cut off slices to dunk in marinara. The classic version substitutes Capicola ham for the vegetables.

The grilled portobello sandwich got its pizazz from sun-dried tomatoes, roasted peppers and a light smear of guacamole. The simple meatball and provolone sandwich would have been better if the garlicky meatballs weren't so firm. Both sandwiches are served on Ricciuti's focaccia bread, which is soft enough not to overwhelm the fillings.

However, the dull, soft focaccia flopped when it was served cold with the creamy spinach and artichoke dip. Even grilled as the base for tomato bruschetta, it was a too soft. We wanted a bread with more depth, flavor and texture.

The best dish of the night was the surprisingly light lasagna, filled with spinach-studded ricotta cheese. We paired this generously sized portion with a house salad of crisp romaine, bell pepper rings and sliced Roma tomatoes. The house balsamic vinaigrette was a winner, too.

Even before we ordered dinner, the kids at our table had decided on the brownie sundae for dessert. With scoops of vanilla gelato and drizzles of fudge sauce, the sundae kept them happy until the chocolate pizza arrived to steal the show. Soft, strudel-like pastry dough formed an oblong pizza, covered in raspberry preserve "sauce," melted white and dark chocolate "cheese," and fresh fruit — "pepperoni" bananas, kiwi slices and strawberries.

Adults may prefer the less-sweet lemon torte, a delicate, sugar-dusted shortcake with lemon custard and pine nuts.

*Kathryn Higham*

# Rocky Run Tap & Grill

*6480 Dobbin Center Way, Columbia • 410-730-6581*
*Hours: Open daily for lunch and dinner*
*Prices: Appetizers, $1.98-$7.39; entrees, $5.39-$16.92*
*Live music: No • Kid's menu: Yes • Waterfront views: No •*
*Wheelchair access: Yes • Reservations: Accepted*

Pumpkin. Cinnamon cranberry. Lemon wheat. No, these aren't suggestions for quick breads. They're some of the seasonal brews at Rocky Run Tap & Grill, a Columbia restaurant and microbrewery.

Brewing beer is a tricky art. You might come up with smooth, assertive beers, like Rocky Run's light and lemon wheat. Or you might concoct something like its cinnamon cranberry ale, a taste combination that's best left untapped.

Beer is not the only card that Rocky Run can play. The food is good and inexpensive, the atmosphere casual and fun. Red-check tablecloths are covered with paper for crayon doodling, and the walls are decorated with rock-music memorabilia.

It's hard to imagine a place like this not serving nachos, chicken wings and potato skins. They are indeed on the menu, but so are some interesting starters. We liked the hint of horseradish in the five fat, bacon-wrapped Bayou shrimp we tried. I would have preferred a chewier focaccia bread for our wedges of bruschetta, but we loved the garlicky topping of chopped tomato, green pepper and red onion.

The crab dip was creamy and full of flaked crab; soft bread sticks were on the side for scooping. Only the "house favorite" Cheddar soup, thick and bright as Velveeta, disappointed.

Ribs are a good choice at Rocky Run. They're cooked long and slow, so that the meat falls off the bone. The popular rib and shrimp combo features half a rack of baby back ribs and a skewer of four enormous shrimp, basted on the grill with garlic butter. Cumin-scented baked beans and a large house salad of fresh romaine were side dishes.

From the pasta category, we ordered the Cajun shrimp penne. A rich butter and cream sauce offset the slight spiciness of the seasoned shrimp.

The Rocky jerk chicken is a house specialty, our waitress told us. Think of it as a fusion burrito: strips of moist, Caribbean-spiced chicken rolled with bacon, mushrooms and Cheddar cheese inside a warm tortilla. The flavor of the jerk-seasoned chicken really comes through in this jumbo burrito, which is served with a house salad and a monster spud topped with sour cream and bacon.

Besides her helpful, honest advice on the menu, our waitress won kudos for being quick to greet us and take our order. Had we asked, maybe she would have warned us about the gelatinous dressing for the Oriental chicken salad, or the dry "mile-high" carrot cake that stands at least 6 inches tall.

Rocky Run's desserts are better in smaller doses, like the normal-sized, tart Key lime pie and the dollop of chocolate mousse in a shot glass that costs less than a dollar.

*Kathryn Higham*

# Romano's Macaroni Grill

*9701 Beaver Dam Road, Timonium • 410-628-7112*
*Hours: Open every day for lunch and dinner*
*Prices: Appetizers, $4.95-$8.95; entrees, $6.75-$16.45*
*Live music: No • Kid's menu: Yes • Waterfront views: No •*
*Wheelchair access: Yes • Reservations: Not accepted*
*Other locations: Yes (national chain)*

Visit the Romano's Macaroni Grill and you'll feel as if a bit of Italy has come to Timonium. Well, almost.

As Chili's is to Southwestern, so Macaroni Grill is to Italian. If you don't mind the crowds and the noise, you can get a decent meal at a reasonable price, and sometimes more than decent. The perfect example is the house salad, 99 cents extra with an entree. You get fresh romaine, croutons, grated Parmesan and a tangy Caesar dressing or balsamic vinaigrette.

The restaurant is one huge room with exposed stone walls, cement floor and open kitchen. But some of it is quite nice: the white linen tablecloths and the arrangements of white gladioli. The tablecloths are covered with white paper, and each table has crayons on it. One of my guests got into the spirit of the thing and drew some beautiful eggplants and tomatoes while we waited. I decided I liked the crayons.

You can get a jug of wine on your table, and on the honor system you total up the number of glasses you've had. Or you can order a bottle of wine from the short list or several respectable wines by the glass. Individual loaves of hot focaccia arrive, along with olive oil for dipping.

The food is straightforward Italian, except for nachos. Imagine fried won tons with an Asiago-cheese white sauce, sausage, diced tomatoes, chopped peppers and olives.

Some of the food has sophistication, like emerald spinach sauteed lightly with garlic and dressed with vinaigrette. Or a complex tomato, leek and cannellini-bean soup.

Not everything worked. Ravioli stuffed with ricotta and minced leek, swimming in a cream sauce, were monotonous, and the shrimp garnish had the chew of a rubber tire. The wood-burning oven didn't produce a crisp a crust on the pizza Napoli; but the combination of pepperoni, vinegary banana peppers, spinach and roasted garlic had lots of verve.

The best bets on the menu are probably the dishes highlighted as being made from a family recipe, like scaloppine di pollo. The strips of chicken breast in their buttery sauce were enhanced by mushrooms, artichoke hearts, capers and pancetta. The same sort of dish, with salmon instead of chicken and capers, diced tomato and fresh basil, also pleased.

Desserts were richer than rich, the best being a liquor-soaked tiramisu. Other possibilities were a good apple-custard cake with a caramel sauce that tasted like liquid brown sugar, and a bland almond mousse.

True, the food here is chain Italian food. But I've had lots worse in homey, family-run restaurants. And as an added attraction: they play Italian-language tapes in the restrooms.

*Elizabeth Large*

# Rootie Kazootie's

*2701 N. Charles St., Charles Village • 410-889-9977*
*Hours: Open daily for lunch and dinner*
*Prices: Appetizers, $2.95-$13.95; entrees, $4.50-$6.99*
*Live music: No • Kid's menu: No • Waterfront views: No •*
*Wheelchair access: Yes • Reservations: Accepted*
*Credit cards: MasterCard, Visa*

We felt older than thirtysomething when we ate at Rootie Kazootie's, a sports-themed bar-restaurant near Johns Hopkins University. We would have felt downright ancient had we arrived after 10 p.m., when the place is packed with college students. A line usually snakes out the door, we're told.

The good news is that you don't have to be a sports fanatic to be comfortable here. The sports theme is hinted at with halved baseball bats affixed to the windows and green football yard-lines painted on the floor. And the televisions are all tuned to college and pro games. But the atmosphere, at least at dinner time, is more that of a low-key neighborhood restaurant than of a jock haven.

You can't run a sports bar-restaurant without the requisite starters, munchies like the crowd-pleasing nine-layer dip, a cheese-covered casserole of black beans, chopped peppers, tomatoes and onions. We scooped up the dip with warm tortilla chips that were served on the side.

Chili was a good pick, too. It was made with ground beef, onions, jumbo beans and not too much tomato. We loved the flavor, which was full of unexpected spices. We actually thought we tasted star anise. The shrimp we tried were larger than expected, lightly spiced and steamed perfectly.

Don't miss the pulled pork sandwich. What makes it special is Rootie Kazootie's dark, complex barbecue sauce, laced with cloves and cinnamon. It's ladled over tender shreds of pork on a soft bun.

Burgers here don't break any new ground. They're not the biggest or juiciest we've ever had, but they have decent grilled flavor. Skip the potato chips that come with all sandwiches and order a side of golden fries, which are edged with potato skin and dusted with Old Bay.

There are a few platters on the menu, among them chicken-fried steak, hot open-faced roast beef and turkey, and chicken Parmesan. We wanted to try the latter, but the kitchen was out of linguine, of all things. Keeping with the Italian theme, we ordered Francesca's pizza instead. The menu said "grandma's" pizza has been served in the D.C. area for 40 years. It had a homemade taste, with a soft, thin crust and long-simmered marinara.

Surprisingly, the London broil sandwich, recommended by our friendly, eager-to-accommodate waiter, was a dud. The meat was tough, even though it had been marinated for what tasted like days in Italian dressing.

Dessert choices are easy at Rootie Kazootie's. It's either apple pie, apple pie or apple pie. Hot and homemade, it's a choice worth making.

*Kathryn Higham*

# Rudys' 2900

*2900 Baltimore Blvd., Finksburg • 410-833-5777*
*Hours: Open Tuesday through Friday for lunch;*
*Tuesday through Sunday for dinner*
*Prices: Appetizers, $3.50-$9.95; entrees, $8.95-$26.95*
*Live music: No • Kid's menu: No • Waterfront views: No •*
*Wheelchair access: Yes • Reservations: Accepted*

Rudys' 2900 is a perennial favorite of people who prefer their food to be more Continental than cutting-edge. Food that's not trendy, or stodgy, but polished.

Throw in an attractive dining room with country-club panache and a gracious staff, and you have an idea of what has made this Finksburg restaurant so popular.

One of the best dishes isn't on the menu, although it's a house specialty. The grouper is succulently moist inside a crisp golden crust of shredded potato. We loved the play of textures and flavors of the pearly white fish and the pool of red-wine butter sauce that's sweetened with a touch of port.

Sauces are standouts at Rudys', especially the creamy green peppercorn sauce we tried with half of a slow-roasted duck. Like velvet against fire, the cream softened the sharpness of the peppercorns. Our waitress, who did a smooth job all night, brought a finger bowl with lemon in case my friend who ordered the duck wanted to gnaw on some of that wonderfully crispy skin.

Another specialty is the smoked shrimp appetizer. Plump shrimp are quickly brined, slowly cold-smoked, grilled to order and placed atop field greens with a triple mustard sauce. Just as impressive are phyllo boats of warm goat cheese teamed with cold ratatouille.

Other entrees included a tender, thick veal chop, covered in an earthy wild-mushroom sauce. The side dishes were perfectly matched — spaghetti squash with caraway seed, a wedge of grilled polenta and buttered green beans.

From the light-fare menu, we tried the penne with grilled shrimp wrapped in prosciutto and basil leaves. The cured Italian meat gave a certain depth of flavor to the pink tomato-cream sauce, and a sprinkling of grated cheese perfected it. We were charmed.

Light-fare entrees aren't served with the small house salad of fresh baby greens that comes with regular entrees. It's the fine vinaigrettes, especially one made with chunks of blue cheese, that make these salads seem special.

But the food at Rudys' stops just short of dazzling. Some seafood, such as an appetizer of seared sea scallops and the grilled shrimp in our pasta dish, was overcooked to the point of toughness. The herb-flecked seafood sausage was moist, but paired with a pale clam sauce, it made a bland starter.

There are some clunkers on the double-tiered dessert cart, too. If the Bavarian cheesecake had been named lemon chiffon cake, maybe we would have appreciated its frothy texture. It reminded us of a whipped gelatin dessert. The deeply flavored chocolate ganache was a better choice.

*Kathryn Higham*

# Rusty Scupper

*Inner Harbor Marina, 402 Key Highway, Federal Hill • 410-727-3678*
*Hours: Open Monday through Saturday, 11: 30 a.m.-3 p.m. for lunch; Monday through Thursday, 5 p.m.-10 p.m. for dinner; Friday, 5 p.m.-11 p.m., Saturday 4 p.m.-11 p.m.; Sunday, 11 a.m.-10 p.m.*
*Prices: Appetizers, $4.75-$8.50; entrees, $13.95-$39.95*
*Live music: Monday to Saturday nights • Kid's menu: Yes •*
*Waterfront views: Yes • Wheelchair access: Yes • Reservations: Suggested*

The renovated Rusty Scupper is Baltimore's newest tourist attraction. It's for all those visitors to the city who want to eat seafood by the water, and don't much care about crowds or cost. But can those of us who live here year-round find happiness (or at least a good crab cake) at the new Rusty Scupper? The answer is a qualified yes.

First of all, the renovations are wonderful. The view of the harbor is great from almost any table, and because the tables are on various levels you don't realize what a food factory the Rusty Scupper really is. Added comfortable seating, touches of aqua and coral, handsome carpeting to keep noise levels down, and charming contemporary lighting that glows gently as dusk falls make everything look fresh and new. The table settings are clean-lined, simple and handsome.

But we're here for the seafood, and much of it is excellent. A spicy seafood gumbo is as flavorful as I've ever had, although it arrives at room temperature before anyone else's first course. Crisply fried calamari served with a remoulade is a pleasing variation on a standard. The crab cakes are gently seasoned and full of lump crab meat. The salmon fillet sits invitingly on a cedar plank, beautifully fresh and perfectly cooked. Snow peas, red pepper strips and new potatoes make an attractive border on the plank.

"Newburg Pie," a specialty, doesn't contain as much seafood as I expected; but the creamy sauce with a touch of brandy is terrific, and the puff pastry on top adds to the decadence. Large shrimp skewered with vegetables are also delicious, with a smoky flavor, and are probably more healthful.

What you want to avoid here are the "Oysters on the James," three fat oysters that are weighted down with ham and a thick blanket of melted Cheddar. Stuffed clams taste like chopped rubber bands baked with bread crumbs. The french fries that come with the crab cakes are fish-belly white, while the coleslaw is sweet enough for dessert.

Speaking of which, save room for a slice of tart Key lime pie, or Toll House pie, which tastes like warm chocolate chip cookie dough in a pie shell. Or my favorite: a rich bread pudding with sun-dried cherries, apples and a bourbon sauce that the waitress pours on at the table.

Speaking of our waitress, it's like having a fourth guest at the table. She jumped right into any conversation we happened to be having while she was serving our food. Still, she got the food on the table and was good-natured about it — something you don't always find, even in the best of restaurants.

*Elizabeth Large*

# Sabatino's

*901 Fawn St., Little Italy • 410- 727-9414.*
*Hours: Open every day for lunch and dinner*
*Prices: Appetizers, $4-$13.50; entrees, $8.95-$33.95*
*Live music: No • Kid's menu: Yes • Waterfront views: No •*
*Wheelchair access: Yes • Reservations: Accepted*

The best of Little Italy's restaurants, like Sabatino's, have an extraordinary quality in common. You can like the place and have a fine time — whether the food is good or not.

Sabatino's has inviting, soothing dining rooms, done in soft, dusty pinks, taupes and cream. The lighting is gentle and the chairs are comfortable. The rooms are always full of people, and everybody is having a good time.

Except the restaurant critic, who wants to love this nice restaurant and is not happy that the bread is stale.

The waitress amiably replaces it with fresher bread; but as it isn't very good to begin with, I'm still unhappy. Especially because I have before me a bottle of excellent Chianti that cries out for some decent bread.

The clams casino that arrive soon after fail to cheer me up: The bread-crumb topping is nicely seasoned, but it can't disguise the unpleasant flavor of the clams. Linguine with red clam sauce is respectable, even though the minced clams aren't much of a presence. Prosciutto and melon starts with perfect slices of honeydew dripping with juice. But wrapped around them are thick, therefore tough, slices of the peppery Italian ham, which should have been paper-thin. Only a cup of Italian egg drop soup is flawless, because it starts with a superb homemade chicken broth, rich and seasoned perfectly.

The shrimp in shrimp Renato have been put in a casserole dish with a winy, buttery sauce, mozzarella and prosciutto and cooked for so long they have the texture of rubber bands. Homemade cheese ravioli are a little tough, but would be fine if they hadn't been drowned in oceans of marinara sauce.

Things look up a little with the braciola, the beef rolled around a stuffing of hard-boiled egg, bread crumbs and cheese, and made tender and flavorful with long, slow braising. And a veal chop is thick, tender, pink-white inside and juicy. I like the sauteed mushrooms on top, and I love the sauteed, diced potatoes, skins still on, served on the side.

Sabatino's makes an excellent decaffeinated cappuccino, a very good decaffeinated regular coffee and bitter decaffeinated espresso. Desserts are the standards, except for a super-rich chocolate cheesecake. The star is the tartufo, a molded ice cream covered with a thick chocolate shell. But the tiramisu and cannoli are worth ordering, too.

There are no dishes that the waitress can say are uniquely Sabatino's, but you will find all the classics: veal saltimbocca, shrimp fra diavolo, chicken cacciatore and so on. My guess is that the regulars have found those dishes that work — if everybody had our experience the place wouldn't be so crowded on a weekday night.

*Elizabeth Large*

# Samos

*600 S. Oldham St., Highlandtown • 410-675-5292*
*Hours: Open daily for lunch and dinner*
*Prices: Appetizers, $2-$6; entrees, $4-$13*
*Live music: No • Kid's menu: Yes • Waterfront views: No •*
*Wheelchair access: No • Reservations: Accepted for large parties •*
*Credit cards: Not accepted*

Appetizers are disarmingly good at Samos, a small Greek restaurant in Highlandtown. There's garlic shrimp with sharp fried cheese on seasoned rice. Orange-spiked sausage tossed with feta, tomatoes, green peppers and red onions. Creamy taramasalata, the Greek fish roe spread on golden pita triangles. Fried calamari, crackle-crisp on the outside and tender inside.

If you face away from the lighted "sub" sign and the colorful potato chip display rack, or if you just close your eyes and taste, you will think you are in a much fancier restaurant. Not that we minded the blue and white plastic tablecloths, the ice water served in plastic foam cups or the metal folding chairs. For appetizers this good, we would have been happy to sit on the floor.

Nicholas Georgalas opened Samos in 1977. He serves a full menu of Greek specialties, plus subs and sandwiches, pizza and Maryland favorites, like crab cakes.

We mostly ordered from the Greek side of the menu, dishes that were served with sizable Greek salads. Our favorite entree was a square of moussaka that dwarfed the small plate on which it was served. All the flavors were distinct, yet all blended perfectly — eggplant, potatoes, custardy bechamel and tomato sauce with ground beef.

Disappointing were overcooked baby lamb chops, with long, greasy logs of oven-roasted potatoes, and chicken that had been baked so long its texture seemed chalky.

The combination platter was fine, with lemon-scented dolmades (grape leaves stuffed with meat and rice), fresh-tasting spinach pie, a skewer of well-seasoned pork souvlaki, and long, thin slices of lamb and beef gyro meat. If you order this platter, save some of your Greek salad to make mini gyro sandwiches; no salad or sauce is served on the plate.

The only dessert that Samos makes in-house is the galatoboureko, a pastry roll filled with light custard. Luckily, you don't have to pronounce it correctly to appreciate its charms.

We also sampled a creamy cheesecake swirled with raspberries; a nutty and crisp baklava; and a chocolate layer cake that was exceedingly light.

Don't expect all of the rules of restaurant etiquette to be adhered to at Samos. For instances, cream will be added to your coffee before it gets to the table, and an entree may arrive with the salad course. This is casual dining.

On the other hand, prices are low and service, to judge by our waitress, is friendly and fast. Most important, the food will transport you to the Greek isles, especially if you start with the terrific appetizers.

*Kathryn Higham*

# San Marco

*Pikesville Hilton, 1726 Reisterstown Road, Pikesville • 410- 653-1100*
*Hours: Open daily for breakfast and dinner,*
    *Monday through Friday for lunch*
*Prices: Appetizers, $4.75-$7.25; entrees, $15.75-$23*
*Live music: No • Kid's menu: Yes • Waterfront views: No •*
*Wheelchair access: Yes • Reservations: Accepted*

At San Marco, you get a pleasant, comfortable dining room without much personality. Mediterranean is suggested obliquely by some vaguely Roman pictures on the wall and by grape leaves under the containers of butter and cheese spread.

One could argue, of course, that any Italian, Spanish or Greek restaurant is Mediterranean. But these days the term is usually reserved for places that serve a dish or two from all those cuisines plus a little North African and Middle Eastern as well. So San Marco has a meze (a selection of dips), ravioli, a Greek casserole (pastitsio), Moroccan chicken and even a fig tartlette for dessert.

I'd seen a menu beforehand, and it was the fig tartlette that caught my imagination and led me to the Pikesville Hilton for dinner — most restaurants' idea of a Mediterranean dessert is tiramisu. (The tartlette was every bit as good as I had hoped, rich and intensely almond-flavored.)

But before we got to dessert, we had a long evening of hits and misses as far as the food was concerned, warm wine, excruciatingly slow service and a major wait for our main courses. Great busboys, though. (If you notice them, they must be snappy at filling water glasses and clearing dirty dishes.)

What kind of generalities can you make about a kitchen that produces a meze where one dip has the look and texture of prune whip and tastes like pure garlic, but two others are excellent: a classic hummus and a cucumber and yogurt dip? Or a kitchen that offers a fine crab soup and a not-so-fine sea trout escabeche with a sauce that tastes like thick crab soup with chunks of potatoes and peppers in it?

Sometimes you get something different from the menu description, but quite good. Mediterranean flounder was supposed to be sauteed with garlic, spinach and feta cheese. Instead, the fresh fillet had a light batter and was placed on a bed of jewel-green spinach with a light, lemony butter sauce.

Sometimes you get exactly what's promised and it's delicious: namely, ravioli stuffed with minced mushrooms in a creamy sauce.

And sometimes you can take or leave what you order: Moroccan chicken that's highly and exotically spiced but otherwise not particularly noteworthy; a thick veal chop with portobello mushrooms and a dark wine sauce.

But give the kitchen extra points for its vegetable of the day, delicious green beans and strips of bell peppers sauteed together. I've been in restaurants with bigger reputations that didn't give half as much thought to its side dishes.

*Elizabeth Large*

# Sascha's Daily

*5 E. Hamilton St., Mount Vernon • 410-659-7606*
*Hours: Open Monday through Friday, 9:30 a.m. to 4 p.m.*
*Prices: Appetizers, $1.75-$2.75; entrees, $4-$8.50*
*Live music: No • Kid's menu: Yes • Waterfront views: No •*
*Wheelchair access: No • Reservations: Not accepted •*
*Credit cards: Not accepted*

If you work downtown, you may want to stroll over to Sascha's Daily for lunch or an early dinner. You're likely to have an interesting, inexpensive meal there.

The catch is that the cafe closes at 6 p.m. and the menu is limited. Step up to the counter to take a look at what Sascha's does serve: Saschette sandwiches wrapped in cellophane and tied with ribbon; crispy topped focaccia sandwiches held together in sheaths of foil; tubs of freshly made salads, like the Tuscan tuna with artichokes and sun-dried tomatoes.

For lunch, there's always a homemade soup and a hot item, like the zesty gazpacho and seafood-studded paella. For dinner, there are three hot entrees, usually available by early afternoon.

Don't expect table service and white linen at Sascha's. This is a casual cafe where you pay in cash at the counter and carry your plastic plate to your own table. You can eat outside, or inside, where a large farmhouse table is the centerpiece. The decor is simple, brightened by Chinese red trim and an exhibition of folk art.

The stellar focaccia is some of the best bread around — crusty on top, fragrant with rosemary, and soft enough inside so that eating a sandwich made with it isn't a chore. Ours was filled with an inspired combination: thinly shaved fresh turkey breast, slivers of red-skinned apples and a smear of chutney.

Even though it looked terrific, we skipped the veggie-filled calzone. Instead, we decided on one of the Saschette hoagies. The Moroccan chicken sandwich was filled with moist chicken, grilled onions and a faintly sweet, cinnamon-laced tomato sauce that gave the sandwich verve. The doughy hoagie roll seemed pedestrian, though, after that focaccia.

There are plenty of prepared salads that you can order by themselves or on a bed of lettuce. We chose an entree salad of Cajun chicken with two sides — thick cuts of grilled vegetables and lentils with the sweet surprise of Mandarin oranges. The chicken salad was made with chunks of chicken breast tossed in a low-fat yogurt-mayonnaise dressing, pink with Cajun spices, yet so mild it seemed bland.

Paella was full of shrimp, chicken, mussels and, unfortunately, breakfast sausage subbing for chorizo, all nestled into a bed of sunny saffron rice. It also included a side of steamed asparagus or one of Sascha's other salads.

There's a home-baked appeal to the desserts, so be sure to save room to try one. We liked them all — a saucer-sized chocolate chip cookie, a slice of sugar-crusted lemon blueberry pie, a cupcake with decadent chocolate frosting and even a simple scone jazzed up with a bit of fresh peach.

*Kathryn Higham*

# Sebastian's

*566A Ritchie Highway, Severna Park • 410-544-4705*
*Hours: Open every day for lunch and dinner*
*Prices: Appetizers, $5.75-$12.50; entrees, $6.75-$25*
*Live music: Tuesday, Friday and Saturday nights • Kid's menu: Yes •*
*Waterfront views: No • Wheelchair access: Call ahead •*
*Reservations: Accepted*

Sebastian's tries to be all things to all eaters, and does a pretty good job of it.

They have bar food. But they try to make it really good bar food. Sebastian's is also a family restaurant, with a children's menu of $3.99 dinners.

Looking for a neighborhood spot where you can get a quick bite after work? Sebastian's has pastas for under $10 and chicken dishes for just a bit more.

And then there's the fairly haute cuisine, like the grilled veal chop, marinated in olive oil and herbs, with wild mushrooms, roasted new potatoes and a demi-glace.

Our meal fell somewhere in between the extremes — not bar food, but not the most expensive dishes on the menu, either. Some of it was standard fare done pretty well, like the eggplant parmigiana layered with soft, hot ricotta cheese. A smooth cream of crab soup with lump crab meat would have been just about perfect if it hadn't been so peppery. Fisherman's pasta featured clams, mussels, scallops and shrimp in a chunky tomato sauce over linguine — good enough, but not particularly notable.

What was notable was a Chicken Marsala Sebastian Style. The tender boneless breast was baked with artichoke hearts and soft, mild cheese, then finished with a creamy sauce tinged with Marsala. It was decorated with rosemary-scented red-skinned potatoes. Not exactly spa cuisine, but delicious.

Equally good were sliced medallions of pork loin with a dark, tart-sweet sauce of apples and rosemary. They came with swirls of buttery mashed potatoes.

An excellent first course of lump crab meat and sliced portobello mushrooms sauteed in butter and finished with brandy was arranged over rounds of French-bread toast.

Dinners come with a fine house salad made with fresh greens, good cherry tomatoes, black olives and peppers and dressed with a sparkling balsamic vinaigrette.

Desserts are made on the premises. My favorite was a spicy pumpkin cheesecake in a cookie crust, but the bread pudding with butterscotch sauce couldn't be faulted, either. Only the apple pie with an inedible crust was a bust.

Sebastian's is a place to keep your eye on, in spite of the fact that the decor makes it look like just another chain restaurant, and the service wasn't great. (Our waiter had too many tables to handle comfortably.)

But the food is good — sometimes better than good — and the prices are reasonable.

*Elizabeth Large*

# Shanghai Lil's

*2933 O'Donnell St., Canton • 410-327-1300*
*Hours: Open daily for lunch and dinner*
*Prices: Appetizers, $2.50-$5.50; entrees, $7.50-$10.25*
*Live music: No • Kid's menu: No • Waterfront views: No •*
*Wheelchair access: No • Reservations: Accepted*

Some restaurants are so much fun that the food is almost secondary. That's kind of how we felt about Shanghai Lil's, a sushi bar and Asian restaurant

The upstairs bar is filled with vintage war memorabilia from the Pacific corridor. Sandblasted bombs serve as table legs, a stretcher hung on the wall does double duty as a menu, and camouflage netting shields the sushi bar. Parts of actual B-17s and B-29s have been painted like the embellished planes of the famed Flying Tigers. In the dining room, the mood is darker and more serene, with the ceiling painted dark purple and the walls a buttery pumpkin. There are wonderful details here as well, from the rice-paper fish hanging from the ceiling to the vintage Asian ads on the walls.

Unfortunately, the food didn't quite measure up to the decor. Part of the problem may be that Shanghai Lil's permanent menu is still in development. The current menu is limited — with a heavy emphasis on Chinese food — while the pan-Asian specials list is more extensive.

When we asked our accommodating waiter for suggestions, he only mentioned dishes on the specials list, like the grilled tuna with ginger, miso and cilantro sauce, and the gingered scallops with snow peas and peppers.

Almost everything we tried on the regular menu had some problems. Excessive saltiness marred both the shiitake-filled hot and sour soup, and the chicken and broccoli with orange peel. The chicken dish had no redeeming qualities other than the tender meat and the crisp vegetables.

Rings of squid, done Kung Pao style, had been cooked perfectly, but they were sitting in a sauce that was strangely soupy, not to mention mild. There's no way this dish needed a star to warn of its spiciness.

We were happier with our specials. The Chinese barbecued salmon was flaky and moist, covered in a glaze that tasted of star anise. It looked pretty, too, sitting on a starburst of fried bean threads next to a cold salad of cooked spinach.

Two angle-cut spring rolls, another special, were full of crab meat seasoned with jalapeno and red chilies. We wished the rolls had been hotter, both in temperature and spice.

Everything was fiery about our gorgeous thunderbolt roll, though. The spicy tuna rolled inside, the garnish of fresh jalapeno and the dot of hot sauce on top, as red and round as the symbol on the flag of Japan.

To squelch the heat at the end of your meal, there's a trio of desserts: a not-too-sweet strawberry tart, and a pair of cheesecakes — one that is faintly tropical with mango, and a less successful ginger version.

*Kathryn Higham*

# Shula's Steak 2

*101 W. Fayette St., Omni Inner Harbor Hotel, Inner Harbor • 410-385-6630*
*Hours: Open daily for breakfast, lunch and dinner*
*Prices: Appetizers, $3.70-$9.80; entrees, $6.90-$20.90*
*Live music: No • Kid's menu: Yes • Waterfront views: No •*
*Wheelchair access: Yes • Reservations: Not accepted*

Shula's Steak 2 is Shangri-la for red-blooded sports fans who have a hankering for red meat. It's served here straight up as steaks and burgers, tossed with fettuccine, wrapped in fajitas, tucked into salads and simmered in soups.

With the music heart-thumpingly loud, and the television display as vast as the electronics department of Circuit City, Shula's Steak 2 sets a new standard for sports bars. Maybe that's because owner Don Shula knows the sports business inside and out. For the uninitiated, he played for the Baltimore Colts and later had a long career as a coach, beginning here.

Capitalizing on his fame, he launched a chain of sports bars and restaurants, with locations in Miami, Cleveland and now Baltimore. Shula's Steak 2 and the more upscale Shula's Steakhouse are both in the Omni Inner Harbor Hotel.

Open the menu and you'll find a team of sports-bar heavy hitters. Among them, wings, skins and chicken fingers. We liked them all on a combination platter called the "Big Deal."

You'll also find some Hungarian oddities, like the gogabvanka pizza filled with meat, goulash-style fettuccine and paprika, and steak soup served in an herbed sourdough bowl, a delicious Hungarian alternative to chili. We can't vouch for the gogabvanka. Our upbeat, skilled waiter did everything in his power to steer us away from it.

The menu's highlight, as you might have guessed, is steak: sirloins, rib-eyes, New York strips, T-bones — even a 22-ounce prime rib. We tried the 12-ounce sirloin, "the 325," named for the game that made Shula "the winningest coach in NFL history." Thick, juicy and unadulterated by marinades or smoky overtones, it was all that a steak should be.

It was served with creamy "smashed" potatoes, spiked with a little too much nutmeg, and floured, pan-fried onions that were so unappealing they deserved to be kicked off the plate and back into the end zone of the kitchen. A side of sour-tasting creamed spinach was even worse.

The steak fajitas are a good deal, but our meat was too heavily sauced and salty. The grilled dolphin was a better pick, cooked perfectly and served on a soft roll. We also liked the sweet-sour tang of the fresh coleslaw, and the thick steak fries that came on the plate. The half-pound burger was terrific, too. It had the distinct flavor and texture of a burger that's never been frozen. Over-cooked "yacko yammers" (or sweet potato fries) weren't worth tackling.

But a few desserts were: warm apple cobbler, rich with butter and cinnamon; and the light, seven-layer chocolate cake crowned with a chocolate football. Score.

*Kathryn Higham*

# Shula's Steakhouse

*101 W. Fayette St., Omni Inner Harbor Hotel, Inner Harbor • 410-752-1100*
*Hours: Open for dinner nightly*
*Prices: Appetizers, $7.95-$12.95; entrees, $15.95-$59.95*
*Live music: No • Kid's menu: Yes • Waterfront views: No •*
*Wheelchair access: Yes • Reservations: Required*

The draw here is beef. Big beef. What do I mean by big? If you finish the 48-ounce porterhouse ($59.95), your name is inscribed on a bronze plaque in the front of the restaurant.

Shula's has truly wonderful beef. Full of juicy flavor, it's cooked precisely as ordered and seasoned perfectly. If my meal had consisted of nothing else but a steak, a baked potato, a simple salad and the restaurant's fine sourdough bread, I would have given the food four stars.

The prime rib is just as good as the steak — with one advantage. You don't have to meet it first. Shula's has one of those carts where the waiter displays staggeringly large slabs of raw beef, lamb chops and even a live lobster for your perusal. This is almost in lieu of a menu because the menu itself is fairly unreadable. It's hand-printed on a regulation football, which is hard to take seriously — especially in such a sumptuous dining room.

With its mahogany paneling, brick-colored walls, handsomely set tables and romantic lighting, the room is gorgeous — except that the pictures in those ornate frames are football photos. Testosterone Baroque, as a friend described it.

But back to the food. If you like nutmeg, you're going to love the Yorkshire pudding with nutmeg, the hash browns with nutmeg, the creamed spinach with cheese and nutmeg and the cream of crab soup with nutmeg. Odd that the kitchen knows to leave well enough alone when it comes to the beef, but over-seasons so much else with that one spice.

Oysters Rockefeller began with superb oysters and ended with good hollandaise but were weighted down with an overly garlicky bread-crumb and spinach mixture. The crab soup was too salty. The best of our first courses was enormous barbecued shrimp, each one wrapped around a fresh basil leaf.

If you don't want beef at Shula's (but why come here if you don't?), you have several seafood choices for a main course. Thick, mild-flavored red snapper fillets with a simple lemon butter sauce had the potential to be out of this world, but the kitchen overcooked them.

We tried several a la carte salads — the nutmeg-laced ones plus telephone-pole-size asparagus and half a head of broccoli, both those last two served with that rich hollandaise by our attentive waiter. (The professionalism of the service is extraordinary at a restaurant that's a step above a sports bar.)

Those who have managed to save room for dessert will be happy with a monster slice of chocolate cake; a delicate, velvety creme brulee; or a tart Key lime pie. But my favorite, was a moist slice of old-fashioned red velvet cake.

*Elizabeth Large*

# Silk Road

*336 N. Charles St., Mount Vernon • 410- 385-9013*
*Hours: Open Monday through Saturday for lunch and dinner,*
*Sunday for dinner only*
*Prices: Appetizers, $2.75-$9.75; entrees, $9.75-$14.95*
*Live music: No • Kid's menu: No • Waterfront views: No •*
*Wheelchair access: Yes • Reservations: Suggested for weekends or groups*

I often wondered why Baltimore had only one Afghan restaurant, when that one was so popular. What I didn't expect was that when a second one, the Silk Road, did open up, it would do so five blocks south of its rival on the same street.

Comparisons are unavoidable, but that really isn't fair to the new place. Even though it doesn't have the sophistication of the Helmand, it has its own virtues. Foremost among them: good and inexpensive ethnic food.

Right off the bat, the Silk Road offers one thing the Helmand doesn't. It's open for lunch. Unfortunately, my visit for that meal underwhelmed me. That's why I put off going back for dinner until recently.

Happily, my second visit was much more successful.

It was a bitterly cold night, and at first the spare main dining area with its few ethnic appointments didn't seem inviting. But we rapidly settled in, because this was exactly the kind of food we needed: hearty, soul-warming and flavorful.

We started with the aush soup. Dark, thick and sumptuous, its bold flavors blended so perfectly it was difficult to pick out the ingredients. It was blazing hot and intriguingly spicy, with a cooling swirl of yogurt on top.

Bulanee kadu was just as good as a starter. The thin, crisp pastry triangles were sandwiched with a delicate pumpkin puree with yogurt on the side.

Also fine were the aushak, tender "ravioli" stuffed with a spiced green-onion filling and napped with a tomato and meat sauce. They come as a first or main course.

The best of our main courses was a chicken dish, lawangi-murgh, made with tender chunks of chicken. I loved its mild, creamy yogurt sauce studded with chickpeas.

For something a bit more exotic, try norange palaw. A mound of saffron rice hid sauteed eggplant and tomatoes. The dish was almost sweet, decorated with pistachios and orange strips and fragrant with rose water and cardamom.

When I had lunched at the Silk Road, I pretty much felt I could take it or leave it. But this evening the only take-it-or-leave-it fare was an expensive kabab-e-qhaburgha, which couldn't hold a candle to the rest of our meal. The chunks of lamb, served with a few grilled vegetables, were highly marinated, a bit tough and overcooked.

I hate to end on a negative note, because so much of our meal was a hit. We should have quit while ahead and not ordered dessert, which consisted of fried dough sprinkled with powdered sugar, a milky pudding flavored with rose water, and baklava that wasn't as fresh as it should have been.

*Elizabeth Large*

# Sin Carne

*1000 Reisterstown Road, Pikesville • 410-486-8811*
*Hours: Open Monday to Saturday for lunch, every night for dinner*
*Prices: Appetizers, $6-$12; entrees, $9-$13*
*Live music: No • Kid's menu: No • Waterfront views: No •*
*Wheelchair access: Yes • Reservations: Accepted*

If you had to pick a healthful cuisine, I'm not sure Tex-Mex would come to mind first. Short on fresh vegetables and long on fatty calories, it also doesn't have much of a gourmet reputation. So you have to give the owners credit for breaking new ground when they opened Sin Carne, a "meatless Mexican cantina."

You may not be able to get a New York strip there, but you can have a glass of wine with your grilled fish. And, yes, you can get a margarita with your quesadillas at Sin Carne.

As for Sin Carne's food, you could substitute tofu for chicken or fish, soy cheese for "our own gourmet Tex-Mex cheese blend" or nonfat yogurt for the sour cream. But if you don't elect any of those substitutions, you'll end up with traditional Tex-Mex food produced with quite a bit of style.

Style is one of Sin Carne's selling points. Like any cantina worth its salt, the focus is the bar. The walls, hung with Ansel Adams photographs, are painted a fine strawberry-margarita red. It works with the chic slate-gray, black and white of the rest of the room. The tables and chairs are casual contemporary — and is that cowhide on the bar stools?

The kitchen is attempting gourmet Mexican here, and it often succeeds. Salsas are homemade. Even side dishes like rice and refried beans are seasoned so they don't have that Tex-Mex monotonous sameness. The lettuce that comes with the fajitas and such is baby greens, not shredded iceberg.

If you crave beef with your Mexican food, you're out of luck. But otherwise you won't notice, except in a positive way, that this food is more healthful than the usual Tex-Mex.

Not everything works. An appetizer paired too-small grilled shrimp with four greasy mini-tacos. Grilled salmon nestled in two white corn tortillas had been overcooked, and the mole verde sauce was so sour it overwhelmed the fish. A side of guacamole sported so much onion you couldn't taste the avocado.

But no one could complain about the crab quesadillas, the flour tortillas filled with impressively big lumps of crab meat, roasted red peppers, caramelized onions and melted cheese. Fajitas came with all the trimmings and strips of flavorful grilled chicken. Pieces of grilled rockfish fillet, fresh and moist, were rolled in soft tortillas with just the right amount of cheese, lettuce and tomatoes. Salsa verde added zing. For greenery, three of us split a Southwestern Cobb salad — mesclun with avocado, tomato, onion, cheese and a spicy-sweet citrus vinaigrette.

For dessert, my advice is to get the chocolate-chip coffee cake, light as a feather and served warm with frozen yogurt and hot fudge sauce.

*Elizabeth Large*

# Sisson's

*36 E. Cross St., Federal Hill • 410-539-2093*
*Hours: Open for lunch Monday through Saturday, brunch Sunday, dinner nightly*
*Prices: Appetizers, $4.50-$7.25; entrees, $11.95-$16.95*
*Live music: No • Kid's menu: Yes • Waterfront views: No •*
*Wheelchair access: Yes • Reservations: Accepted*

Sisson's is the granddaddy of Baltimore brew pubs, and also the city's first Cajun restaurant.

Baltimoreans know Sisson's is more than a scruffy little Federal Hill bar; but walk into the dim, noisy, crowded bar and you'd never guess there's a pleasant dining room in back where you can get crawfish spring rolls with a mango dipping sauce or salmon fillet with a smoked salmon and horseradish crust and warm fennel potato salad.

The menu has much to recommend it, including its moderate prices. While Cajun and Creole still have pride of place, there are more nonspicy choices available than before, such as the salmon fillet mentioned above. The fish, with its tangy, horseradish-sparked "crust," was fresh, moist and rich, and set off admirably by the warm potato salad.

The Cajun food, though, is still a big draw at Sisson's — at least judging by the couple sitting at the table next to us. They had ordered crawfish. My friend ordered the Cajun Sampler: blackened chicken and catfish, shrimp etouffee and red beans and rice. But I caught her looking longingly at my golden-crusted soft-shell crabs. They were nestled on a bed of perfectly cooked angel-hair pasta and jewel-green broccoli florets and had a buttery sauce studded with capers.

As for the Cajun Sampler, I liked it well enough, although blackening both the chicken and the catfish gave the plate a certain sameness. The fat shrimp swam in a dark, heady sauce; the red beans and rice were fine.

Sandwiches with a spicy slaw are also an option. One of us had a chicken salad sandwich made with roast chicken tossed lightly with barbecue sauce. Other choices include a smoked crawfish cake and a couple of different po' boys.

We began our meal with popcorn crawfish, fried crusty with a zingy remoulade (mayonnaiselike, but more highly seasoned). We also had crawfish in crisp spring rolls, a spectacular first course. Less spectacular, but perfectly decent, were large shrimp fried in a coconut batter with a Creole orange sauce that tasted like melted marmalade.

When I last ate at Sisson's, the choices were either Cajun food or dishes cooked with beer. A pork chop Marble Ale is still on the menu, but that's about it for beer as an ingredient — except for the porter ice cream. The porter flavor is delicate, but the ice cream is good. You can have it by itself or on a brownie with hot fudge sauce.

Desserts are all homemade. A chocolate chip derby pie tasted unbaked, as did the pecan pie. But Sisson's bread pudding is out of this world.

*Elizabeth Large*

# Snyder's Willow Grove

*841 N. Hammonds Ferry Road, Linthicum • 410-789-1149*
*Hours: Open daily for lunch and dinner*
*Prices: Appetizers, $1.95-$11.95; entrees, $8.50-$26.95*
*Live music: No • Kid's menu: Yes • Waterfront views: No •*
*Wheelchair access: Yes • Reservations: Accepted*

Standing outside Snyder's, listening to the roar of Beltway traffic, it's hard to imagine the stand of weeping willows that once stood here. Those graceful trees inspired "Bumps" Snyder and his wife, Sis, to name their Linthicum restaurant Snyder's Willow Grove in 1937. Despite two hurricanes and one devastating fire, the restaurant survives, not because it has kept up with the times, but because in some ways it's a throwback to the past.

The music is so muted it's barely audible. The veteran staff is made up of quiet, efficient pros. And the attractive dining rooms, dressed in crisp green and white, are full of cushy, curved banquettes. Another draw is the size of the portions. We watched in awe as a waitress delivered a stunningly large prime rib. The customer only managed to eat a third of it.

Snyder's' ad in the phone book says seafood is its specialty. What the ad really should say is "Home of world-class cream of crab soup." Served piping hot, it is a cupful of pure bliss, made of nothing but sweet crab and sweet cream, or so it seems. The soup's thin consistency, smooth and free of thickeners, is what really sets it apart. Other crab dishes are handled well, including a light-textured dip with scallions and a golden crab cake full of lumps, which would be even better with fewer bread crumbs and parsley flakes.

But our grilled tuna with a side of buttery caper sauce was overcooked, and an appetizer of skewered barbecued shrimp was tough. The other seafood we tried was even worse — clams casino covered in grease-laden crumbs and leaden fried oysters weighed down in heavy breading. With none of the plump freshness of just-shucked oysters, they were as flat as chicken fingers.

Meat may be a better choice at Snyder's. A man seated opposite us leaned over to recommend the filet mignon special, a tall, tender filet wrapped in bacon. Cooked perfectly, ours had wonderful flavor and a crispy grilled crust.

Filet mignon is on the regular menu, either plain or stuffed with crab imperial, along with porterhouse and strip steaks, and the prime rib that could feed a family of four.

Garnished with a spiced-apple slice, all dinners are served with two choices: a simple iceberg salad, potato or vegetable, like fresh broccoli with cheese sauce. The sauteed button mushrooms swimming in oil aren't worth the extra cost.

At the end of our meal, our waitress brought over a tray filled with desserts, none made in-house. The creamy peanut-butter cheesecake and rich mousse-filled chocolate cake were satisfying, but lemon meringue pie had the kind of old-fashioned appeal that suited our night at Snyder's.

*Kathryn Higham*

# SoBo Cafe

*6-8 W. Cross St., Federal Hill • 410-752-1518*
*Hours: Open daily for lunch and dinner*
*Prices: Appetizers, $2.50-$4.50; entrees, $7-$10*
*Live music: No • Kid's menu: No • Waterfront views: No •*
*Wheelchair access: Yes • Reservations: Accepted for large parties*

Baltimore's SoBo may never be as famous as New York's SoHo, the arty area south of Houston Street, or as trendy as Miami's SoBe, the art-deco jewel of South Beach. But South Baltimore has an appeal of its own, and so does Brent Ludtke's SoBo Cafe.

It's hard not to have an immediate positive response walking into the bright and airy SoBo, with its gauzy curtains, paddle fans and sunflower-colored walls hung with bold artworks. Some are pretty funny, like Phil Wiley's surfing alien who also hangs 10 on the oversized blackboard above the wide stretch of SoBo's wooden bar.

That's where the menu, which changes daily, is written in chalk. The menu is a beautiful sight, not only because entrees like shrimp in chili sauce, and curried chicken with caramelized vegetables, sound enticing, but also because few items costs more than $10.

There are a few things that are always available, including the potpie, soup of the day and the Cincinnati five-way chili. You can also order either the meat or vegetarian chili plain. We tried the chunky veggie version with corn. It comes on a plate of nachos, a sunburst of loaded chips topped with melted Cheddar.

The chicken potpie was served in a large casserole topped with buttery puff pastry embellished with the name of the cafe. Inside, big hunks of red-skinned potatoes, moist slivers of chicken, bright peas and hand-cut carrots and celery were nestled in a seasoned white sauce. Like the delicious broccoli soup we tried, creamy with whole florets, the potpie might be a little heavy for a summer night, unless you're in the mood for comfort food.

The linguine with mussels and clam sauce was a lighter choice. We loved the flavor of the sauce, with its soft sauteed peppers, celery and thyme. The dill the blackboard touted was undetectable. It did show up as a nice surprise in the spinach pie appetizer, a phyllo-topped square filled with baby spinach and feta cheese. It was almost as light as a souffle.

We also tried SoBo's salmon, a small, flaky-moist fillet. It was served with a creamy roasted garlic sauce that won raves, artichoke hearts that somehow clashed with the fish, and sides of yellow rice and roasted carrots and zucchini.

Aside from those artichokes, there were few misses at SoBo. In the kitchen and out front, the staff clearly is paying attention to details.

That includes pastry chef Joanne Goshen, who spoons whipped cream next to her blueberry pie and sits her tall cheesecake on a delectable, inch-thick chocolate-chip crust.

*Kathryn Higham*

# Sotto Sopra

*405 N. Charles St., Mount Vernon • 410- 625-0534*
*Hours: Open Sunday through Thursday, 5:30 p.m. to 9:30 p.m.;*
*Friday and Saturday, 5:30 p.m. to 11:30 p.m.*
*Prices: Appetizers, $6.75-$13; entrees, $10-$25*
*Live music: No • Kid's menu: No • Waterfront views: No •*
*Wheelchair access: Yes • Reservations: Suggested*

Sotto Sopra is a restaurant that sizzles.

The dining room is wonderfully theatrical; the food, trendy and expensive — although not outrageously so. A customer breaks, full voice, into an aria, to the amazement of the rest of the room. It's a trip. (If you want to hold a quiet conversation over dinner here, you're out of luck.)

The room where other eateries once were has been strikingly redone. Only the cracked tile floors remain, giving the restaurant a touch of ruined elegance. At night the dining room has a golden glow. Murals of cafe scenes and mirrors stretch to the high ceiling; and the appointments, from the maitre d's stand to the whirly, wiry chandeliers, are stunning.

Image is everything at Sotto Sopra. Only image isn't everything. How's the food?

Some of it, I'm happy to say, lives up to the fabulous surroundings — and the prices. Some of it doesn't.

Start with vitello tonnato — the star among our first courses. Tissue-thin slices of veal were fanned in a circle, then gilded with a silky sauce of pureed tuna, cream and anchovies. A crisp-crusted pizza layered with mozarella, prosciutto and arugula would have been almost as good, but the greens were excessively salty. The salad with balsamic vinaigrette arranged with the zingy scallop seviche was oversalted, the mixed greens with green beans that decorated the fine grilled swordfish were oversalted — you get the idea.

Come to think of it, the vegetables around the sauteed veal chop, including artichokes, cauliflower, potatoes and red pepper, had been seasoned with a heavy hand as well.

But the homemade spinach ravioli stuffed with ricotta and decorated with a pretty, subtle tomato sauce couldn't have been more delicate. Gnocci made with ricotta in a pink cream of a red pepper sauce were also very good but would work better as a half-order first course than a main dish. A large plate of them got a little monotonous.

It's hard to resist dessert when you see what other customers have ordered, all sauced and swirled and spangled with powdered sugar. The tiny profiteroles with pastry cream and chocolate sauce pleased us, and the sampler of truffles and cookies was lovely; but the mixed berries with zabaglione and vanilla ice cream imported from Italy carried the day.

No, not everything was perfect; but some of it, like the vitello tonnato, came pretty close. Sotto Sopra will eventually have to add more casual food to its menu and lower its prices. But right now Sotto Sopra is flying high, with every table filled on a rainy Tuesday night.

*Elizabeth Large*

# Spike & Charlie's

*1225 Cathedral St., Mount Vernon • 410-752-8144*
*Hours: Open Tuesdays to Sundays for dinner*
*Prices: Entrees, $15-$24*
*Live music: No • Kid's menu: No • Waterfront views: No •*
*Wheelchair access: Yes • Reservations: Suggested*

If you think Baltimore is a stodgy city, visit the ultra-hip Spike & Charlie's Restaurant and Wine Bar. Sit down in the bar, with its autumnal colors, contemporary art and gauzy curtains. Or go back to the multilevel, minimalist dining room. No candles, no flowers, plain white table linen — nothing to detract from the seriously decorative plates to come.

You never know with hip places: Sometimes the food is more style than substance; good food is simply a bonus.

Not at Spike & Charlie's.

The looks of the chilled asparagus soup with red pepper puree were noteworthy: a yin and yang of cool green puree balanced with a curve of soft red, a thin white line or two of cream traced through them. Beautiful, and the two-toned flavors were remarkably pleasing.

A sea scallop and littleneck clam stew may sound pedestrian, but the reality was anything but. The expertly cooked shellfish was afloat in an aromatic broth, rich with tomatoes, sliced okra and chickpeas. A pretty chunk of fresh rockfish was an unexpected bonus, and jewel-green baby asparagus spears added bright color as well as flavor.

Not everything that came out of Spike & Charlie's kitchen reached the heights of these two dishes; but nothing we tried was an out-and-out failure except a green salad with cardboard tomato wedges, an unexceptional vinaigrette, pine nuts and one long dark hair.

The Vidalia onion soup, with a thin, crisp fennel-seed crouton made of sourdough bread is a sophisticated relative of good old French onion soup, without the thick crust of melted cheese, but with plenty of flavor.

Our tres trendy pizza had a thin, crisp crust that sported a topping of succulent chicken, homemade mozzarella and spinach. A fresh-tasting ratatouille graced four al dente ravioli stuffed with goat cheese. Slices of marinated pork loin were laid on a pretty bed of diced sweet potato and red beans. I loved the accompaniments and the richly seasoned sauce, but the pork itself was a bit tough and flavorless.

Spike & Charlie's has many pluses: style, serious food, excellent bread, an expertly chosen wine list. It also has minuses, including service with an attitude, and a lemon cream dessert that wasn't sweet, lemony or custardy enough.

In spite of that last, desserts in general are one of the restaurant's greatest strengths: fresh, imaginative, delicate and unique. The delicious peach clafouti, a cakelike pudding, came with homemade cinnamon ice cream. But we fought over the banana tarte — a puff pastry topped with banana slices, a drizzle of caramel and fresh banana ice cream.

*Elizabeth Large*

# Suburban House

*911 Reisterstown Road, Pikesville • 410-484-7775*
*Hours: Open daily for breakfast, lunch and dinner*
*Prices: Appetizers, $2.50-$5; entrees, $3.50-$9.95*
*Live music: No • Kid's menu: Yes • Waterfront views: No •*
*Wheelchair access: Yes • Reservations: Accepted for large parties*

There's a funny glossary of Yiddish words on the paper place mats at Suburban House, but to get the jokes, you have to speak the language. Goy was one of the few words we recognized. Definition: someone who buys retail.

I can, however, recognize a great pastrami when I taste it, and this restaurant serves it. We tried the lean, thinly sliced meat instead of corned beef in Reuben variation.

But you'll find more than deli favorites like pastrami at Suburban House, which has been around in one form or another for 50 years. They offer an extensive menu, full of typical diner fare like hot turkey platters and ethnic specialties such as kippered salmon and kasha. Though it's not kosher, Suburban House does offer a Friday night Shabbos dinner.

It's also home to the biggest matzo ball we'd ever seen. The size of a softball, the moist, light dumpling sat in a bowl of yellow broth. However, the soup didn't have the same homemade flavor as the rich puree of split pea we tried.

It isn't hard to love a latke when the potato pancakes are crisp and golden, as they were here. A combination of creamy chocolate mousse and rich, crumbly cheesecake also was a hit. We polished off the enormous slice one bite at a time.

Not everything we tried was as good. Bland chopped liver needed something to boost its flavor. We chose what we thought would be a hit from the list of specials: cabbage rolls. But they were disappointing, stuffed with a ground-turkey mixture and covered in gelatinous sweet and sour sauce.

Crab cakes, another dinner special, looked like hockey pucks, commercially pressed and deep fried to a dark brown. The specials were served with soup or a fresh iceberg salad, and a choice of vegetable and dessert.

Our waitress said the peach cake was homemade and wonderful. It turned out to be peach slices in a sweet apricot goo on a thin sheet of pastry.

So while the specials look like a bargain, sandwiches here may be a better choice. They're served with crunchy half-sour pickles and a delightful slaw, lightly dressed. There are so many sandwiches to choose from — hot and cold, open faced and triple-decker — you may have trouble deciding.

Don't look to your waitress for help, though. Ours seemed tired and impatient. But the whole staff snapped to attention when a baby spilled a bowl of soup. They quickly cleaned the mess and calmed the child. This seems like a good place to bring the family.

The restaurant is spare, yet bright, with mirrors to give the illusion of roominess. And there are lots of cushy upholstered booths to settle into when those pastrami cravings start.

*Kathryn Higham*

# Sushi Sono

*10215 Wincopin Circle, Columbia • 410-997-6131*
*Hours: Open for lunch and dinner Monday through Saturday*
*Prices: Appetizers, $2.95-$11.95; entrees, $10.95-$35*
*Live music: No • Kid's menu: Yes • Waterfront views: Yes •*
*Wheelchair access: Yes • Reservations: Accepted*

Sushi Sono, the new restaurant and sushi bar in Columbia, has good Japanese food, no better and certainly no worse than most of Baltimore's Japanese restaurants. So why is it worth making the trip from Baltimore to Columbia to eat there? I can tell you in one word. Well, two.

The view.

Sushi Sono is right on the lake, very near Clyde's and the Tomato Palace. But those are restaurants where a lot is happening. At Sushi Sono you can sit very quietly in the serene blond-wood dining room and contemplate the water, the branch of a pine tree, a family of ducks floating calmly by.

And, of course, enjoy food like Sushi Sono's spicy crab roll. The lump crab and avocado mixture is rolled in sticky rice and spiked with pickled ginger and wasabi. It's a happy alternative to the usual imitation crab meat California roll.

A more adventuresome first course, though, is the shredded jelly fish salad, with its marvelous texture and tangy sauce. Or try the seaweed salad, a beautiful crystalline green studded with sesame seeds. Its texture is as interesting as its flavor. (The iceberg lettuce salad that comes with Sushi Sono's dinners is a bow to American tastes, and not much thought has been put into it.)

As for main courses, sukiyaki can only be ordered for two and you have to do the work of cooking it yourself, but that allows you to pace your meal. Vegetables and fragile rice noodles were brought to the table simmering in a flavorful, slightly sweet broth. We added the paper-thin slices of beef and cooked them just till they changed color. (I would have been happier with more vegetables and fewer of the red-edged processed cakes made from various kinds of fish).

Sushi Sono has a fine tempura, crisply battered and almost grease-free, with vegetables and enormous shrimp. But the chef's specialty is a handsome assortment of sushi and sashimi — 12 pieces of impeccably fresh raw fish and nine pieces of nigiri, raw fish layered with rice. I've seen such assortments that were more works of art; this was decorated simply with shredded daikon radish and real maple leaves. But there were no complaints about freshness or flavor.

Sushi Sono is a restaurant where you'd do best to avoid concessions to American tastes. Have sake or Japanese beer; skip the nameless Chardonnay sold by the glass. And don't end your meal with the green tea ice cream or tempura ice cream (vanilla surrounded by fried batter) — the two dessert choices. Both are fairly tasteless. Have instead a steaming cup of green tea.

*Elizabeth Large*

# Suzie's Soba

*1009 W. 36th St., Hampden • 410-243-0051*
*Hours: Open daily for dinner*
*Prices: Appetizers, $3.50-$9; entrees, $6-$17; no liquor license*
*Live music: No • Kid's menu: No • Waterfront views: No •*
*Wheelchair access: Yes • Reservations: Accepted for large parties •*
*Other locations: 1023 N. Charles St., Mount Vernon • 410-244-0055*

Sue Hi Hong, known about town as Suzie, is a little bit superstitious. So she took it as a sign when she found an ornamental gong that was a perfect fit for a restaurant space she was considering in Hampden. The location, Hong knew, was just right for Suzie's Soba.

The restaurant's interior features seafoam-green walls painted softly with undulating grasses, wild grapevines entwined with tiny lights and mosses, and fish sculpted out of foam core to create an underwater world. It's magical.

So is much of the fare at Suzie's Soba, from a tempura-fried maki roll filled with shrimp and basil to a simple house salad with impeccably fresh baby greens, pickled ginger and marinated shiitake mushroom slivers that explode with flavor.

The shiitakes also turned up in our tuna donburi, a Japanese dish layered with slivers of carrots, snow peas, green onions and red peppers over short-grain rice. An egg had been broken over the top, cooking as it mixed with the soy-based sauce, hot fish, rice and vegetables. Chopped cilantro and thin strips of nori, the seaweed wrapper for sushi rolls, added another dimension of flavor. It would have been perfect if the tender sushi-grade tuna hadn't been overcooked.

Besides several donburi dishes, entrees fall into two categories: sauteed noodles and soup-based noodles. Our sauteed soba dish of dried wild spinach, garlic and pine nuts looked like a plate of linguine and pesto. We loved the earthy flavor of the wild spinach, brought out even more by cha soba, a wheat noodle with the delicate taste of green tea.

A pale, fat noodle was used in the Oriental chicken soba, slathered with a spicy-sweet sauce and studded with sesame seeds. Everything was cut into bite-size bits, slivers and shreds, from the boneless chicken to the broccoli, snow peas, red bell pepper and carrots.

We tried the Korean-style yook gye jang soup, which combined thin cellophane noodles, shredded beef, green onions, Napa cabbage and bean sprouts in a tangy broth flavored with kimchee, the spicy Korean condiment. It had a rustic simplicity and a more traditional flavor than other dishes.

For starters, there are a few sushi rolls on the menu. We preferred the flavor of the tempura shrimp roll to a standard tekka maki, made with pale pink tuna. Other options include a simple salad of Napa cabbage seasoned with fresh kimchee, and crisp fried dumplings filled with cabbage and sprouts.

Desserts aren't made in-house, and they're not Asian-inspired. But you can always go the minimalist route and satisfy your sweet tooth with a cup of green tea.

*Kathryn Higham*

# Tapestry

*1705 Aliceanna St., Fells Point • 410-327-7037*
*Hours: Open Monday through Friday 4 p.m. to 11 p.m., Saturday and*
*   Sunday 2 p.m. to midnight*
*Prices: Appetizers, $6-$8; entrees, $9-$15*
*Live music: No • Kid's menu: No • Waterfront views: No •*
*Wheelchair access: No • Reservations: Accepted*

In many ways Tapestry is very much like other Fells Point restaurants. The setting, particularly the bar, has lots of funky charm. The narrow dining room is appealing, although it won't sound like it when I describe the color scheme as acorn-squash yellow and dark green.

On a Sunday night, with every table taken, there's one waiter and one cook. "We didn't think it would be this busy," our waiter tells us. Dishes aren't removed unless we pile them on one corner to show that we're finished with them. Water glasses remain unfilled. Only one dessert is available this night because last night they sold out. All this is part of the appeal of eating in Fells Point. Charming. But funky.

Of course, the corollary of charming and funky is interesting and reasonably priced food. That's why we get grumpier as we see that appetizers average $7 and entrees average $15.

Three things save the day. First, the food is interesting and pretty good. Second, Tapestry serves the world's greatest mashed potatoes. Third, the appetizers really function as small meals. So you can get a Creole crab cake, which is fat with lump crab meat and has a fiery remoulade sauce and enough vegetable garnishes to qualify as supper.

A Middle Eastern plate with warm, miniature pitas, a fine hummus and a zippily seasoned eggplant dip comes with couscous and various salad-like garnishes. Plump, unusually grit-free mussels are bathed in a saffron-scented sauce made with white wine, butter and a bit of fresh corn and tomatoes. Delicious, especially with bread to dip in the sauce.

If that isn't enough food for you, order the boneless chicken breast stuffed with lobster covered in a fine, thick mushroom gravy labeled "morel sauce" on the menu. It comes with those great whipped potatoes, mashed with some of their skin, and tender asparagus spears.

The pan-fried alligator tail supposedly tastes like chicken but doesn't really. (The flavor is mild and unlike anything else.) It's lavishly treated with roasted red pepper, slices of andouille sausage and lumps of crab.

Our other entree doesn't live up to the rest of our meal. Tuna encrusted with black and white sesame seeds comes medium rare, as our waiter warned us. Because the fish is notably fresh, it doesn't bother me. What does bother me is a wasabi sauce so fiery it has to be avoided .

We can end with any dessert we want as long as it's the pretty passion fruit mousse-and-cake concoction. Luckily, it would be my choice for dessert — if there were any choice.

*Elizabeth Large*

# The Tavern at Centre Park

*8808 Centre Park Drive, Columbia • 410-884-7001*
*Hours: Open daily for lunch and dinner, Sunday for brunch*
*Prices: Appetizers, $1.95-$11.95; entrees, $6.95-$19.95*
*Live music: No • Kid's menu: Yes • Waterfront views: No*
*Wheelchair access: Yes • Reservations: Accepted*

Deciding what to order is difficult when a restaurant's menu is as interesting as the one at the Tavern. It took awhile just to wade through the nearly two dozen appetizers.

So, it was a good thing executive chef Henry Pertman made his way to our table before we ordered. He pointed out some Tavern specialties, the crab dip and Florentine mixed grill, and his own favorites, the smoked fish and duck.

Enclosed in smoked glass, the expansive dining room has a dark, contemporary feel, with an open display kitchen, exposed ceiling painted black and cushy booths upholstered with a splash of color.

Like the decor, the menu has an up-to-date feel, and gets its inspiration from lots of different places — the Pacific Rim, California, Italy and the Southwest. Interesting ingredients, like the Southwestern spices in the crab cake, give dishes a different twist.

Golden edged, with the faintest flavor of cumin, this phenomenal crab cake practically fell apart into big, sweet lumps. You can order it as a sandwich on a Portuguese roll, or as a platter, with mashed potatoes and diced vine-ripe tomatoes drizzled with honeyed balsamic vinaigrette.

Duck is served two ways: smoked, encrusted with herbs and baked, or the way we tried it, roasted simply with Oriental seasonings. A thin oyster-garlic sauce had been used to baste the half-duck, making it aromatic and moist. There was no gamy flavor and no grease.

The popular Florentine mixed grill pairs chunks of tender steak with jumbo shrimp in a cream sauce with wilted spinach. The cream sauce brings the other ingredients together harmoniously without overpowering them.

Sauces stood out among our appetizers, too. Honey-barbecue-mustard sauce and creamy horseradish-dill remoulade had been swirled into a starburst pattern of red and white on the smoked fish platter.

Subtle, buttery and fine is the way we'd describe the wild mushroom-wine sauce served with our grilled portobello. The thick crab and artichoke dip was subtle as well, made with lumps of crab, cream cheese and a smattering of capers.

We had only a few minor problems, mainly with our side dishes: garlic mashed potatoes that needed more garlic; squash slices so heavily seasoned they tasted dirty.

Our waiter, a model of efficiency and helpfulness all night, suggested the chocolate fantasy cake for dessert. We tried it but it didn't have the intensity of flavor we expected. It, like the rest of the desserts, was not made in-house.

*Kathryn Higham*

# Teranga African Restaurant

*20 W. 21st St., Baltimore • 410-783-0780*
*Hours: Open Monday through Saturday for lunch and dinner*
*Prices: Entrees, $8.99-$11.99*
*Live music: No • Kid's menu: No • Waterfront views: No •*
*Wheelchair access: Yes • Reservations: Accepted*

Some restaurants are worth talking about for what they are, others for what they might be.

Teranga African Restaurant, serving food from Senegal, is a small spot with plenty of promise. Since opened by restaurant veteran Fode Kande, Teranga has not had an easy time.

Kande started with a complete Senegalese menu, including peanut butter-infused stews; marinated, grilled meats; and thiebou dieun, a baked bluefish that is Senegal's national dish. He offered a full complement of desserts, from American sweets like cheesecake to exotic-sounding mamongo cake.

But few diners came. So Kande dropped the menu and switched to a lunch and dinner buffet. He says it is easier for people who don't know Senegalese cooking to see a dish first.

There has been a bit more action at Teranga, as some former Peace Corps workers and people in the area's Senegalese community found out about the restaurant. Almost everyone asks for thiebou dieun, the bluefish dish. It remains the one entree that can be ordered from the original menu.

Covered in a golden batter, the fish is sauteed, baked, then placed back in the pan with a thin, seasoned tomato sauce. The sauce also coats the sliced eggplant, yucca, cabbage and mound of rice that accompany the fish.

The moist fish is spiked with a powerful filling of parsley, pepper and onion. Senegal natives prefer a hotter version than Teranga's, but we loved the dish just as it was. If you like fiery food, you can request the dish the authentic way.

The night we visited, the buffet featured maffe Saloum, beef stew in a peanut butter and tomato sauce; beef Teranga, a stew in a tomato sauce with yams and carrots; and yassa Diola, marinated chicken with olives. It was hard to tell the difference between the two stews. Both had tender cubes of beef in a full-bodied tomato gravy. With carrots and cabbage, the maffe may have had a slightly creamier texture, but we couldn't detect any peanut flavor. The Teranga was a bit brighter on the tongue, with its cubes of yams and carrots. We tried the maffe over couscous, and the beef Teranga over rice.

The chicken yassa, wings and thighs chopped into small pieces, had a wonderful, tangy flavor. It came in an unctuous sauce — with green olives and sliced onions — but we didn't mind because it was authentic. We would have preferred the promised breast meat rather than the wings, though.

If you haven't tried Senegalese cuisine, Teranga is worth a trip. Where else will you be able to sip sorrel bissap, a sweet drink that looks like grape juice but has a tang similar to cranberries? Or zingy, uncarbonated ginger ale — the real stuff extracted from fresh ginger?

*Kathryn Higham*

# Tiffin

*1341 University Blvd. East, Langley Park • 301-434-9200*
*Hours: Open daily for lunch and dinner*
*Prices: Appetizers, $2.50-$7.95; entrees, $6.50-$13.95; daily lunch buffet, $5.95 weekdays, $7.95 weekends*
*Live music: No • Kid's menu: No • Waterfront views: No • Wheelchair access: Yes • Reservations: Accepted*

We opened our dinner menus at Tiffin to read that the name of this Indian restaurant translates as lunch. Sure enough, a long serving table stood against one wall, ready for the next day's elaborate lunch buffet.

If you're going to travel to eat at Tiffin, go for the lunch buffet, a terrific deal that includes soup, appetizers, dessert and a half-dozen freshly made meat and vegetarian dishes.

One thing you won't find on the buffet line is bread. That's because it's brought fresh and steaming hot to your table. Our waitress served us a basket filled with wedges of naan, plus a small pancake made with fresh vegetables and herbs.

The doting service and tranquil, open atmosphere are part of what makes Tiffin special. The dining room has an upscale feel, and so does the buffet — mainly because the staff manages to keep everything looking and tasting like it all just came from the kitchen.

When we visited for lunch, the buffet started with a mild and creamy tomato soup and two appetizers — spicy chickpeas in a thick, fragrant paste and soft potato fritters. We also spooned out portions of pungent lemon pickle, mild cucumber and yogurt raita, and green coriander chutney.

Onto a bed of basmati rice, we ladled tender curried goat in a dark, fiery sauce; chicken on the bone cooked in a less-spicy vindaloo sauce with chunks of potatoes; and juicy pieces of tandoori chicken. Vegetable dishes included seasoned chopped greens and potatoes; smooth yellow lentil dal; and curried button mushrooms and green peppers cooked with cinnamon and spices.

Our dinner at Tiffin wasn't quite as smooth as our lunch. Bitter baby eggplant served in a thick, bland curry sauce was disappointing, and the tandoori chicken at lunch was more flavorful than the a la carte appetizer platter at dinner. The dish also included fried, potato-filled samosas, vegetable fritters and herb-flecked sausages that were all fairly ordinary.

We preferred creamy mulligatawny lentil soup and chunks of fried fish splashed with vinegar hot sauce as starters.

Among our entrees, we had to work to get the moist flesh of a small, bony rockfish. But big chunks of lamb and potatoes done vindaloo-style required nothing more than an appreciation of sauces. We sopped up the vindaloo with pieces of fried poori and onion kulcha, two of Tiffin's outstanding breads.

For dessert, you can try the squares of pressed cheese in pistachio cream or a cone of saffron ice cream topped with rice noodles. But gulab jamun, fried cheese balls soaked in honey, is the traditional crowd-pleaser.

*Kathryn Higham*

# Timber Creek Tavern

*10092 Belair Road, Kingsville • 410-529-7999*
*Hours: Open every day for lunch and dinner*
*Prices: Appetizers, $3.50-$7.50; entrees, $7.50-$16*
*Live music: Tuesday, Wednesday, Friday and Saturday nights •*
*Kid's menu: Yes • Waterfront views: No • Wheelchair access: Yes •*
*Reservations: Accepted*

Looks are deceiving. The Timber Creek Tavern appears to be a backwoods bar. The parking lot is filled with pickup trucks and four-wheel drives. Inside the large dining room next to the bar, people are smoking, and one man is smoking a pipe. And when was the last time you ate salmon Portofino with lump crab, scallions, sun-dried tomatoes and a white wine sauce in the same room where people were playing pool?

Families with kids eat here because the food is good and the prices are reasonable. The tavern is an interesting combination of bar, family dining and, yes, a little haute cuisine.

The menu is made up mostly of burgers, sandwiches, pizzas and salads, but you can also get some elegant entrees. A fat, grilled pork chop, even though it was cooked a little too long, had a fabulous smoky flavor. Its apple-horseradish relish added plenty of zing, and on the side came the two vegetables of the day, red-skinned potatoes roasted with herbs and whole baby carrots sauteed with fresh broccoli.

Even better was my superb filet mignon, buttery tender and rare, with a great grilled flavor. It lay on a bed of slivered and sauteed red, green and yellow peppers, and had an intriguing bit of sauce tinged with soy. Salmon Portofino was beautifully grilled and topped with fat lumps of crab and a buttery wine sauce, while sun-dried tomatoes gave the dish spark. The crab cakes were nicely done with plenty of lump crab and a good balance of seasonings and binder.

Timber Creek's appetizers are mostly classic bar food, like a half-pound of shrimp. These were steamed with potatoes, onions and enough spices to set your hair on fire. But there are other choices. Mussels in white wine with garlic toast pleased us, as did the flavorful cream of mushroom soup.

The special appetizer that night was made up of layers of fried eggplant, fresh tomatoes, mozzarella and spinach with a delicate blush-pink sauce. Good, but it could have doubled as a main course with a salad.

We finished off with Timber Creek's piece de resistance, a banana wrapped in phyllo pastry and deep-fried, then served with homemade chocolate chip ice cream and chocolate sauce. (The other choices weren't bad either: a rum-scented bread pudding and a banana chocolate chip poundcake.)

As for those niceties like polished service and a good wine list — well, you don't expect them in a country bar. But the truth is, I've had a lot worse service at a lot fancier places.

This is value dining, but you aren't shortchanged on anything but atmosphere at the Timber Creek Tavern — both figuratively and literally (if you mind people smoking).

*Elizabeth Large*

# Tio Pepe's

*10 E. Franklin St., downtown • 410- 539-4675.*
*Hours: Open Monday through Friday for lunch, every day for dinner*
*Prices: Appetizers, $5.75-$10.75; entrees, $14.50-$23.25*
*Live music: no • Kid's menu: no • Waterfront views: No •*
*Wheelchair access: Yes • Reservations: Required*

People still complain about having to wait for a table at Tio Pepe's when they have a reservation. But after they've been seated, they know they'll be waited on with lots of flourishes and great Spanish charm.

We were seated in one of the endless number of basement rooms — snug rooms with whitewashed brick walls, lots of shawls and gaily painted pottery, fresh flowers, handsomely appointed tables placed quite close together. Everyone is having a good time, so we didn't mind being seated right next to another table.

We started with the suave seafood bisque, full of cream and a touch of sherry. We tried the house specialty, shrimp in garlic sauce, which was exactly the way it always is: lots of shrimp, a killer amount of garlic, a sauce that begs to be sopped up with an inordinate amount of bread. Best of all our first courses was chewy-tender squid stuffed with minced veal and ham in an intensely flavored, inky sauce.

If all these sound a bit heavy as starters, begin with the special salad with romaine, watercress, tomatoes, artichoke hearts and beets in a vinaigrette sparked with chopped olives.

Roast suckling pig appears on the menu periodically as a special. The presentation is simple: big, juicy chunks of flavorful pork and a side dish of excellent black beans. If you want a little greenery with this, have the a la carte spinach sauteed with green grapes and pine nuts. The roast suckling pig was about as close to regional Spanish cuisine as we got, except for pollo y langosta a la Catalana, a combination of leg and thigh of chicken and lobster meat in a creamy sherry-flavored sauce reminiscent of that seafood bisque.

Much of the menu is Continental food served in enormous portions. You wouldn't, for instance, think of rockfish and crab meat in champagne sauce as a particularly Spanish dish. The good seafood was mounded high under a devastatingly rich sauce of butter, cream and wine. With it were perfectly cooked green beans. Pheasant Alcantara is a classic example of what makes Tio Pepe so successful. Tender slices of white meat decorated with green grapes lay in a lake of highly seasoned, winy sauce, and a mountain of wild and long-grain rice.

Everybody usually saves room for one of the rolled sponge cakes, gooey with custard or laden with whipped cream. The pine nut cake is the most popular, with its spongecake, thick custard and heavy coating of pignolias. But don't overlook the chocolate roll, something like a fallen chocolate souffle wrapped around whipped cream. You can also get strawberries and raspberries with a sabayon sauce (basically egg yolks, sugar and wine).

*Elizabeth Large*

# Tonino's

*2 Hanover Road, Reisterstown • 410-833-2070*
*Hours: Open daily for lunch and dinner*
*Prices: Appetizers, $2.95-$6.95; entrees, $4.40-$14.95*
*Live music: No • Kid's menu: Yes • Waterfront views: No •*
*Wheelchair access: Yes • Reservations: Not accepted*

We went to Tonino's in Reisterstown in search of what we heard was a great house dressing, and found much more. This family-friendly Italian restaurant handles pasta, pizza and subs as smoothly as it tosses its salads.

The house dressing is incredible: Think of a lemon-less Caesar dressing with four times the Parmesan cheese. We tried the dressing on the Tonino's salad, a large Italian-style chef's salad, with jumbo shrimp nestled in cups of provolone and salami, sliced vegetables and artichoke hearts.

You might not want to order a salad, though, if you're having an entree. The complimentary house salad is big enough to share and comes with plenty of Tonino's wonderful dressing. Instead, order an appetizer of mushrooms Provencale, a bowlful of button mushroom caps in a luscious golden broth of garlic, wine and fresh tomatoes. Make sure to ask for extra bread to sop up the Provencale sauce.

Bruschetta and crostini are on the regular menu, but we tried the bruschetta special with goat cheese, slivers of grilled eggplant and diced red-ripe tomatoes. It was the big lumps of creamy goat cheese that really made this starter stand out.

Goat cheese? Grilled eggplant? Mushrooms Provencale? That's right. This is no ordinary pizzeria. Jesse Issa opened Tonino's 10 years ago with his brother, Michael, a chef who trained at the Baltimore International College.

The look is Mediterranean, with muted Italian tile, arched niches outlined in brick and artwork that calls to mind the charms of Venice and Italian seaside towns. Tonino's is pretty enough for a weekend dinner and comfortable enough to bring the kids for midweek subs and pizza.

Tonino's pizza has a wonderful crust with fresh, yeasty flavor and a bright-tasting tomato sauce that's not too acidic. The sub expert at our table declared the chicken parmigiana sub a winner. Sauce to cheese ratio, perfect. Breading, not greasy. Chicken breast, generously portioned and moist.

The pasta primavera substituted spaghetti for fettuccine, but we didn't mind. We liked the mix of six large, tender shrimp with slivers of carrots, sun-dried tomatoes, mushroom slices and crisp florets of broccoli; and the way the barest amount of cream enriched the tomato sauce.

Desserts aren't made in-house and, aside from a cannoli with lovely cinnamon-flavored ricotta cream, they're mostly forgettable.

Stick with what Michael Issa prepares in the kitchen and don't be shy about taking leftovers with you. The staff is smart, quick and willing to oblige requests for doggie bags.

*Kathryn Higham*

# The Trolley Stop

*6 Oella Ave., Ellicott City • 410-465-8546*
*Hours: Open daily for breakfast, lunch and dinner*
*Prices: Appetizers, $1.50-$5.95; entrees, $5.50-$11.95*
*Live music: No • Kid's menu: Yes • Waterfront views: No •*
*Wheelchair access: Yes • Reservations: Accepted •*
*Credit cards: MasterCard, Visa*

There are people who would never consider going to the Trolley Stop, a rustic eatery on the edge of historic Ellicott City. Some might get as far as the cigarette haze at the bar, take a look at the year-round Christmas decorations and the rough wood floors and decide the Trolley Stop is not for them.

They wouldn't even have to know this place was once a biker's bar with a bad reputation. That was before Joe Morea bought the 19th-century tavern in 1981 and started focusing more on food than drink. A few locals can still be found at the bar, but people now come mainly to eat, filing in for nightly specials, like the $9.95 lobster on Tuesday nights.

"Cheap eats" is the reason, says Mary Fields, who manages the restaurant with her brother, John, and father, Bob. The food here isn't just cheap, though. It's remarkably good, and so is the service. Our waitress managed to be funny, smart, efficient and full of helpful information.

One of the best things she recommended was the thick turkey and Swiss cheese sandwich grilled on rounds of sourdough bread. The thinly sliced turkey breast was freshly roasted and moist, accented with honey mustard for a touch of sweetness. Served with pickle chips and a tumble of golden fries, this sandwich was a bargain at $4.25.

The crab cake platter, another of the waitress' picks, featured a small, firm crab cake with more filler than crab-cake connoisseurs would like, but with enough backfin lumps to compensate. It was served with a salad and baked potato.

Platters and sandwiches make up most of the regular menu, with different entrees, sandwiches and often appetizers on the specials list each day.

We tried the Cajun-blackened New York strip steak, which was juicy and flavorful under a thick coating of fiery spices; a half-pound of plump shrimp, cooked perfectly with crab spice; and pasta shells stuffed with tender morsels of sea scallops, shrimp and crab meat. The seafood was fine, but the sauce the menu described as "lobster cream" tasted a lot like the creamy seafood soup we had for starters.

As a soup, it was quite good — creamy without being too thick, with bits of crab, chopped clam and shrimp. Crunchy, crusty-coated jalapeno poppers filled with cream cheese, and a Caesar salad with a homemade dressing full of anchovy bits and slivers of Parmesan were our other appetizers.

Individual tubs of not-quite-butter and fake plants are as much a part of the Trolley Stop's charm as the exposed beams of Tennessee black oak and the homey desserts baked by a local woman and brought in fresh each afternoon.

Be sure to try at least one dessert.

*Kathryn Higham*

# Tuscany Grill

*2047 York Road, Timonium • 410-252-3353*
*Hours: Open for lunch Monday through Friday, for dinner nightly*
*Prices: Appetizers, $6.25-$9.25; entrees, $9.95-$21*
*Live music: No • Kid's menu: No • Waterfront views: No •*
*Wheelchair access: Yes • Reservations: Suggested*

I worry about the Tuscany Grill, the new Italian restaurant in Timonium. I'd like to think its very good food will overcome its disadvantages (mainly, its location), but I'm mildly pessimistic.

Don't let the Tuscany Grill's exterior fool you. It looks like any one of those pleasant but unmemorable Italian eating places set along a busy highway. The interior doesn't give you much of a clue either — nice enough but not at all striking. And with no carpet, draperies or even tablecloths to absorb sound, it can get deafeningly noisy. People dress casually here, and the service can be equally casual.

The food, however, is often quite elegant. Tuscany Grill has a well-conceived menu of traditional dishes produced with imagination and verve. Bruschetta started with crisp toasts, and each topping was more appealing than the last: fresh tomatoes, a tangy olive spread, savory bean puree.

Mussels here seem fresher and more grit-free than most, their wine and chopped fresh tomato sauce a little more flavorful. A green salad, elegant in its simplicity, sported summer tomatoes, Belgian endive and a fine balsamic dressing.

Our most spectacular first course was a huge crab cake, worthy of any Chesapeake Bay cook, on a bed of fruity slaw. The plate was decorated prettily with a piping of fresh tomato sauce and dots of tartar sauce. Have this with the restaurant's good focaccia and a glass of wine, and you won't need anything else.

The Tuscany Grill's buttery risotto is at once creamy, dense and just slightly chewy — a perfect foil for fat shrimp and tiny, tender-crisp asparagus spears. Juicy charred chicken breasts were further enhanced by their bed of spinach sauteed with garlic and golden raisins. Strips of "oven cured" (a k a sun-dried) tomatoes added colorful contrast.

The fish of the day, mahi mahi, was wonderfully fresh and moist; its lentil salad, the perfect summer accompaniment. And I loved a quartet of rib lamb chops bathed in a sophisticated sauce of olive oil, chopped fresh parsley and garlic. (The chops, however, weren't pink as ordered.) They came with a swirl of whipped potatoes and sauteed vegetables, including bell peppers, snow peas and onions.

The Tuscany Grill's desserts are all homemade. Some work, some don't. Hazelnut gelato most definitely did; so, too, the tartufo with its chocolate mousse-like filling. But a chocolate mousse cake contained no chocolate mousse, and was somewhat gummy besides. As for the fresh fruit: Strawberries and blueberries swam in a tasteless zabaglione, as if the kitchen had forgotten the Marsala that night.

*Elizabeth Large*

# The Union Hotel

*1282 Susquehanna Road, Port Deposit • 410-378-3503*
*Hours: Open for lunch and dinner Tuesday through Sunday*
*Prices: Appetizers, $4.95-$9.95; entrees, $13.95-$28.95*
*Live music: No • Kid's menu: Yes • Waterfront views: Yes •*
*Wheelchair access: Yes • Reservations: Suggested*

The Union Hotel, built in the late 18th century, isn't a hotel but a restaurant. It has a log-cabin feel to it — an elaborate log cabin, with lots of cozy nooks, beamed ceilings, fireplaces and candlelight. A front porch overlooking the river is decorated for the season with pumpkins and chrysanthemums.

The waitresses wear period costumes a la Williamsburg, but there's no attempt to be rigidly authentic in decor or food. Owner Janet Dooling says she wants to introduce foods that "were common in the early years of our country, but which have faded into obscurity." That doesn't stop her from also having lobster ravioli in vodka tomato sauce on the menu.

The Union Hotel isn't a restaurant I would normally drive over an hour to just for the food. But as a pleasant place to eat after an afternoon at the nearby Perryville outlet mall, or after biking or hiking or antiques shopping in Port Deposit — that I could see.

Not that there's anything much wrong with the food. There's enough wrong, however, given the prices. Take the oysters Calvert. They were baked on a bed of stewed watercress and chopped onions. I say stewed because their Parmesan cream sauce separated, and the dish ended up being unpleasantly watery. Pan-fried Camembert was covered with apple slices sweetened with maple syrup. It tasted more like dessert than an appetizer. Of our first courses, only a well-seasoned, not-too-thick salmon chowder really hit the mark.

As for main courses, if you don't want to spend major money for prime rib or lobster tails, there are plenty of pastas in the $14 to $18 range. A special of the day paired tenderloin tips with shrimp in a quite spicy marinara sauce over linguine. Not bad. From the seafood selections, shrimp and scallops flavored with sambuca, an anise-flavored liqueur, worked pretty well but wasn't memorable.

The best of our entrees was an old-fashioned Maryland combination of tender boneless chicken breast, salty country ham and rich and mayonnaisey crab imperial with some nice lumps of crab.

Dinners came with potato or wild rice and fresh green beans with Oriental seasonings. Either a house or a watercress salad with good dressings like sesame seed or Dijon vinaigrette is also part of the package.

Skip the Ms. Desserts cheesecakes and other store-bought pastries in favor of the homey apple dumpling in puff pastry with lots of good vanilla ice cream, or the old-fashioned "hotel cake," yellow cake with a custard filling, smooth white icing and chopped walnuts on top. But forget the peach cobbler — this time of year it's made with canned peaches.

*Elizabeth Large*

# Vera's Bakery and Cafe

*548 Baltimore-Annapolis Blvd., Severna Park • 410-647-3337*
*Hours: Open for dinner Thursday through Saturday; breakfast, lunch served Tuesday through Sunday; high tea served Wednesday*
*Prices: Appetizers, $2.50-$8.95; entrees, $12.95-$18.95. No liquor license. There's a $3 corkage fee if you bring your own wine.*
*Live music: Friday night and Sunday afternoon • Kid's menu: No •*
*Waterfront views: No • Wheelchair access: Yes • Reservations: Accepted*

Vera's specializes in Brazilian food and freshly baked breads and desserts. But the charm of eating here is that owner Vera Hasler Port and her husband make you feel as if you're a guest in their home.

They serve breakfast, lunch, dinner and high tea in their small dining room opposite the bakery cases up front. The walls are papered in a wide lemon stripe, and tropical landscapes are hung in gold frames. The effect is pretty and polished, down to the red tablecloths and long-stemmed roses.

With Brazilian music playing softly in the background, we started our meal by devouring the contents of the bread basket — a dense raisin bread and a soft white bread with crystallized sugar on the crust. That's when Vera, in her chef whites, appeared for the first time, toting a hot babka. There's nothing quite like eating this sweet yeast bread when the ribbon of cream cheese that runs through it is still molten.

Of our appetizers, we loved the crab soup, rich with cream and flavored with sherry. Other choices include a skewer of five tender shrimp with vegetables done in a spice rub; and two bruschetta slices topped with sliced tomatoes and flavorful garlic and oil. We enjoyed the fresh flavors of the tropical salad, dotted with banana, grapes, pineapple, pear and guava.

The Brazilian muqueca featured lots of expertly cooked shrimp in a Creole-like sauce of tomatoes and coconut milk. It was ladled around a mound of seasoned yellow rice.

The flavorful strip steak was a particularly fine cut, topped with grilled onions and an intensely flavored demi-glace.

It took a little work to order the feijoada, Brazil's most famous dish. Vera had the waiter bring a cup of the rich meat and black bean stew for my friend to taste. Apparently, some diners have been disappointed with this platter of black beans, rice, farofa and collards. We thought it was superb.

Only the Maryland crab cakes, dense and dry, were below par. Asparagus with fresh hollandaise and buttery potatoes were served with both the crab cakes and the steak.

Orange mousse cake, with delicate citrus flavor, and chocolate mousse cake, with billows of soft mousse spilling from between chocolate sponge layers, were delightful. We liked the tiny, raspberry-filled petit four, though it was achingly sweet.

Best of all was the way the Ports made us feel as though we were regulars, telling us stories about their family, and even tucking a loaf of raisin bread into our hands as we left.

*Kathryn Higham*

# Victor's Cafe

*801 Lancaster St., Pier 7, Inner Harbor • 410- 244-1722*
*Hours: Sunday through Thursday 11 a.m. to 10 p.m.,*
*Friday and Saturday 11 a.m. to 11 p.m.*
*Prices: Appetizers, $4.25-$8.95; entrees, $9.95-$17.95*
*Live music: Friday and Saturday nights • Kid's menu: Yes •*
*Waterfront views: Yes • Wheelchair access: Yes •*
*Reservations: Suggested on weekends*

Given the amount of money that must have been poured into Victor's Cafe, hardly anyone seems to know about it, and that's too bad.

Its upper and lower decks offer some of Baltimore's best waterside tables.

It hardly matters how the food is when you've got a view like Victor's. But as a matter of fact, the food is quite decent.

You'd think Victor's would be packing them in. All the hottest trends are represented here: Straightforward grilled food with Mediterranean and Southwestern touches. Farfalle and penne. (Those are pastas if you're not feeling very with-it.) Garlic mashed potatoes. And, of course, tiramisu and bread pudding for dessert.

Some of it doesn't work very well, like a flavorful but too thick potato chowder in a large bowl made of a French loaf called boule. If you ate all this you wouldn't have room for anything else. Or cinnamon shrimp Granados, featuring beautiful, large shrimp around a timbale of orzo (rice-shaped pasta). The sauce, based on a cinnamon liqueur, is too sweet.

Some of the food is over-hyped, like the appetizer described as a "unique seafood delicacy" (i.e., fried calamari) with a "special dipping sauce" (a k a marinara).

But hey. It was very good fried calamari.

Still, the kitchen has grilling down pat, which takes care of a large part of the menu. The seafood, like the twin grilled swordfish steaks, is fresh and well-prepared.

Tender boneless chicken and large shrimp are grilled just long enough, with just enough Cajun spices to furnish a kick. They come with a tropical fruit salsa made of chopped pineapple, red sweet pepper and such.

Sauces are sometimes too thick and too heavy, such as the cream sauce on the swordfish and the marsala sauce on the tender veal scaloppine. They are, however, beautifully seasoned and have lots of flavor. Victor's is short on subtlety but long on flavor.

For dessert, our waitress recommended the pastries. We tried a chocolate mousse cake and a tiramisu cake, which were fine; but the moist raisin and nut bread pudding made on the premises was every bit as good.

*Elizabeth Large*

# Weber's on Boston

*845 S. Montford Ave., Canton • 410-276-0800*
*Hours: Open Monday through Saturday for lunch, Sunday for brunch, every night for dinner*
*Prices: Appetizers, $4.25-$7.95; entrees, $12.95-$17.95*
*Live music: Friday nights • Kid's menu: Yes • Waterfront views: No • Wheelchair access: Yes • Reservations: Accepted*

The evolution of Weber's on Boston has been gradual. When Denis Manneville took over the turn-of-the-century tavern, you had a feeling he wasn't going to be satisfied serving a pub menu of wings and burgers forever.

These days, Weber's is becoming a French bistro and my guess is that Weber's will succeede for two reasons: The food is good, and it's reasonably priced. Oh, it could be tweaked a bit. A lovely shrimp bisque, delicate but full-flavored and creamy, arrived only lukewarm. Broccoli was substituted for the promised sauteed spinach without a word. Chocolate pate for dessert was gritty with undissolved sugar.

But on the whole, we had a fine meal. A gorgeous hunk of tenderloin was napped with a dark, winy sauce, while a sensational mushroom risotto held court to one side. An enormous pork chop was just about as good, with crisp chunks of potato to complement it.

Like any bistro worth its salt, Weber's has homey dishes such as cassoulet and coq au vin. The kitchen's take on the classic French chicken in red wine dish was a good one, with a full-bodied sauce, tender poultry, fresh mushrooms and pearl onions. Grilled polenta gave it untraditional pizazz.

As befitting a place this close to the water, Weber's has plenty of seafood as well. Le saumon grille showcases the chef's talent, with a fresh fillet draped over aromatic fennel topped with crisply fried slivers of leek. A delicate beurre blanc sparked with mustard swirled around it.

A beurre blanc also graced the best of our first courses, la tour de courgette, a "tower" built of spaghetti squash, lumps of crab meat and bits of ham and shallots. The tower may have been our favorite, but we also liked a warm tart of flaky pastry filled with sauteed onions and creme fraiche.

Desserts were the most uneven part of our meal. That gritty chocolate pate and an overcooked creme brulee with not enough topping were the downside, in contrast to chocolate crepes filled with luscious banana mousse and an agreeable chocolate mousse cake.

Weber's has always been a pleasant restaurant; with the new menu, it's become better than that. The fine food is served in a comfortable dining room of exposed brick, dark wood, pressed-tin ceiling and period light fixtures. The mahogany bar is magnificent, and it's flanked by original marble fireplaces. Add to the relaxing setting a thoughtful wine list and good service — nothing fancy, just competent staff — and you have the makings of an admirable restaurant.

*Elizabeth Large*

# Wharf Rat

*206 W. Pratt St., downtown • 410-244-8900*
*Hours: Open for lunch and dinner every day*
*Prices: $2.95-$17.95*
*Live music: No • Kid's menu: Yes • Waterfront views: No • Wheelchair access: Yes • Reservations: Wait list*

The Wharf Rat near Camden Yards is so serious about its beer you have to be an expert just to understand the menu. That's the beer menu, not the food menu.

This brewery-pub takes its food seriously as well. I'm not a beer drinker, but I have one unscientific observation to make: Microbreweries serve good food. I don't know if that's because beer is a great cooking ingredient. I don't have a large sampling to base my conclusions on, but I'll stick by them.

Everybody around us was ordering fish and chips, and it looked great: crisply fried fillets of orange roughy with hand-cut fried potatoes, served British-style with vinegar. I know the fries were hot and crisp because we had them with a hamburger. But the kitchen had run out of fish by the time our waiter had put in our order, so we didn't get to try them.

The Wharf Rat models itself on a British pub, which mostly means spelling fare "fayre" and calling shrimp prawns. Buffalo wings are R.A.F. wings. The six large, fresh shrimp (sorry, prawns) had been steamed to order, so they were pleasantly warm despite being served on ice. The wings were huge and meaty, with lots of fiery sauce, celery and an excellent blue cheese dressing.

Not to be missed is the Wharf Rat's English beer and onion soup. If you're used to getting onion soups with canned beef broth as the base, you'll love this intensely flavorful version with homemade croutons and real Stilton cheese. More of that good Stilton was the topping for a fine hamburger, lean beef cooked rare as ordered. A fried chicken salad wedded Stilton with fried chicken breast pieces and crumbled bacon as a topping for mixed greens.

It's hard to make a shrimp salad sandwich sound British, and the Wharf Rat doesn't try. You'll get big pieces of well-seasoned shrimp on a fat kaiser roll.

Not everything is a sandwich or pub fayre, and not everything works. A London broil dinner looked beautiful, with mashed potatoes and fresh broccoli, but I wasn't wild about the meat's marinade — it had an off taste. As for the broccoli, it could have been cooked a bit longer and buttered or otherwise seasoned. It was like having a small bush plonked down on the plate. Good mashed potatoes, though.

The Wharf Rat has a handsome space, with exposed brick, expanses of wood and lots of beer memorabilia around. Good food, good atmosphere — but terrible service. Our waiter was the only one working the whole room that night. That was bad enough, but when we wanted our check we had to go find him at the bar where he was drinking a beer.

*Elizabeth Large*

# Wharfside

*1600 Frederick Road, Catonsville • 410-788-1400*
*Hours: Open every day for lunch and dinner*
*Prices: Appetizers, $5.95-$7.95; entrees, $12.95-$23*
*Live music: No • Kid's menu: Yes • Waterfront views: No •*
*Wheelchair access: Yes • Reservations: Accepted*

The Wharfside in Catonsville operates on a simple concept. It offers a staggering selection of seafood dishes that are reasonably priced, if not exactly inexpensive.

To give you some idea of what I mean by a staggering selection, the menu has 10 lobster dishes and 23 fresh-fish choices, from mako shark to tile. Plus much more.

From our experience, though, you'd do best to stick to the daily specials. A bowl of seafood chowder was simple and satisfying, chock-full of crab and shrimp and fish, the soup base creamy and flavorful. Shad with shad roe and bacon was also well done. The huge whole fish was completely boned, and its sweet flesh had been cooked to firm perfection. A refined lemon butter sauce finished it off. The roe was a little overcooked, but was fresh and good-tasting, and the bacon strips with it were crisp and smoky.

If only the mussels had tasted as fresh as the clams, oysters and shrimp in the steamed combination appetizer, it would have been superb. Everything was nicely cooked, and there was enough shellfish to make a complete meal. The two broiled crab cakes were mammoth and full of backfin, but they lacked pizazz. We didn't try some of the more elaborate concoctions, but the delicacy of the shad's lemon butter sauce and the nicely done bearnaise on a first course of artichoke hearts and crab made me pretty sure the Wharfside kitchen could carry them off if it didn't overcook the seafood.

The low point of our meal was the Wharfside broiled combination: a fillet of orange roughy, crab imperial, scallops, shrimp, a clam casino and an oyster Rockefeller. It tasted as if everything had been broiled together for the same long length of time, so that some of the seafood had practically shriveled up, and all of it was overcooked.

A generous salad or vegetables come with each meal. Sauteed summer squash turned out to be not-very-good zucchini in a cream sauce, but fat homemade french fries and fresh coleslaw pleased us all. Desserts, handsome ones, are offered (we tried a super-fudge chocolate bourbon cake); but will anyone show any interest in them after such a huge dinner?

The Wharfside has a lot going for it, including excellent service, but one thing it doesn't have is atmosphere. It's a big, plain restaurant with almost no personality. The dropped ceiling makes it feel a little closed in, and the colors are bland. Only the etched-glass panels have a nautical theme.

The seafood case in the front is the restaurant's most striking feature. All the items on the menu are available raw, making the Wharfside a seafood market as well as a restaurant.

*Elizabeth Large*

# Windows

*Renaissance Harborplace Hotel, Inner Harbor • 410-685-8439*
*Hours: Open daily for breakfast, lunch and dinner*
*Prices: Appetizers, $3.95-$7.95; entrees, $12.95-$26.95*
*Live music: No • Kid's menu: No • Waterfront views: Yes •*
*Wheelchair access: Yes • Reservations: Accepted*

Some of the prettiest restaurants in Baltimore can be found in the hotels that hug the Inner Harbor. Windows, at the Renaissance Harborplace Hotel, is a lovely place to dine, especially if you reserve a table overlooking Pratt Street.

Floor-to-ceiling windows let in the bright lights and bustle of the harbor. Mirrors, blond wood and crystal chandeliers create an atmosphere of modern, streamlined elegance.

The menu at Windows emphasizes fresh seafood and Chesapeake-region specialties. Our waiter, who was as polished and attentive as they come, said the crab cakes and the crab chowder were not to be missed.

Both crab dishes were fine, but they were short of exceptional. The chowder was a little skimpy on crab meat, but looked appealing served in a sourdough boule. Two jumbo lump crab cakes, broiled to within seconds of being overdone, were full of beautiful lump crab meat and served with steamed vegetables and lime tartar sauce. A white nugget of crab turned up on the baked oysters, under a lemony sauce.

Our favorite starter was the salad of mixed greens featuring tender, smoky rounds of chicken breast and a lovely pepper vinaigrette. Tiny pancetta squares and roasted vegetables gave the pan-roasted mussels appetizer an interesting turn.

From the quartet of fish selections cooked over a wood-fired grill, we tried an enormous tuna steak. It arrived on a mound of saffron risotto, garnished with asparagus spears. Even though it was cooked just as we asked, with a hint of pink inside, the tuna was slightly tough. We loved the smoky flavor the grill imparted, though, and the pool of fragrant basil oil that lined the plate. The wood-fired grill is not reserved for fish alone. If you prefer a filet mignon, a custom-cut steak, or even grilled vegetables, the chef will oblige.

To judge from the rack of lamb, meat is handled exceptionally well at Windows. Tender, rare and rubbed with jerk spices for a Caribbean slow burn, the lamb chops paired nicely with pineapple chutney and whipped sweet potatoes.

Among the specials, the halibut was given a buttery crumb topping spiked with fresh horseradish. A creamy pink sauce made with smoked tomatoes and buttered haricots verts added to the dish; lukewarm mashed potatoes did not.

As for dessert, we liked the texture of the tall, creamy pumpkin cheesecake, the raspberry glaze on the chocolate mousse cake, and the peanut-studded whipped cream of the rich chocolate gateau.

Ultimately, though, we felt about these desserts as we had the rest of our meal: They were fine but not extraordinary.

*Kathryn Higham*

# Women's Industrial Exchange

*333 N. Charles St., downtown • 410-685-4388.*
*Hours: Open Mondays to Fridays for breakfast and lunch*
*Prices: Entrees, $3.50-$6.50*
*Live music: No • Kid's menu: No • Waterfront views: No •*
*Wheelchair access: No • Reservations: Not accepted •*
*Credit cards: Not accepted*

Breakfast is an overlooked meal these days. Too many of us grab a slice of toast as we head out the door, in spite of what our mothers told us about starting the day right. Every once in a while, though, you wish you knew about a restaurant that serves a good breakfast. Not brunch. Breakfast.

Here, then, is a breakfast places that has its own small-scale charm. The Women's Industrial Exchange is known as a homey lunch spot, a sort of time capsule with food and atmosphere from a different, and gentler, era. It's not so widely known that the Exchange serves breakfast, starting at 7 a.m. Mondays to Fridays.

Is anyone in Baltimore not familiar with this genteel tearoom? Its deferential doorman?

The shop in front that sells hand-crocheted afghans and cross-stitched christening gowns?

The 90-year-old waitress who's better at her job than many 50 years younger?

The scuffed black and white linoleum floor, the faded mural and the plain little tables?

At lunchtime the Women's Industrial Exchange is often crowded and noisy, but at breakfast the mood is much more leisurely.

I'm not sure why it even opens for breakfast. There are just enough customers for one waitress to handle with ease — and she serves as cashier as well. (In fact, one morning when the cook called in sick, she made us a bacon and egg sandwich and an order of toast.)

While the menu isn't normally as limited as that, it is limited. But simple food is sometimes exactly what you want at breakfast. Fresh eggs ($1.75) were scrambled deliciously soft, and didn't taste as if they had been cooked in day-old grease. Crusty home-fried potatoes came on the side.

Be sure to have a biscuit with your eggs instead of toast; they're so charmingly misshapen they have to be homemade, and are wonderfully short and tender.

Excellent, mildly spiced link sausages ($1.40) were split and grilled so they weren't a bit greasy.

While the menu promises weekly breakfast specials, what that translates to is — according to our waitress, Charlotte — "Sometimes we have creamed chip beef on Wednesdays."

No, thank you. I'll settle for "petite pancakes," juice and tea or coffee for $2.25. The pancakes were hardly my idea of petite — they were almost as big as the plate — very plain but tender and tasting made-from-scratch. Coffee isn't extraordinary, but it is good and hot and keeps on coming.

*Elizabeth Large*

# Woodfire

*Park Plaza Shopping Center, Severna Park • 410-315-8100*
*Hours: Open for lunch and dinner daily*
*Prices: Appetizers, $5.95-$9.50; entrees, $14.95-$22.95*
*Live music: No • Kid's menu: Yes • Waterfront views: No •*
*Wheelchair access: Yes • Reservations: Not accepted*

I like a restaurant that sets out to do one thing, and does it well. If only Woodfire would stick to grilling.

You walk into the restaurant, fragrant with wood smoke, and you start salivating. It makes you want to order the biggest, juiciest steak on the menu. The smell of the place is maybe the best part of the ambience.

Not that Woodfire isn't attractive. It would actually be fairly chic except for all the red neon. It has that slightly edgy decor typical of late-'90s restaurants: at once somewhat dressy and casual.

Woodfire's ribs have great flavor and a fine barbecue sauce, but ours weren't very meaty. They come with thin, crisp fries and celery seed-infested coleslaw.

We had no complaints about the Delmonico steak, smoky and flavorful, blackened with Cajun spices that don't overpower the juicy pink meat. A thick cloud of whipped potatoes and fresh green beans finish a picture-perfect plate.

Start with an appetizer pizza cooked over the wood fire, its honey-wheat crust crisp at the edges and loaded down with caramelized onions, a smoky tomato sauce, mozzarella and thick bacon. Or share the Woodfire smoked sampler. Strips of chicken and salmon were good, but the fork-tender tenderloin was nothing short of fabulous. On the side were three sauces, two of them sweet, but the food didn't need them.

Woodfire has good seafood, judging from the tuna we tried. It was thick and fresh, cooked rare at the center. There was no hint, however, of the promised "rosemary marinade," nor was the tuna blackened as promised. Instead, it had a buttery sauce, rice and excellent grilled vegetables.

Those same grilled vegetables came with my seafood strudel. The phyllo dough was supposed to contain crab, smoked salmon and shrimp. I did come across a few shrimp, but it was mostly a thick, cheesy filling that made the strudel taste like an expensive Greek cheese pie.

Although this is a restaurant with a simple concept — meat and fish grilled over wood — the kitchen loves to gussy up everything else. The mashed potatoes are goosed with Cheddar and garlic. The butter is laced with garlic. Not to mention the berries on the house salad.

All this is OK, but when it comes to the desserts, too much is too much. The strawberry shortcake, made with a good old-fashioned sweet biscuit, already has strawberries and whipped cream. Why drizzle it with chocolate? Why pour caramel sauce over a slice of Grand Marnier cake already frosted with butter cream? Some things are better left alone.

*Elizabeth Large*

# Ze Mean Bean Cafe

*1739-41 Fleet St., Fells Point • 410-675-5999*
*Hours: Open every day for lunch and dinner, brunch on weekends*
*Prices: Appetizers, $4.25-$8.95; entrees, $6.95-$19.95*
*Live music: Every night and Sunday brunch • Kid's menu: No •*
*Waterfront views: No • Wheelchair access: Yes • Reservations: Accepted •*
*Credit Cards: Master Card, Visa*

As the world fills up with more and more coffee bars, Ze Mean Bean Cafe has made a wise decision. The funky Fells Point coffee bar has changed into a full-scale restaurant.

Oh, you can still linger over a latte here while you listen to live music nightly. And the Slavic specialties (pierogi, goulash and mushroom soup) are still on the menu. What's new is chef Kevin Miller, who's added a full dinner menu to the mix with dishes like roasted duck breast and Moroccan lamb stew.

Also new is a charming second-story dining room. If you want to have a conversation while you eat, it puts you just far enough away from the live music to enjoy it but still talk.

But the food is the story here. Miller has quite a repertoire. It isn't dainty fare — the large portions lack a certain elegance — but who's complaining? It's imaginative and good.

Not everything works. The mussels were gritty in the seafood pasta, an otherwise pleasing combination of monkfish, scallops and shrimp with linguine. And saffron dominated the dish's tomato saffron broth. Borscht was oversalted and not quite hot enough when it arrived at the table.

The grilled-apple and brandy-infused duck sausage is sliced in half and placed in all its greasy glory on top of the mesclun salad (which also boasts warm new potatoes, caramelized red onions and sliced pear). The flavors were fine, but it was a hefty first course.

All our other dishes were very good, particularly a tender duck breast. It was roasted perfectly, so it had just the faintest flush of pink and stayed juicy, with a bit of crisp skin and almost no fat. Its orange-cranberry relish flavored with port gave it just the right edge of sweetness. It was draped on an intriguing potato torta layered with butternut squash puree, and broccoli florets added bright color to the plate.

Moroccan lamb stew, a special that night, was served over herb-infused couscous. Tomatoes, eggplant, apricots, red wine, mint leaves and a touch of garlic had been cooked down to an aromatic sauce for the tender chunks of meat.

Equally good was the smoked pork chop, although it didn't taste smoked, though its sweet-potato hash had plenty of smoky flavor. A spicy pear chutney and fresh spinach sauteed with garlic rounded out a handsome plate with bold flavors.

Chef Miller's signature dessert is pumpkin bread pudding with homemade cinnamon ice cream and caramel sauce. It's excellent, and there's enough for four. We also tried the mincemeat-like apple pie and a light but very sweet banana-pineapple cake. Neither rises to the heights of the bread pudding, but they are pleasant enough.

*Elizabeth Large*

# Zodiac

*1726 N. Charles St., Charles Village • 410-727-8815*
*Hours: Open daily for dinner*
*Prices: Appetizers, $5-$7.50; entrees, $5-$18.*
*Live music: Weeknights • Kid's menu: Yes • Waterfront views: No •*
*Wheelchair access: Yes • Reservations: Accepted •*
*Credit cards: MasterCard, Visa*

The stars must have been properly aligned when Zodiac opened. But whether it's celestial forces or a talented kitchen staff, we predict this restaurant has a glowing future.

The bar, the curved aqua banquettes, the crystal chandelier hanging in the second-floor dining room, were all Art Moderne treasures rescued from doomed Baltimore landmarks.

If the decor says 1940s, the menu says '90s. Among the entrees, culinary influences range from Italian to Indian, Tex-Mex to Thai. There's also lighter fare like burgers, tortillas and buckwheat crepes; all are executed well.

We dug into freshly baked bread, warm from the oven, with tapenade and herb butter to spread on top. That held us over until our enchilada appetizer arrived, napped with tomatillo salsa, pico de gallo and vinegar-dressed slaw. Inside were bay scallops, small shrimp and bits of charred tomatoes and zucchini. It was surprisingly light, with a deliciously smoky edge.

Rosemary and sun-dried tomato gave the polenta appetizer intense flavor. While the herbal punch of fresh rosemary was strong, it didn't overwhelm the thick cornmeal triangles served on a tangy paste of roasted red peppers. Our last appetizer was a mixed field greens salad, spiked with grilled tomatoes, cucumbers, macadamia nuts and cinnamon-fried plantains. The flavors married nicely with a papaya-nectar dressing.

Our waiter, who was upbeat and full of information, suggested the Norwegian salmon. The fillets were wonderfully moist, seared inside a crust of black and golden sesame seeds. We loved the salads that were mounded high on the same plate — a spicy one with cold buckwheat noodles, and a sweet Asian mix of julienne carrots, red peppers and cucumbers.

Equally impressive was the boneless breast of duck, grilled dark on the edges and rare inside. Sliced into medallions, it was served with Zodiac's orange "voodoo" sauce. Presentation didn't suffer, either, with a tower of black quinoa and capers adding visual punch to the plate.

We liked the look of the buckwheat crepe, too, folded flat like a large square envelope. Drizzled with thin wasabi aioli, it was so pretty it looked like dessert. Inside each dark, crisp-edged bite of crepe were thin layers of smoked salmon, wilted kale and cream cheese.

Desserts didn't have the same pizazz. Mango and blackberry sorbets were too sweet. Chocolate mousse was fudgy but unremarkable. Only a light layer cake, soaked with lime and tequila and layered with kiwis, satisfied us . The combination of ingredients was surprising, the flavors powerful. That pretty much sums up the rest of the meal, too.

*Kathryn Higham*

# Zorba's

*4710 Eastern Ave., Greektown • 410-276-4484*
*Hours: Open every day for dinner*
*Prices: Appetizers, $2.50-$9.95; entrees, $8.95-$16.95*
*Live music: No • Kid's menu: Yes • Waterfront views: No •*
*Wheelchair access: No • Reservations: Accepted*

The Black Olive, which opened this past spring in Fells Point, reminded Baltimoreans how much they like good Greek food. At least it reminded me; I'm guessing about the rest of you because the new restaurant has been successful.

The reason I bring it up is that my meal at the Black Olive inspired me to return recently to the one other Greek restaurant in the city that specializes in grilled meat and fish, Zorba's on Eastern Avenue.

When Zorba's opened in 1992, it, too, got a lot of favorable press. I had a fine meal there, but never got back till now.

My first thought when I entered the narrow dining room, dominated by a handsome oak bar in front and an open rotisserie in back, was how little Zorba's has changed. The tables sport the same blue-and-white checked tablecloths, or so it seems. The same black-and-white stills from the movie "Zorba the Greek" decorate the walls. The same plastic grapevines entwine the banister.

Now, though, it all seems a bit faded. What was a very pretty restaurant has turned into a neighborhood hangout, a little worn around the edges, with two TVs going. But I happen to like neighborhood hangouts, especially when every table is taken on a Tuesday night. I figure all those people must know something.

They must come for the rotisserie chicken, half a bird per serving, herb-scented and juicy under its crisp skin.

They must come for the "Greek Village Salad," generous with wedges of ripe tomato, red onions, green peppers, cucumbers, Greek olives and feta cheese.

They must come for the basket of warm, freshly grilled bread. It's delicious with a chilled bottle of Santorini; some garlicky eggplant salad; and Zorba's charred and sliced octopus, served cold with a squeeze of lemon.

But Zorba's is one of those restaurants where if you don't know what to order you could end up with a mediocre meal. Thin fillets of grilled swordfish had a faintly fishy taste. On my last visit there, the lamb was superb. This time around, my grilled lamb chops were greasy and strong-flavored. Vegetables were even more overdone than they are traditionally in Greek cooking.

Our spirits picked up with dessert, though. I've had enough of the chocolate pate death decadence instant heart attack desserts to last a lifetime. These were a welcome change. An ugly but tasty rice pudding, fresh baklava, and the milky custard and pastry dessert called galaktoboureko saved the day.

*Elizabeth Large*

# The Indexes

# Restaurants A to Z

| | |
|---|---|
| Acropolis | 1 |
| Akbar Palace | 2 |
| Aldo's | 3 |
| Ambassador Dining Room | 4 |
| Angelina's | 6 |
| Annapurna | 5 |
| Antrim 1844 Country Inn | 7 |
| Ashley M's | 8 |
| Azeb's Ethiopian Restaurant | 9 |
| Bandaloops | 10 |
| Bare Bones | 11 |
| Barn Restaurant & Crab House | 12 |
| Bay Cafe | 13 |
| Bayou Blues Cafe | 14 |
| Bill Bateman's Bistro | 15 |
| The Black Olive | 16 |
| Blue Garden | 17 |
| Bo Brooks | 18 |
| Boomerang | 19 |
| The Brass Elephant | 20 |
| Burke's Cafe | 21 |
| Cactus Willies | 22 |
| Cafe Isis | 23 |
| Cafe Madrid | 24 |
| Cafe Normandie | 25 |
| Cafe Pangea | 26 |
| Cafe Troia | 27 |
| California Pizza Kitchen | 28 |
| Candle Light Inn | 29 |
| Capitol City Brewing Company | 30 |
| Capriccio | 31 |
| Carney Crab House | 32 |
| Carrabba's Italian Grill | 33 |
| Carrol's Creek | 34 |
| Charleston | 35 |
| Charred Rib | 36 |
| Chiapparelli's | 37 |
| Chris' Charcoal Pit | 38 |
| Ciao | 39 |
| Ciao Bella | 40 |
| City Cafe | 41 |
| Cockey's Tavern | 42 |
| Coho Grill | 43 |
| Corks | 44 |
| Da Mimmo | 45 |
| Della Notte | 46 |
| Doc's Eastside | 47 |
| Donna's Coffee Bar | 48 |
| Dooby's Bar & Grill | 49 |
| Due | 50 |
| Edo Sushi | 51 |
| El Azteca | 52 |

| | |
|---|---|
| Ellicott Mills Brewing Company | 53 |
| ESPN Zone | 54 |
| Ethel & Ramone's | 55 |
| G & M | 56 |
| Gampy's | 57 |
| Geckos Bar & Grille | 58 |
| Germano's | 59 |
| Golden Gate Noodle House | 60 |
| Hamilton's | 61 |
| Hampton's | 62 |
| Han Sung | 63 |
| Hard Rock Cafe Baltimore | 64 |
| Hard Times | 65 |
| Harryman House | 66 |
| Haussner's | 67 |
| The Helmand | 68 |
| Hunt Valley Szechuan | 69 |
| Hunters Lodge | 70 |
| Ikaros | 71 |
| J. Paul's | 72 |
| Joung Kak | 73 |
| Joy America Cafe | 74 |
| La Tavola | 75 |
| Ladew Topiary Gardens Cafe | 76 |
| Lennys Chop House | 77 |
| Linwood's | 78 |
| Little Havana | 79 |
| Lord Baltimore Grill | 80 |
| Louie's the Bookstore Cafe | 81 |
| M. Gettier's Orchard Inn | 82 |
| Main Street Blues | 83 |
| Maison Marconi's | 84 |
| Mangia | 85 |
| Mangia Mangia | 86 |
| McCafferty's | 87 |
| McCormick & Schmick's | 88 |
| Mediterranean Palace | 89 |
| Micah's | 90 |
| Michaelangelo | 91 |
| Mill Towne Tavern | 92 |
| Milton Inn | 93 |
| Morton's of Chicago | 94 |
| Mount Washington Tavern | 95 |
| Nacho Mama's | 96 |
| Needful Things | 97 |
| No Way Jose Cafe | 98 |
| North Star | 99 |
| Obrycki's | 100 |
| O'Learys | 101 |
| Olive and Sesame | 102 |
| Olney Ale House | 103 |
| Oregon Grille | 104 |
| The Owl Bar | 105 |
| Pecora's | 106 |

| | |
|---|---|
| Piccolo's | 107 |
| Pinebrook Chinese Restaurant | 108 |
| Pisces | 109 |
| Planet Hollywood | 110 |
| Ralphie's Diner | 111 |
| Red Brick Station | 112 |
| Red River Barbecue and Grille | 113 |
| Reisters Country Inn | 114 |
| Restaurant Columbia | 115 |
| Ricciuti's Brick Oven Pizza | 116 |
| Rocky Run Tap & Grill | 117 |
| Romano's Macaroni Grill | 118 |
| Rootie Kazootie's | 119 |
| Rudys' 2900 | 120 |
| Rusty Scupper | 121 |
| Sabatino's | 122 |
| Samos | 123 |
| San Marco | 124 |
| Sascha's Daily | 125 |
| Sebastian's | 126 |
| Shanghai Lil's | 127 |
| Shula's Steak 2 | 128 |
| Shula's Steakhouse | 129 |
| Silk Road | 130 |
| Sin Carne | 131 |
| Sisson's | 132 |
| Snyder's Willow Grove | 133 |
| SoBo Cafe | 134 |
| Sotto Sopra | 135 |
| Spike & Charlie's | 136 |
| Suburban House | 137 |
| Sushi Sono | 138 |
| Suzie's Soba | 139 |
| Tapestry | 140 |
| The Tavern at Centre Park | 141 |
| Teranga African Restaurant | 142 |
| Tiffin | 143 |
| Timber Creek Tavern | 144 |
| Tio Pepe's | 145 |
| Tonino's | 146 |
| The Trolley Stop | 147 |
| Tuscany Grill | 148 |
| The Union Hotel | 149 |
| Vera's Bakery and Cafe | 150 |
| Victor's Cafe | 151 |
| Weber's On Boston | 152 |
| Wharf Rat | 153 |
| Wharfside | 154 |
| Windows | 155 |
| Women's Industrial Exchange | 156 |
| Woodfire | 157 |
| Ze Mean Bean Cafe | 158 |
| Zodiac | 159 |
| Zorba's | 160 |

# Community

## Annapolis
- Cafe Normandie .................................................................25
- Carrol's Creek ....................................................................34
- Chris' Charcoal Pit ............................................................38
- Ciao .....................................................................................39
- Mangia ...............................................................................85
- Michaelangelo ..................................................................91
- O'Learys ..........................................................................101

## Canterbury
- Ambassador Dining Room ..............................................4

## Canton
- Bay Cafe ............................................................................13
- Doc's Eastside .................................................................47
- Dooby's Bar & Grill .........................................................49
- Geckos Bar & Grille ........................................................58
- Mangia Mangia ................................................................86
- Nacho Mama's .................................................................96
- Needful Things ................................................................97
- Shanghai Lil's ................................................................127
- Weber's On Boston .......................................................152

## Catonsville
- Candle Light Inn .............................................................29
- Wharfside .......................................................................154

## Charles Village
- Donna's Coffee Bar .........................................................48
- Rootie Kazootie's ..........................................................119
- Zodiac ..............................................................................159

## Clarksville
- El Azteca ..........................................................................52

## Columbia
- Coho Grill .........................................................................43
- Hard Times ......................................................................65
- Piccolo's .........................................................................107
- Red River Barbecue and Grille ..................................113
- Ricciuti's Brick Oven Pizza ........................................116
- Rocky Run Tap & Grill .................................................117
- Sushi Sono .....................................................................138
- The Tavern at Centre Park .........................................141

## Downtown / Inner Harbor
Azeb's Ethiopian Restaurant .................................................9
Burke's Cafe ...........................................................................21
California Pizza Kitchen .......................................................28
Capitol City Brewing Company............................................30
Charleston .............................................................................35
ESPN Zone .............................................................................54
Hampton's ..............................................................................62
Hard Rock Cafe Baltimore ...................................................64
J. Paul's ..................................................................................72
Lennys Chop House ..............................................................77
Lord Baltimore Grill .............................................................80
McCormick & Schmick's .......................................................88
Morton's of Chicago ..............................................................94
Pisces ...................................................................................109
Planet Hollywood ................................................................110
Shula's Steak 2 ....................................................................128
Shula's Steakhouse .............................................................129
Tio Pepe ...............................................................................145
Victor's Cafe ........................................................................151
Wharf Rat ............................................................................153
Windows ..............................................................................155
Women's Industrial Exchange ...........................................156

## Easton
Restaurant Columbia .........................................................115

## Ellicott City
Bare Bones.............................................................................11
Carrabba's Italian Grill.........................................................33
Ellicott Mills Brewing Company .........................................53
Han Sung ...............................................................................63
Hunters Lodge ......................................................................70
Main Street Blues .................................................................83
Mill Towne Tavern ................................................................92
The Trolley Stop .................................................................147

## Federal Hill
Bandaloops............................................................................10
Joy America Cafe ..................................................................74
Little Havana ........................................................................79
No Way Jose Cafe .................................................................98
Rusty Scupper ....................................................................121
Sisson's ................................................................................132
SoBo Cafe ............................................................................134

## Fells Point
The Black Olive.....................................................................16
Boomerang ............................................................................19
Cafe Madrid ..........................................................................24

166 | Dining in Baltimore

| | |
|---|---|
| Corks | 44 |
| Hamilton's | 61 |
| Tapestry | 140 |
| Ze Mean Bean Cafe | 158 |

## Finksburg
| | |
|---|---|
| Rudys' 2900 | 120 |

## Gardenville
| | |
|---|---|
| Bo Brooks | 18 |

## Glen Burnie
| | |
|---|---|
| Blue Garden | 17 |

## Greektown
| | |
|---|---|
| Acropolis | 1 |
| Zorba's | 160 |

## Hampden
| | |
|---|---|
| Cafe Pangea | 26 |
| Pinebrook Chinese Restaurant | 108 |
| Suzie's Soba | 139 |

## Highlandtown
| | |
|---|---|
| Haussner's | 67 |
| Ikaros | 71 |
| Samos | 123 |

## Hunt Valley
| | |
|---|---|
| Hunt Valley Szechuan | 69 |
| Oregon Grille | 104 |

## Kingsville
| | |
|---|---|
| Timber Creek Tavern | 144 |

## Langley Park
| | |
|---|---|
| Tiffin | 143 |

## Linthicum
| | |
|---|---|
| G & M | 56 |
| Snyder's Willow Grove | 133 |

## Little Italy

| | |
|---|---|
| Aldo's | 3 |
| Capriccio | 31 |
| Chiapparelli's | 37 |
| Ciao Bella | 40 |
| Da Mimmo | 45 |
| Della Notte | 46 |
| Germano's | 59 |
| La Tavola | 75 |
| Pecora's | 106 |
| Sabatino's | 122 |

## Lutherville

| | |
|---|---|
| Charred Rib | 35 |

## Monkton

| | |
|---|---|
| Ladew Topiary Gardens Cafe | 76 |

## Mount Vernon

| | |
|---|---|
| Ashley M's | 8 |
| The Brass Elephant | 20 |
| City Cafe | 41 |
| Gampy's | 57 |
| The Helmand | 68 |
| Louie's the Bookstore Cafe | 81 |
| Maison Marconi's | 84 |
| The Owl Bar | 105 |
| Sascha's Daily | 125 |
| Silk Road | 130 |
| Sotto Sopra | 135 |
| Spike & Charlie's | 136 |

## Mount Washington

| | |
|---|---|
| Ethel & Ramone's | 55 |
| McCafferty's | 87 |
| Mount Washington Tavern | 95 |

## Northwest Baltimore

| | |
|---|---|
| Joung Kak | 73 |
| Micah's | 90 |
| Teranga African Restaurant | 142 |

## Olney

| | |
|---|---|
| Olney Ale House | 103 |

## Owings Mills
Due .................................................................................... 50
Linwood's ............................................................................ 78

## Parkville
Angelina's .............................................................................. 6
Barn Restaurant & Crab House ........................................ 12
Carney Crab House ............................................................ 32

## Pikesville
Annapurna ............................................................................ 5
Olive and Sesame ............................................................. 102
San Marco .......................................................................... 124
Sin Carne ........................................................................... 131
Suburban House ............................................................... 137

## Port Deposit
The Union Hotel ................................................................ 149

## Randallstown
Akbar Palace ......................................................................... 2

## Reisterstown
Harryman House ................................................................. 66
North Star ............................................................................ 99
Reisters Country Inn ......................................................... 114
Tonino's .............................................................................. 146

## Severna Park
Sebastian's ........................................................................ 126
Vera's Bakery and Cafe .................................................... 150
Woodfire ............................................................................. 157

## Sparks
Milton Inn ............................................................................ 93

## Taneytown
Antrim 1844 Country Inn ..................................................... 7

## Timonium
Cafe Isis ............................................................................... 23
Edo Sushi ............................................................................ 51
Ralphie's Diner .................................................................. 111
Romano's Macaroni Grill .................................................. 118
Tuscany Grill ..................................................................... 148

---

Dining in Baltimore | 169

## Towson
Bill Bateman's Bistro ............................................................. 15
Cactus Willies ...................................................................... 22
Cafe Troia ............................................................................ 27
Golden Gate Noodle House ................................................. 60
M. Gettier's Orchard Inn ...................................................... 82
Mediterranean Palace .......................................................... 89

## Westminster
Cockey's Tavern .................................................................... 42

## White Marsh
Bayou Blues Cafe ................................................................. 14
Red Brick Station ............................................................... 112

# Cuisine

## Afghani
The Helmand ..................................................................68
Silk Road ....................................................................130

## American
Antrim 1844 Country Inn ................................................7
Bandaloops .....................................................................10
Bare Bones .....................................................................11
Bill Bateman's Bistro ....................................................15
The Brass Elephant .......................................................20
Burke's Cafe ..................................................................21
Cactus Willies ................................................................22
Candle Light Inn ...........................................................29
Carrabba's Italian Grill .................................................33
City Cafe ........................................................................41
Cockey's Tavern ............................................................42
Coho Grill ......................................................................43
Corks ..............................................................................44
Doc's Eastside ................................................................47
Donna's Coffee Bar .......................................................48
Dooby's Bar & Grill .......................................................49
Ellicott Mills Brewing Company ..................................53
ESPN Zone ....................................................................54
Ethel & Ramone's .........................................................55
G & M ............................................................................56
Gampy's .........................................................................57
Hard Rock Cafe Baltimore ...........................................64
Hard Times ....................................................................65
Harryman House ...........................................................66
Hunters Lodge ...............................................................70
J. Paul's ..........................................................................72
Lennys Chop House ......................................................77
Lord Baltimore Grill .....................................................80
M. Gettier's Orchard Inn ..............................................82
Main Street Blues ..........................................................83
McCafferty's ..................................................................87
Mill Towne Tavern ........................................................92
Milton Inn ......................................................................93
Mount Washington Tavern ...........................................95
North Star ......................................................................99
Olney Ale House .........................................................103
The Owl Bar .................................................................105
Planet Hollywood ........................................................110
Ralphie's Diner ............................................................111
Red Brick Station ........................................................112
Reisters Country Inn ...................................................114
Rocky Run Tap & Grill ................................................117
Rootie Kazootie's .........................................................119
SoBo Cafe .....................................................................134
Suburban House ..........................................................137

Dining in Baltimore | 171

| | |
|---|---|
| Tapestry | 140 |
| Timber Creek Tavern | 144 |
| The Trolley Stop | 147 |
| Union Hotel | 149 |
| Wharf Rat | 153 |
| Women's Industrial Exchange | 156 |

## Australian

| | |
|---|---|
| Boomerang | 19 |

## Bakeries

| | |
|---|---|
| Sascha's Daily | 125 |
| Vera's Bakery and Cafe | 150 |

## Barbecue/Ribs

| | |
|---|---|
| Bill Bateman's Bistro | 15 |
| Charred Rib | 36 |
| Han Sung | 63 |
| Red River Barbecue and Grille | 113 |

## Bars/Pubs

| | |
|---|---|
| Angelina's | 6 |
| Ashley M's | 8 |
| Barn Restaurant & Crab House | 12 |
| Bay Cafe | 13 |
| Bill Bateman's Bistro | 15 |
| Boomerang | 19 |
| The Brass Elephant | 20 |
| Burke's Cafe | 21 |
| Candle Light Inn | 29 |
| Capitol City Brewing Company | 30 |
| Carney Crab House | 32 |
| Carrabba's Italian Grill | 33 |
| Charleston | 35 |
| Charred Rib | 36 |
| Ciao | 39 |
| Doc's Eastside | 47 |
| Dooby's Bar & Grill | 49 |
| Ellicott Mills Brewing Company | 53 |
| ESPN Zone | 54 |
| Gampy's | 57 |
| Geckos Bar & Grille | 58 |
| Hard Times | 65 |
| Haussner's | 67 |
| Hunters Lodge | 70 |
| J. Paul's | 72 |
| Lennys Chop House | 77 |
| Little Havana | 79 |

172 | Dining in Baltimore

| | |
|---|---|
| McCafferty's | 87 |
| McCormick & Schmick's | 88 |
| Mill Towne Tavern | 92 |
| Nacho Mama's | 96 |
| No Way Jose Cafe | 98 |
| Olney Ale House | 103 |
| The Owl Bar | 105 |
| Red Brick Station | 112 |
| Red River Barbecue and Grille | 113 |
| Rocky Run Tap & Grill | 117 |
| Rootie Kazootie's | 119 |
| Rusty Scupper | 121 |
| Sisson's | 132 |
| SoBo Cafe | 134 |
| Sotto Sopra | 135 |
| Spike & Charlie's | 136 |
| Tapestry | 140 |
| The Trolley Stop | 147 |
| Victor's Cafe | 151 |
| Weber's On Boston | 152 |
| Wharf Rat | 153 |
| Windows | 155 |
| Zorba's | 160 |

## Beef

| | |
|---|---|
| Lennys Chop House | 77 |
| McCafferty's | 87 |
| Morton's of Chicago | 94 |
| Oregon Grille | 104 |
| Shula's Steak 2 | 128 |
| Shula's Steakhouse | 129 |
| Snyder's Willow Grove | 133 |
| Woodfire | 157 |

## Brew Pubs

| | |
|---|---|
| Bare Bones | 11 |
| Capitol City Brewing Company | 30 |
| Ellicott Mills Brewing Company | 53 |
| Red Brick Station | 112 |
| Sisson's | 132 |

## Cafes/Coffeehouses

| | |
|---|---|
| Cafe Pangea | 26 |
| City Cafe | 41 |
| Donna's Coffee Bar | 48 |
| Louie's the Bookstore Cafe | 81 |
| Needful Things | 97 |
| SoBo Cafe | 134 |
| Ze Mean Bean Cafe | 158 |

## Cajun/Creole
Bayou Blues Cafe ..................................................................14
Main Street Blues ..................................................................83
Sisson's ..................................................................................132

## Chinese/Japanese/Korean
Blue Garden ...........................................................................17
Edo Sushi ...............................................................................51
Golden Gate Noodle House ..................................................60
Han Sung ................................................................................63
Hunt Valley Szechuan ...........................................................69
Joung Kak ..............................................................................73
Olive and Sesame ................................................................102
Pinebrook Chinese Restaurant ...........................................108
Shanghai Lil's ......................................................................127
Silk Road ..............................................................................130
Sushi Sono ...........................................................................138
Suzie's Soba ........................................................................139

## Continental
Cafe Normandie .....................................................................25
Corks ......................................................................................44
Hampton's ..............................................................................62
Maison Marconi's ...................................................................84
Rudys' 2900 .........................................................................120

## Crab House
Barn Restaurant & Crab House .............................................12
Bo Brooks ..............................................................................18
Carney Crab House ...............................................................32
Obrycki's ..............................................................................100

## Deli
Suburban House ..................................................................137

## Diner
Ralphie's Diner ....................................................................111

## Eclectic
Angelina's ................................................................................6
Ashley M's ................................................................................8
Bandaloops ............................................................................10
Cafe Pangea ..........................................................................26
Ciao .........................................................................................39
Corks ......................................................................................44
Donna's ..................................................................................48
Ladew Topiary Gardens Cafe ................................................76
Louie's the Bookstore Cafe ...................................................81

174 | Dining in Baltimore

| | |
|---|---|
| M. Gettier's Orchard Inn | 82 |
| Main Street Blues | 83 |
| Pisces | 109 |
| The Tavern at Centre Park | 141 |
| Weber's On Boston | 152 |
| Zodiac | 159 |

## Ethiopian
| | |
|---|---|
| Azeb's Ethiopian Restaurant | 9 |
| Teranga African Restaurant | 142 |

## French
| | |
|---|---|
| Cafe Normandie | 25 |
| M. Gettier's Orchard Inn | 82 |
| Maison Marconi's | 84 |
| Weber's On Boston | 152 |

## German
| | |
|---|---|
| Haussner's | 67 |

## Greek
| | |
|---|---|
| Acropolis | 1 |
| The Black Olive | 16 |
| Chris' Charcoal Pit | 38 |
| Ciao | 39 |
| G & M | 56 |
| Ikaros | 71 |
| Samos | 123 |
| San Marco | 124 |
| Zorba's | 160 |

## Indian
| | |
|---|---|
| Akbar Palace | 2 |
| Ambassador Dining Room | 4 |
| Annapurna | 5 |

## Italian
| | |
|---|---|
| Aldo's | 3 |
| Angelina's | 6 |
| Cafe Troia | 27 |
| Capriccio | 31 |
| Carrabba's Italian Grill | 33 |
| Chiapparelli's | 37 |
| Chris' Charcoal Pit | 38 |
| Ciao Bella | 40 |
| Da Mimmo | 45 |
| Della Notte | 46 |
| Due | 50 |

| | |
|---|---|
| Ethel & Ramone's | 55 |
| Germano's | 59 |
| La Tavola | 75 |
| Mangia | 85 |
| Mangia Mangia | 86 |
| Michaelangelo | 91 |
| Pecora's | 106 |
| Piccolo's | 107 |
| Romano's Macaroni Grill | 118 |
| Sabatino's | 122 |
| Sebastian's | 126 |
| Sotto Sopra | 135 |
| Tiffin | 143 |
| Tonino's | 146 |
| Tuscany Grill | 148 |
| Victor's Cafe | 151 |

## Mediterranean & Middle Eastern
| | |
|---|---|
| Cafe Isis | 23 |
| Mediterranean Palace | 89 |
| Michaelangelo | 91 |
| San Marco | 124 |

## Mexican/Southwestern
| | |
|---|---|
| El Azteca | 52 |
| Geckos Bar & Grille | 58 |
| Hard Times | 65 |
| Nacho Mama's | 96 |
| No Way Jose Cafe | 98 |
| Sin Carne | 131 |

## New American
| | |
|---|---|
| Corks | 44 |
| Hamilton's | 61 |
| Joy America Cafe | 74 |
| Linwood's | 78 |
| Milton Inn | 93 |
| Restaurant Columbia | 115 |

## Pizza
| | |
|---|---|
| Cafe Isis | 23 |
| California Pizza Kitchen | 28 |
| Dooby's Bar & Grill | 49 |
| Ricciuti's Brick Oven Pizza | 116 |

## Seafood

| | |
|---|---|
| Angelina's | 6 |
| Barn Restaurant & Crab House | 12 |
| Bay Cafe | 13 |
| Bayou Blues Cafe | 14 |
| Bill Bateman's Bistro | 15 |
| Bo Brooks | 18 |
| Carney Crab House | 32 |
| Carrol's Creek | 34 |
| McCafferty's | 87 |
| McCormick & Schmick's | 88 |
| Obrycki's | 100 |
| O'Learys | 101 |
| Oregon Grille | 104 |
| Pisces | 109 |
| Rudys' 2900 | 120 |
| Rusty Scupper | 121 |
| Snyder's Willow Grove | 133 |
| Tapestry | 140 |
| Victor's Cafe | 151 |
| Wharfside | 154 |
| Windows | 155 |

## Southern

| | |
|---|---|
| Charleston | 35 |
| Micah's | 90 |

## Spanish

| | |
|---|---|
| Cafe Madrid | 24 |
| Tio Pepe | 145 |

## Vegetarian/Health Food

| | |
|---|---|
| Ethel & Ramone's | 55 |

# Entree pricing

## Under $5

- Barn Restaurant & Crab House .................................... 12
- Bill Bateman's Bistro .................................................... 15
- Bo Brooks ..................................................................... 18
- Burke's Cafe ................................................................. 21
- Cafe Isis ....................................................................... 23
- Carney Crab House ..................................................... 32
- Chris' Charcoal Pit ...................................................... 38
- Donna's Coffee Bar ..................................................... 48
- Dooby's Bar & Grill ..................................................... 49
- Gampy's ....................................................................... 57
- Geckos Bar & Grille .................................................... 58
- Golden Gate Noodle House ........................................ 60
- Hard Times .................................................................. 65
- Mediterranean Palace ................................................. 89
- Micah's ........................................................................ 90
- Nacho Mama's ............................................................. 96
- Needful Things ............................................................ 97
- Olney Ale House ........................................................ 103
- Pinebrook Chinese Restaurant ................................. 108
- Ralphie's Diner .......................................................... 111
- Rootie Kazootie's ....................................................... 119
- Samos ........................................................................ 123
- Sascha's Daily ............................................................. 12
- Suburban House ....................................................... 137
- Tonino's ..................................................................... 146
- Wharf Rat .................................................................. 153
- Women's Industrial Exchange .................................. 156
- Zodiac ........................................................................ 159

## $6 — 11

- Acropolis ....................................................................... 1
- Akbar Palace ................................................................. 2
- Ambassador Dining Room ............................................ 4
- Annapurna .................................................................... 5
- Angelina's ...................................................................... 6
- Ashley M's ..................................................................... 8
- Azeb's Ethiopian Restaurant ........................................ 9
- Bare Bones .................................................................. 11
- Barn Restaurant & Crab House .................................. 12
- Bay Cafe ...................................................................... 13
- Bayou Blues Cafe ........................................................ 14
- Bill Bateman's Bistro .................................................. 15
- Blue Garden ................................................................ 17
- Bo Brooks .................................................................... 18
- Boomerang .................................................................. 19
- Burke's Cafe ................................................................ 21
- Cactus Willies ............................................................. 22
- Cafe Isis ...................................................................... 23

178 | Dining in Baltimore

| | |
|---|---|
| Cafe Normandie | 25 |
| Cafe Pangea | 26 |
| Cafe Troia | 27 |
| California Pizza Kitchen | 28 |
| Carney Crab House | 32 |
| Carrabba's Italian Grill | 33 |
| Charred Rib | 36 |
| Chiapparelli's | 37 |
| Chris' Charcoal Pit | 38 |
| Ciao Bella | 40 |
| City Cafe | 41 |
| Coho Grill | 43 |
| Della Notte | 46 |
| Doc's Eastside | 47 |
| Donna's Coffee Bar | 48 |
| Dooby's Bar & Grill | 49 |
| Due | 50 |
| Edo Sushi | 51 |
| Ellicott Mills Brewing Company | 53 |
| ESPN Zone | 54 |
| Ethel & Ramone's | 55 |
| G & M | 56 |
| Gampy's | 57 |
| Geckos Bar & Grille | 58 |
| Golden Gate Noodle House | 60 |
| Han Sung | 63 |
| Hard Rock Cafe Baltimore | 64 |
| Hard Times | 65 |
| Haussner's | 67 |
| The Helmand | 68 |
| Hunt Valley Szechuan | 69 |
| Hunters Lodge | 70 |
| Ikaros | 71 |
| J. Paul's | 72 |
| Joung Kak | 73 |
| Ladew Topiary Gardens Cafe | 76 |
| Little Havana | 79 |
| Louie's the Bookstore Cafe | 81 |
| Main Street Blues | 83 |
| Mangia | 85 |
| Mangia Mangia | 86 |
| McCormick & Schmick's | 88 |
| Mediterranean Palace | 89 |
| Micah's | 90 |
| Mill Towne Tavern | 92 |
| Nacho Mama's | 96 |
| Needful Things | 97 |
| No Way Jose Cafe | 98 |
| North Star | 99 |
| Olive and Sesame | 102 |
| Olney Ale House | 103 |
| The Owl Bar | 105 |
| Pecora's | 106 |
| Piccolo's | 107 |

| | |
|---|---|
| Planet Hollywood | 110 |
| Ralphie's Diner | 111 |
| Red Brick Station | 112 |
| Red River Barbecue and Grille | 113 |
| Reisters Country Inn | 114 |
| Ricciuti's Brick Oven Pizza | 116 |
| Rocky Run Tap & Grill | 117 |
| Romano's Macaroni Grill | 118 |
| Rootie Kazootie's | 119 |
| Rudys' 2900 | 120 |
| Sabatino's | 122 |
| Samos | 123 |
| Sascha's Daily | 125 |
| Sebastian's | 126 |
| Shanghai Lil's | 127 |
| Shula's Steak 2 | 128 |
| Silk Road | 130 |
| Sin Carne | 131 |
| Snyder's Willow Grove | 133 |
| SoBo Cafe | 134 |
| Sotto Sopra | 135 |
| Spike & Charlie's | 136 |
| Suburban House | 137 |
| Sushi Sono | 138 |
| Suzie's Soba | 139 |
| Tapestry | 140 |
| The Tavern at Centre Park | 141 |
| Teranga African Restaurant | 142 |
| Tiffin | 143 |
| Timber Creek Tavern | 144 |
| Tonino's | 146 |
| The Trolley Stop | 147 |
| Tuscany Grill | 148 |
| Victor's Cafe | 151 |
| Wharf Rat | 153 |
| Ze Mean Bean Cafe | 158 |
| Zodiac | 159 |
| Zorba's | 160 |

## $12 — $19

| | |
|---|---|
| Acropolis | 1 |
| Akbar Palace | 2 |
| Aldo's | 3 |
| Ambassador Dining Room | 4 |
| Annapurna | 5 |
| Angelina's | 6 |
| Ashley M's | 8 |
| Bandaloops | 10 |
| Bare Bones | 11 |
| Barn Restaurant & Crab House | 12 |
| Bay Cafe | 13 |
| Bayou Blues Cafe | 14 |
| Bill Bateman's Bistro | 15 |

| | |
|---|---|
| The Black Olive | 16 |
| Blue Garden | 17 |
| Bo Brooks | 18 |
| Boomerang | 19 |
| Burke's Cafe | 21 |
| Cafe Isis | 23 |
| Cafe Madrid | 24 |
| Cafe Normandie | 25 |
| Cafe Pangea | 26 |
| Cafe Troia | 27 |
| Candle Light Inn | 29 |
| Capitol City Brewing Company | 30 |
| Capriccio | 31 |
| Carrabba's Italian Grill | 33 |
| Carrol's Creek | 34 |
| Charleston | 35 |
| Charred Rib | 36 |
| Chiapparelli's | 37 |
| Chris' Charcoal Pit | 38 |
| Ciao | 39 |
| Ciao Bella | 40 |
| City Cafe | 41 |
| Cockey's Tavern | 42 |
| Coho Grill | 43 |
| Corks | 44 |
| Da Mimmo | 45 |
| Della Notte | 46 |
| Doc's Eastside | 47 |
| Dooby's Bar & Grill | 49 |
| Due | 50 |
| Edo Sushi | 51 |
| El Azteca | 52 |
| Ellicott Mills Brewing Company | 53 |
| ESPN Zone | 54 |
| Ethel & Ramone's | 55 |
| G & M | 56 |
| Gampy's | 57 |
| Geckos Bar & Grille | 58 |
| Germano's | 59 |
| Hamilton's | 61 |
| Han Sung | 63 |
| Hard Rock Cafe Baltimore | 64 |
| Harryman House | 66 |
| Haussner's | 67 |
| The Helmand | 68 |
| Hunt Valley Szechuan | 69 |
| Hunters Lodge | 70 |
| Ikaros | 71 |
| J. Paul's | 72 |
| Joung Kak | 73 |
| Joy America Cafe | 74 |
| La Tavola | 75 |
| Lennys Chop House | 77 |
| Linwood's | 78 |

| | |
|---|---|
| Little Havana | 79 |
| Lord Baltimore Grill | 80 |
| Louie's the Bookstore Cafe | 81 |
| M. Gettier's Orchard Inn | 82 |
| Main Street Blues | 83 |
| Maison Marconi's | 84 |
| Mangia | 85 |
| Mangia Mangia | 86 |
| McCafferty's | 87 |
| McCormick & Schmick's | 88 |
| Michaelangelo | 91 |
| Mill Towne Tavern | 92 |
| Milton Inn | 93 |
| Morton's of Chicago | 94 |
| Mount Washington Tavern | 95 |
| Nacho Mama's | 96 |
| No Way Jose Cafe | 98 |
| North Star | 99 |
| Obrycki's | 100 |
| O'Learys | 101 |
| Olive and Sesame | 102 |
| Olney Ale House | 103 |
| Oregon Grille | 104 |
| The Owl Bar | 105 |
| Pecora's | 106 |
| Piccolo's | 10 |
| Pisces | 109 |
| Planet Hollywood | 110 |
| Ralphie's Diner | 111 |
| Red Brick Station | 112 |
| Red River Barbecue and Grille | 113 |
| Reisters Country Inn | 114 |
| Restaurant Columbia | 115 |
| Rocky Run Tap & Grill | 117 |
| Romano's Macaroni Grill | 118 |
| Rudys' 2900 | 120 |
| Rusty Scupper | 121 |
| Sabatino's | 122 |
| Samos | 123 |
| San Marco | 124 |
| Sebastian's | 126 |
| Shula's Steak 2 | 128 |
| Shula's Steakhouse | 129 |
| Silk Road | 130 |
| Sin Carne | 131 |
| Sisson's | 132 |
| Snyder's Willow Grove | 133 |
| Sotto Sopra | 135 |
| Spike & Charlie's | 136 |
| Sushi Sono | 138 |
| Suzie's Soba | 139 |
| Tapestry | 140 |
| The Tavern at Centre Park | 141 |

| | |
|---|---|
| Tiffin | 143 |
| Timber Creek Tavern | 144 |
| Tio Pepe | 145 |
| Tonino's | 146 |
| Tuscany Grill | 148 |
| The Union Hotel | 149 |
| Vera's Bakery and Cafe | 150 |
| Victor's Cafe | 151 |
| Weber's On Boston | 152 |
| Wharf Rat | 153 |
| Wharfside | 154 |
| Windows | 155 |
| Women's Industrial Exchange | 156 |
| Woodfire | 157 |
| Ze Mean Bean Cafe | 158 |
| Zodiac | 159 |
| Zorba's | 160 |

## $20 – $25

| | |
|---|---|
| Acropolis | 1 |
| Aldo's | 3 |
| Angelina's | 6 |
| Ashley M's | 8 |
| Azeb's Ethiopian Restaurant | 9 |
| Barn Restaurant & Crab House | 12 |
| Bayou Blues Cafe | 14 |
| The Black Olive | 16 |
| Blue Garden | 17 |
| Boomerang | 19 |
| The Brass Elephant | 20 |
| Burke's Cafe | 21 |
| Cafe Madrid | 24 |
| Cafe Normandie | 25 |
| Cafe Troia | 27 |
| Candle Light Inn | 29 |
| Capriccio | 31 |
| Carney Crab House | 32 |
| Carrol's Creek | 34 |
| Charleston | 35 |
| Chiapparelli's | 37 |
| Ciao | 39 |
| Ciao Bella | 40 |
| Corks | 44 |
| Da Mimmo | 45 |
| Due | 50 |
| Ethel & Ramone's | 55 |
| G & M | 56 |
| Germano's | 59 |
| Hamilton's | 61 |
| Han Sung | 63 |
| Harryman House | 66 |
| Haussner's | 67 |
| Hunt Valley Szechuan | 69 |

| | |
|---|---|
| Hunters Lodge | 70 |
| Joung Kak | 73 |
| Joy America Cafe | 74 |
| La Tavola | 75 |
| Lennys Chop House | 77 |
| Linwood's | 78 |
| Lord Baltimore Grill | 80 |
| M. Gettier's Orchard Inn | 82 |
| Maison Marconi's | 84 |
| McCafferty's | 87 |
| McCormick & Schmick's | 88 |
| Michaelangelo | 91 |
| Milton Inn | 93 |
| Morton's of Chicago | 94 |
| Obrycki's | 100 |
| O'Learys | 101 |
| Olive and Sesame | 102 |
| Oregon Grille | 104 |
| The Owl Bar | 105 |
| Pecora's | 106 |
| Pisces | 109 |
| Restaurant Columbia | 115 |
| Rudys' 2900 | 120 |
| Rusty Scupper | 121 |
| Sabatino's | 122 |
| San Marco | 124 |
| Sebastian's | 126 |
| Shula's Steak 2 | 128 |
| Shula's Steakhouse | 129 |
| Snyder's Willow Grove | 133 |
| Sotto Sopra | 135 |
| Spike & Charlie's | 136 |
| Sushi Sono | 138 |
| Tio Pepe | 145 |
| Tuscany Grill | 148 |
| The Union Hotel | 149 |
| Wharfside | 154 |
| Windows | 155 |
| Woodfire | 157 |

# $26 and up

| | |
|---|---|
| Aldo's | 3 |
| Antrim 1844 Country Inn | 7 |
| The Black Olive | 16 |
| The Brass Elephant | 20 |
| Carney Crab House | 32 |
| Da Mimmo | 45 |
| Due | 50 |
| G & M | 56 |
| Hampton's | 62 |
| Joung Kak | 73 |
| Joy America Cafe | 74 |
| Lennys Chop House | 77 |

| | |
|---|---|
| Linwood's | 78 |
| Lord Baltimore Grill | 80 |
| McCafferty's | 87 |
| McCormick & Schmick's | 88 |
| Milton Inn | 93 |
| Morton's of Chicago | 94 |
| O'Learys | 101 |
| Oregon Grille | 104 |
| Pecora's | 106 |
| Pisces | 109 |
| Restaurant Columbia | 115 |
| Rudys' 2900 | 120 |
| Rusty Scupper | 121 |
| Sabatino's | 122 |
| Shula's Steakhouse | 129 |
| Snyder's Willow Grove | 133 |
| Sushi Sono | 138 |
| The Union Hotel | 149 |
| Windows | 155 |

# Crab prices

Barn Restaurant & Crab House .................................... 12
*$24- $45 per dozen*

Bo Brooks .................................................................... 18
*$20-$42 per dozen*

Carney Crab House ..................................................... 32
*$20-$48 per dozen*

Obrycki's .................................................................... 100
*$20-$60 per dozen*

# Live music

Akbar Palace .................................................................2
Angelina's .....................................................................6
Antrim 1844 Country Inn...............................................7
Ashley M's .....................................................................8
Azeb's Ethiopian Restaurant ........................................9
Bare Bones.................................................................. 11
Barn Restaurant & Crab House ................................. 12
Bay Cafe ......................................................................13
Bayou Blues Cafe ........................................................14
Cafe Isis ......................................................................23
Candle Light Inn .........................................................29
Charred Rib ................................................................36
Cockey's Tavern ..........................................................42
Da Mimmo ...................................................................45
El Azteca .....................................................................52
Hunters Lodge ............................................................70
Louie's the Bookstore Cafe .........................................81
M. Gettier's Orchard Inn ............................................82
Main Street Blues .......................................................83
McCafferty's ................................................................87
North Star ...................................................................99
Oregon Grille .............................................................104
Pecora's .....................................................................106
Piccolo's .....................................................................107
Pisces ........................................................................109
Red Brick Station ......................................................112
Rusty Scupper ...........................................................121
Sebastian's ................................................................126
Timber Creek Tavern ................................................144
Vera's Bakery and Cafe ............................................150
Victor's Cafe ..............................................................151
Weber's On Boston ....................................................152
Ze Mean Bean Cafe ...................................................158
Zodiac ........................................................................159

# Children's menu

Ashley M's .................................................................8
Bare Bones................................................................11
Barn Restaurant & Crab House ...........................12
Bayou Blues Cafe ..................................................14
Bill Bateman's Bistro ............................................15
Blue Garden ...........................................................17
Bo Brooks ...............................................................18
Burke's Cafe ..........................................................21
Cafe Isis .................................................................23
Cafe Normandie ....................................................25
California Pizza Kitchen .....................................28
Capitol City Brewing Company .........................30
Capriccio ................................................................31
Carney Crab House ..............................................32
Carrabba's Italian Grill .......................................33
Carrol's Creek .......................................................34
Charred Rib ...........................................................36
Chiapparelli's ........................................................37
Chris' Charcoal Pit ...............................................38
Coho Grill ..............................................................43
Della Notte ............................................................46
Dooby's Bar & Grill ..............................................49
El Azteca ................................................................52
Ellicott Mills Brewing Company ........................53
ESPN Zone ............................................................54
G & M .....................................................................56
Germano's ..............................................................59
Hamilton's ..............................................................61
Hard Rock Cafe Baltimore .................................64
Hard Times ............................................................65
Hunters Lodge ......................................................70
J. Paul's ..................................................................72
Joung Kak .............................................................73
Joy America Cafe .................................................74
Little Havana ........................................................79
Lord Baltimore Grill ............................................80
Mangia ....................................................................85
McCormick & Schmick's ......................................88
Micah's ...................................................................90
Mill Towne Tavern ................................................92
North Star .............................................................99
O'Learys ...............................................................101
Oregon Grille .......................................................104
Pecora's .................................................................106
Piccolo's ..................................................................10
Pisces ....................................................................109
Planet Hollywood ................................................110
Ralphie's Diner ....................................................111
Red Brick Station ................................................112
Red River Barbecue and Grille ........................113
Reisters Country Inn .........................................114

Dining in Baltimore | 187

| | |
|---|---|
| Restaurant Columbia | 115 |
| Ricciuti's Brick Oven Pizza | 116 |
| Rocky Run Tap & Grill | 117 |
| Romano's Macaroni Grill | 118 |
| Rusty Scupper | 121 |
| Sabatino's | 122 |
| Samos | 123 |
| San Marco | 124 |
| Sascha's Daily | 125 |
| Sebastian's | 126 |
| Shula's Steak 2 | 128 |
| Shula's Steakhouse | 129 |
| Sisson's | 132 |
| Snyder's Willow Grove | 133 |
| Spike & Charlie's | 136 |
| Suburban House | 137 |
| Sushi Sono | 138 |
| The Tavern at Centre Park | 141 |
| Timber Creek Tavern | 144 |
| Tonino's | 146 |
| The Trolley Stop | 147 |
| The Union Hotel | 149 |
| Victor's Cafe | 151 |
| Weber's On Boston | 152 |
| Wharf Rat | 153 |
| Wharfside | 154 |
| Woodfire | 157 |
| Zodiac | 159 |
| Zorba's | 160 |

# Waterfront views

| | |
|---|---|
| Bay Cafe | 13 |
| California Pizza Kitchen | 28 |
| Capitol City Brewing Company | 30 |
| Carrol's Creek | 34 |
| ESPN Zone | 54 |
| Hard Rock Cafe Baltimore | 64 |
| J. Paul's | 72 |
| Joy America Cafe | 74 |
| Lennys Chop House | 77 |
| Little Havana | 79 |
| McCormick & Schmick's | 88 |
| O'Learys | 101 |
| Pisces | 109 |
| Planet Hollywood | 110 |
| Rusty Scupper | 121 |
| Sushi Sono | 138 |
| Suzie's Sobo | 139 |
| The Union Hotel | 149 |
| Victor's Cafe | 151 |
| Windows | 155 |

# Wheelchair accessible

| | |
|---|---|
| Acropolis | 1 |
| Akbar Palace | 2 |
| Aldo's | 3 |
| Annapurna | 5 |
| Angelina's | 6 |
| Antrim 1844 Country Inn | 7 |
| Bandaloops | 10 |
| Bare Bones | 11 |
| Barn Restaurant & Crab House | 12 |
| Bay Cafe | 13 |
| Bayou Blues Cafe | 14 |
| Bill Bateman's Bistro | 15 |
| The Black Olive | 16 |
| Blue Garden | 17 |
| Bo Brooks | 18 |
| Boomerang | 19 |
| Burke's Cafe | 21 |
| Cafe Isis | 23 |
| Cafe Troia | 27 |
| California Pizza Kitchen | 28 |
| Candle Light Inn | 29 |
| Capitol City Brewing Company | 30 |
| Carney Crab House | 32 |
| Carrabba's Italian Grill | 33 |
| Carrol's Creek | 34 |
| Charleston | 35 |
| Charred Rib | 36 |
| Chiapparelli's | 37 |
| Chris' Charcoal Pit | 38 |
| Ciao | 39 |
| City Cafe | 41 |
| Coho Grill | 43 |
| Corks | 44 |
| Della Notte | 46 |
| Doc's Eastside | 47 |
| Due | 50 |
| Edo Sushi | 51 |
| El Azteca | 52 |
| Ellicott Mills Brewing Company | 53 |
| ESPN Zone | 54 |
| G & M | 56 |
| Geckos Bar & Grille | 58 |
| Germano's | 59 |
| Golden Gate Noodle House | 60 |
| Hamilton's | 61 |
| Hampton's | 62 |
| Han Sung | 63 |
| Hard Rock Cafe Baltimore | 64 |
| Hard Times | 65 |
| Harryman House | 66 |
| Haussner's | 67 |

| | |
|---|---|
| The Helmand | 68 |
| Hunt Valley Szechuan | 69 |
| Hunters Lodge | 70 |
| Ikaros | 71 |
| J. Paul's | 72 |
| Joung Kak | 73 |
| Joy America Cafe | 74 |
| La Tavola | 75 |
| Ladew Topiary Gardens Cafe | 76 |
| Lennys Chop House | 77 |
| Linwood's | 78 |
| Little Havana | 79 |
| Lord Baltimore Grill | 80 |
| Louie's the Bookstore Cafe | 81 |
| M. Gettier's Orchard Inn | 82 |
| Mangia | 85 |
| Mangia Mangia | 86 |
| McCafferty's | 87 |
| McCormick & Schmick's | 88 |
| Mediterranean Palace | 89 |
| Micah's | 90 |
| Michaelangelo | 91 |
| Mill Towne Tavern | 92 |
| Milton Inn | 93 |
| Morton's of Chicago | 94 |
| Nacho Mama's | 96 |
| North Star | 99 |
| O'Learys | 101 |
| Olive and Sesame | 102 |
| Olney Ale House | 103 |
| Oregon Grille | 104 |
| The Owl Bar | 105 |
| Piccolo's | 107 |
| Pinebrook Chinese Restaurant | 108 |
| Pisces | 109 |
| Planet Hollywood | 110 |
| Ralphie's Diner | 111 |
| Red Brick Station | 112 |
| Red River Barbecue and Grille | 113 |
| Reisters Country Inn | 114 |
| Ricciuti's Brick Oven Pizza | 116 |
| Rocky Run Tap & Grill | 117 |
| Romano's Macaroni Grill | 118 |
| Rootie Kazootie's | 119 |
| Rudys' 2900 | 120 |
| Rusty Scupper | 121 |
| Sabatino's | 122 |
| San Marco | 124 |
| Sebastian's | 126 |
| Shula's Steak 2 | 128 |
| Shula's Steakhouse | 129 |
| Silk Road | 130 |
| Sin Carne | 131 |
| Sisson's | 132 |

| | |
|---|---|
| Snyder's Willow Grove | 133 |
| SoBo Cafe | 134 |
| Sotto Sopra | 135 |
| Spike & Charlie's | 136 |
| Suburban House | 137 |
| Sushi Sono | 138 |
| Suzie's Soba | 139 |
| The Tavern at Centre Park | 141 |
| Teranga African Restaurant | 142 |
| Tiffin | 143 |
| Timber Creek Tavern | 144 |
| Tio Pepe | 145 |
| Tonino's | 146 |
| The Trolley Stop | 147 |
| Tuscany Grill | 148 |
| The Union Hotel | 149 |
| Vera's Bakery and Cafe | 150 |
| Victor's Cafe | 151 |
| Weber's On Boston | 152 |
| Wharf Rat | 153 |
| Wharfside | 154 |
| Windows | 155 |
| Woodfire | 157 |
| Ze Mean Bean Cafe | 158 |
| Zodiac | 159 |

# Reservations

| | |
|---|---|
| Acropolis | 1 |
| Akbar Palace | 2 |
| Aldo's | 3 |
| Ambassador Dining Room | 4 |
| Annapurna | 5 |
| Angelina's | 6 |
| Antrim 1844 Country Inn | 7 |
| Ashley M's | 8 |
| Azeb's Ethiopian Restaurant | 9 |
| Bandaloops | 10 |
| Bare Bones | 11 |
| Barn Restaurant & Crab House | 12 |
| Bay Cafe | 13 |
| Bayou Blues Cafe | 14 |
| Bill Bateman's Bistro | 15 |
| The Black Olive | 16 |
| Bo Brooks | 18 |
| Boomerang | 19 |
| The Brass Elephant | 20 |
| Burke's Cafe | 21 |
| Cafe Isis | 23 |
| Cafe Madrid | 24 |
| Cafe Normandie | 25 |
| Cafe Pangea | 26 |
| Cafe Troia | 27 |
| Candle Light Inn | 29 |
| Capitol City Brewing Company | 30 |
| Capriccio | 31 |
| Carney Crab House | 32 |
| Charleston | 35 |
| Charred Rib | 36 |
| Chiapparelli's | 37 |
| Ciao | 39 |
| Ciao Bella | 40 |
| City Cafe | 41 |
| Cockey's Tavern | 42 |
| Corks | 44 |
| Da Mimmo | 45 |
| Della Notte | 46 |
| Doc's Eastside | 47 |
| Due | 50 |
| Edo Sushi | 51 |
| El Azteca | 52 |
| Ellicott Mills Brewing Company | 53 |
| Ethel & Ramone's | 55 |
| G & M | 56 |
| Gampy's | 57 |
| Geckos Bar & Grille | 58 |
| Germano's | 59 |
| Golden Gate Noodle House | 60 |
| Hamilton's | 61 |

| | |
|---|---|
| Hampton's | 62 |
| Han Sung | 63 |
| Hard Times | 65 |
| Harryman House | 66 |
| Haussner's | 67 |
| The Helmand | 68 |
| Hunt Valley Szechuan | 69 |
| Hunters Lodge | 70 |
| Ikaros | 71 |
| J. Paul's | 72 |
| Joung Kak | 73 |
| Joy America Cafe | 74 |
| La Tavola | 75 |
| Ladew Topiary Gardens Cafe | 76 |
| Lennys Chop House | 77 |
| Linwood's | 78 |
| Little Havana | 79 |
| Lord Baltimore Grill | 80 |
| Louie's the Bookstore Cafe | 81 |
| M. Gettier's Orchard Inn | 82 |
| Main Street Blues | 83 |
| Maison Marconi's | 84 |
| McCafferty's | 87 |
| McCormick & Schmick's | 88 |
| Mediterranean Palace | 89 |
| Michaelangelo | 91 |
| Mill Towne Tavern | 92 |
| Milton Inn | 93 |
| Morton's of Chicago | 94 |
| Mount Washington Tavern | 95 |
| No Way Jose Cafe | 98 |
| North Star | 99 |
| O'Learys | 101 |
| Olive and Sesame | 102 |
| Olney Ale House | 103 |
| Oregon Grille | 104 |
| The Owl Bar | 105 |
| Pecora's | 106 |
| Piccolo's | 107 |
| Pinebrook Chinese Restaurant | 108 |
| Pisces | 109 |
| Planet Hollywood | 110 |
| Ralphie's Diner | 111 |
| Red Brick Station | 112 |
| Reisters Country Inn | 114 |
| Restaurant Columbia | 115 |
| Rocky Run Tap & Grill | 117 |
| Rootie Kazootie's | 119 |
| Rudys' 2900 | 120 |
| Rusty Scupper | 121 |
| Sabatino's | 122 |
| Samos | 123 |
| San Marco | 124 |
| Sebastian's | 126 |

| | |
|---|---|
| Shanghai Lil's | 127 |
| Shula's Steakhouse | 129 |
| Silk Road | 130 |
| Sin Carne | 131 |
| Sisson's | 132 |
| Snyder's Willow Grove | 133 |
| SoBo Cafe | 134 |
| Sotto Sopra | 135 |
| Spike & Charlie's | 136 |
| Suburban House | 137 |
| Sushi Sono | 138 |
| Suzie's Soba | 139 |
| Tapestry | 140 |
| The Tavern at Centre Park | 141 |
| Teranga African Restaurant | 142 |
| Tiffin | 143 |
| Timber Creek Tavern | 144 |
| Tio Pepe's | 145 |
| The Trolley Stop | 147 |
| Tuscany Grill | 148 |
| The Union Hotel | 149 |
| Vera's Bakery and Cafe | 150 |
| Victor's Cafe | 151 |
| Weber's On Boston | 152 |
| Wharfside | 154 |
| Windows | 155 |
| Ze Mean Bean Cafe | 158 |
| Zodiac | 159 |
| Zorba's | 160 |

# Area classics

Angelina's ............................................................... 6
Antrim 1844 Country Inn ........................................ 7
Burke's Cafe ......................................................... 21
Cockey's Tavern ................................................... 42
Haussner's ........................................................... 67
Louie's The Bookstore Cafe ................................. 81
Maison Marconi .................................................... 84
Obrycki's ............................................................ 100
Rudy's 2900 ....................................................... 120
Sabatino's .......................................................... 122
Snyder's Willow Grove ....................................... 133
Tio Pepe's .......................................................... 145
The Union Hotel ................................................. 149
Women's Industrial Exchange ........................... 156